"... the soaps are the only place on television where you may see adult topics—rape, alcoholism, frigidity, the plight of the professional woman who doesn't want children, racism, sexism, even incest—explored in dramatic context as if they were problems of real people."

—The New York Sunday Times

THE *INSIDE* STORY

At last, there's a book that takes the soap operas seriously . . . a complete guide to that fabulous world of daytime television.

The devoted soap fans—whether they have been following the serials for six weeks, eight months or even twenty years —will relish every fact-filled chapter in the book. No aspect of the phenomenon has been overlooked—everything is here in one giant volume!

Must Reading for 50 Million Soap Fans!

The
Wonderful
World
Of
TV
Soap Operas

Robert LaGuardia

BALLANTINE BOOKS · NEW YORK

Front cover:
    illustrations by Don R. Smith
    photograph from the author's personal collection

Back cover:
    photograph of John Beradino, courtesy of ABC
    photograph of Mary Stuart and Anthony George, courtesy
        of CBS
    photograph of Rosemary Prinz, courtesy of CBS
    photograph of Eileen Fulton, by Charles McLarty

Pictures in the photo section were obtained from the following sources:

    ABC: 5 bot., 12 bot., 13 bot., 14 top, bot., 16 bot.
    Author: 1
    CBS: 3 top, bot. left, 4 bot. right, 5 top right, 6, 7, 8 top,
        bot., 10, 11, 12 top left & right, 15 bot.
    Group W Productions: 13 top, mid.
    NBC: 2, 3 bot. right, 4 top, bot. left, 5 top left, 9, 14 mid.,
        15 top, mid., 16 top

ISBN 0-345-27283-8

Manufactured in the United States of America

First Edition: September 1974
Second Printing: May 1975

First Special Printing: February 1976
Second Special Printing: April 1977

For my parents

CONTENTS

ACKNOWLEDGMENTS

My gratitude goes to all of the people in daytime dramatic television (actors, producers, writers, directors, et al.) who gave freely of their time; without their cooperation this book could never have been written. They granted interviews, racked their brains to remember historical facts, read semi-complete portions of manuscript for accuracy, and were generally so pleasant about things that even "hard core" research almost became fun.

Among those who did far more than their fair share to help were: Charita Bauer, whose memory for details was extraordinary; Mart Hulswit and Bruce Cox, who supplied invaluable documentary material; Don MacLaughlin, who painted vivid images of a bygone era; Val Dufour, who is a marvelous raconteur and offered dozens of funny stories; and Virginia Dwyer, whose no-holds-barred frankness was appreciated.

To Barbara Schrank: who twice had to suggest that I write this book before the idea caught on.

To Donald Lovell, for making available to me his large and important collection of daytime serial memorabilia.

Special thanks also to all those who helped with the seemingly impossible task of compiling story synopses of all the daytime serials: Mary Bonner, assistant producer (*Another World*); Eileen Fulton, Don MacLaughlin, Rosemary Prinz, and Helen Wagner (*As the World Turns*); Wesley H. Kenney, producer (*Days of Our Lives*); Joseph Stuart, producer, and Hugh McPhillips, associate producer (*The Doctors*); Teri Keane, Maeve McGuire, and

Erwin Nicholson, producer (*The Edge of Night*); James Young, producer, and Kylie Masterson, associate producer (*General Hospital*); Charita Bauer (*The Guiding Light*); Larry Auerbach, director (*Love of Life*); Doris Quinlan, producer (*One Life to Live*); Mary Stuart, and Mary-Ellis Bunim, associate producer (*Search for Tomorrow*); Jada Rowland (*The Secret Storm*); Michael Andrews and Georgann Johnson (*Somerset*); and Karen L. Palmer (*The Young & The Restless*).

❦ I ❧

The Daytime Dramas of
Yesterday and Today

ON THE GREAT stage of the Palace the fabulous Garland was scoring yet another triumph. All through her performance a sort of low-keyed anticipation was felt by the audience. Garland incorporated this excitement into her act, ingeniously using her own status as a legend for effect. Crooning "Over the Rainbow," a sob in her throat, she galloped down the aisle of the Palace, head held high, slightly pompous, while adoration swirled about her. It was her prescribed ritual. Yet suddenly, on this particular night, the great Garland brought her glorious exodus to a grinding halt. The magic lady had spotted someone in the audience. All the glory drained from her face—the star had become a mere fan. She cried out to a special person seated in the theater, "I know you. I see you every day on television. You're Connie Ford—Ada!"

That was not an isolated incident; it happens constantly: celebrities making fools of themselves in public over a handful of people whose reputations, you would think, couldn't even get them a seat at Hollywood's Brown Derby, let alone stop a Judy Garland in her tracks. Harry Belafonte was in a TV studio one day when in

walked plain old Virginia Dwyer, the backbone of moral-
ity and uprightness on *Another World.* "Mary Matthews!
Mary Matthews!" shouted the calypso artist. "What are
you doing here? This is such a thrill."

The serials—soap operas—have been going strong for
thirty years on radio and twenty-four years on television,
and from all indications they will probably last for as long
as broadcasting lasts. Today's daytime TV dramas have
never before been as appealing, as elaborate, as well
honed, or as avidly followed by its far-from-disinterested
viewers. Nielsen Ratings, Inc. reveals that twenty million
people daily watch these shows, which are aired each
weekday from about noon until late afternoon. They are
watched devotedly, sometimes clandestinely (hurriedly
switched off when the doorbell rings), sometimes with the
greatest abandon. Sometimes the soaps are viewed close-
up, hands clasped in laps, tears and laughter alternating;
or they are watched from a sick bed, or the kitchen table,
or from behind ironing boards and potato peelings. Sometimes viewers have as much of an interest in their favorite actors as in the story line itself. These actors are
frequently objects of unbelievable involvements on the
part of viewers—involvements that sometimes lead to hate
or love mail, or long-distance phone calls to offer advice
(during murder trials, for example), or booties and bas-
sinets sent to pregnant characters on the shows. Viewers
have been known to stage large wedding parties in their
homes (complete with wedding cake) when characters
marry; and they have even, though rarely, physically attacked the actors themselves. Some years back, one actor
who played a miscreant on *The Secret Storm* was reportedly shot by a viewer; another time the famous Eileen
Fulton, who plays the now much-loved, though once-
hated, Lisa on *As the World Turns,* was struck by an angry lady who called her a "terrible woman." She had to
have police protection going to and from her TV studio
when she began receiving threats on her life in the mail.

One of the first things you learn about the emotional
world of TV's afternoon-installment fiction is that so
many people—not just the late Garland or the great

Belafonte, or even fellow celebrities like Bette Davis, Van Cliburn, Patrick Dennis, P. G. Wodehouse, Dizzy Gillespie, the late Tallulah Bankhead, but nearly everyone who watches serials—make fools of themselves over the afternoon soaps, if only in little ways. Love and tears are catching. People don't just watch the shows as they would movies or plays; they live them. They react to them as if real life were being pumped into their living rooms every day.

And the fact of the matter is that the shows *are* real. This is the important point, which soap opera's numerous critics all over culture-dom always seem to forget. What other form of art lets you in on the day-to-day activities of a family, or select members of a town? In the movies the cowboy and the heroine ride off into the billowy orange sunset, conveying the impression that all will forever be well—but we all know that life isn't like that. Happiness comes only in stretches, and no one, not even the cowboy and his girl, is immune to the heartaches of broken marriages, disease, and even death. Soaps don't pretend. On the serials, misfortune can strike anyone and everyone, even the best of us. As in the plays of the ancient Greeks, the very noblest man can be tormented by fate— with only his own awareness of the ultimate meaning of his life and the viewers' own grief giving his fate any justification at all.

- The serials involve their viewers because they present life as an unknown quantity; viewers can expect only the unexpected. The prospect of one's finding happiness tomorrow is as "certain" as a weather forecast or as finding a penny on the ground. The serials are also entertaining, even in the face of a bad performance on Tuesday or a few jumbled lines of dialogue on Wednesday. And they seem to generate a kind of human compassion. Watching over a long period of time leads to an understanding of what makes a certain character tick—why he or she will seem conniving at times and at other times unselfish. Plays and movies may give an insight into what people are like when they are caught in a certain specific situation—but only soaps can show what people are like in a thousand different situations.

Fate is the only real villain of daytime serials—and that point is brought home again and again by the deaths of "good" characters and the sudden sadnesses inflicted on happy families. In real life people are trapped by fate, and *that* is upsetting. It's upsetting not to know how long parents will live or if a beautiful child will someday turn into a grotesque heroin addict. All viewers implicitly understand these parallels and react to the serials the way they react to life. Several years ago, *Love of Life*'s viewers suffered for months while Bill Prentiss (played by Gene Bua) wasted from leukemia. Still, they hoped. They wrote letters of great concern for his life, sometimes even begging the producers and writers to spare him. Bill—a good, sympathetic character who was perhaps the ideal son— died anyway. Thousands of angry letters poured into *Love of Life*'s production offices, as had happened countless times before over the death, divorce, or sudden misfortune of other characters: "How could you let Bill die? I've liked your show up until now . . ." It was as if people were saying, "I've liked *life*—until now." As the weeks passed and one character after another wept—Tess Prentiss cried over the coffin; Bill's father broke down, telling Bill's mother the news over the phone; concerned friends grieved—viewers silently shared this grief. In the end no one really blamed *Love of Life*. It was just *life*.

The classic example occurred a number of years ago on *The Edge of Night* when detective Mike Karr's wife, Sarah, played by Teal Ames, was killed by an automobile while saving the life of her daughter, Laurie Ann. The phones at CBS were tied up for hours, and special operators had to be called in to handle the hundreds of listeners' complaints about the cruel and unjust fate of the character they loved. The show's rating did not drop, however—it increased. Deep down, people were not angry at the producer of *The Edge of Night* but at the real world, which the show mirrored. No other form of art offers this education in reality—certainly not those insipid, once-a-week nighttime TV serials in which the heroes never have real trouble or wind up dead, lest the series lose its bigger-than-life character.

The snobs, those self-appointed censors of public taste, have always sneered at the soaps. On the basis of a few random samplings, a couple of highly charged emotional scenes, and a preconceived idea of "woman's stuff," critics have pooh-poohed the shows as emotional gibberish. In many cases, however, these critics are somewhat inhibited and easily offended by forthright emotionalism. But the American housewife, who has had a passion-filled love affair with the serials for more than forty-four years, knows the virtues of her daytime stories.

They've given her much. The serials have been her own special brand of entertainment; as the form has changed, she has changed. In a way, the American housewife has grown up with the soap opera. The "tune-in-tomorrow" show has offered her education, social theory, emotional support, and an appreciation for an art form whose standards of excellence have been surprisingly high, despite its purely soap-selling economic motivations and the unbelievable haste in which it must be produced. America's housewives have found great peace of mind through identification with characters like Stella Dallas of the old radio show, Joanne Tate of *Search for Tomorrow,* and the Bauers of *The Guiding Light.*

The daytime soaps were important ego-builders for women long before anyone ever heard of Women's Liberation and even before the appearance of books like *The Second Sex* or *The Feminine Mystique,* which supposedly began the Movement. Women on serials have always been portrayed as doctors, nurses, lawyers, judges, teachers, social workers, and even a senator once. The serials have helped fight the trend of putting down women in movies and especially on nighttime television, where women are portrayed as having little effect on the social order, outside of their sexual role. The average nighttime TV show shows male professionals, like Dr. Joe Gannon of *Medical Center,* or Marcus Welby, M.D., or Lt. McGarrett of *Hawaii Five-O,* undertaking all the important work, while women on these shows do all the interfering, attracting, or suffering. In fact, at this writing, not one nighttime TV series features a woman in a prominent professional role—and yet in reality the professions are filled with women.

Soaps are much more realistic on this point, as in so many other areas. On *Search for Tomorrow,* Kathy Phillips (played by Courtney Sherman) is an ambitious lawyer; Julie Franklin (Rosemary Prinz) is a psychotherapist on *How to Survive a Marriage;* and Althea Davis (Liz Hubbard) is as important a doctor as any man on *The Doctors.* A recent ABC ninety-minute afternoon play even featured a woman judge. The examples of women professionals on the serials are countless.

The serials are also more realistic in their portrayal of current problems of both sexes. *How to Survive a Marriage* is going much further than nighttime TV has ever gone in discussing such delicate subjects as male impotence, promiscuity, female masochism, the effect of divorce on children, and the so-called "swinging singles" life. *The Young and the Restless* recently performed a valuable service to its millions of viewers when it showed Chris Brooks (Trish Stewart), a young rape victim, bear witness against her attacker in court and then lose the case—for unfortunately this is exactly what happens in real life. In nine times out of ten the rapist goes free either because his victim is too ashamed to tell the police, or because the law, which is male dominated, usually favors the man. A recent nighttime TV drama, *Cry Rape!,* purported to be about the same subject (it starred Andrea Marcovicci, who played Betsy Chernak on the old *Love Is a Many Splendored Thing*). In this show, however, the whole issue of the woman's normally handicapped position in a rape trial was subverted by a cloying story of mistaken identity and the very unreal conclusion of the rapist finally being brought to justice. The rape story on *The Young and the Restless,* in which the young female victim was defeated by the system, was far more true to life.

Soap writers and producers, unlike most of their counterparts on the evening shows, are socially concerned enough to run story lines with the specific purpose of conveying socially important information to the viewers. There are many examples. On *The Guiding Light*, Bert Bauer was suspected of having vaginal cancer, and numerous discussions took place of the importance of having a Pap smear test. On *One Life to Live*, Cathy Craig became a teen-aged drug addict and was rehabilitated in real-life therapy sessions taped at Odyssey House with actual teen-aged drug addicts. Later, the same character wrote an article for the town's newspaper, *The Banner*, in which the subject of venereal disease was discussed. The viewers were asked to write in for free copies of the article, which the show's writer, Agnes Nixon, carefully researched and authored with the aim of helping people obtain necessary information on a taboo subject. The program was swamped with requests.

Social enlightenment is one thing; art is quite another. Joanne Woodward was recently asked where she thought the best acting on television was, and Miss Woodward replied, "Why, on the daytime serials. If I ever went back to television it would be on a soap." A veteran of live nighttime television in the fifties, Miss Woodward, like many other actors, recognizes that the daytime serials are the only remaining form of television that still retains the old values of the Golden Age of Television, when drama—as opposed to situation comedy or crime series—was the most important vehicle. The daytime soaps are the only form of consistently appearing drama left that is written expressly for television. Just before *As the World Turns* begins every day, announcer Dan McCullough says, "And now live for the next thirty minutes . . ." producing the same sort of excitement that *Lux Video Theater* and *Studio One* created in the fifties. One always knew then that he was going to see an ensemble of actors performing *pure drama*. Now, on nighttime TV, we are bombarded by ugly, crime-centered shows, or unfunny-funny sitcoms about spritely women who are about as real as Alice in Wonderland. But where are the old dramatic values? Where has the TV studio play gone? To daytime, of course.

Like the old dramas of the Golden Age, the serials bring forth superior acting talent and give work to accomplished actors who might otherwise have to sell out and work in dreary offices. The list of soap-opera graduates is long and impressive. On radio: Orson Welles, Macdonald Carey, Don Ameche, Van Heflin, Agnes Moorehead, Mercedes McCambridge, Jeanette Nolan, Art Carney, Gary Merrill, Paul Ford, Anne Francis, Richard Widmark, And from the televised daytime fare have emerged: Jack Lemmon, Eva Marie Saint, Tony Randall, Efrem Zimbalist, Jr., Sandy Dennis, Roy Thinnes, Beverly Garland, David Birney. The serials have made an amount of money equal to the treasury of a small Fort Knox for their sponsors and have created lively broadcasting during the day. Countries like England, which have not tried to create a serial form of afternoon broadcasting for people at home, have either a nonexistent or an impoverished form of daytime broadcasting.

Yet despite these virtues and achievements, the daytime soap opera has, in the past, been more maligned and undervalued than any other form of entertainment—with the possible exception of hard-core pornography. Campaigns against the soaps have been unending. Back in the old radio days, a New Rochelle women's club announced a We-Don't-Listen-to-Serials-Week, with numerous other "socially conscious" women's clubs quickly following suit, claiming that the fifteen-minute programs were psychologically dangerous for housewives. A New York novelist-psychiatrist caused a maelstrom of criticism and countercriticism that almost amounted to a war, when, in 1942, he published a widely publicized report on the serials: "Pandering to perversity," he said, "and playing out destructive conflicts, these serials furnish the same release for the emotionally distorted that is supplied to those who desire satisfaction from a lynching bee, lick their lips at the salacious scandals of the *crime passionel,* and who in the unregretted past cried out in ecstasy at witch burnings." He also accused the serials of causing such awesome physical symptoms as "tachycardia, arithmias, increase in blood pressure, profuse perspiration, tremors, vasomotor instability, nocturnal frights, vertigo, and gastro-intestinal disturbances."

James Thurber once told the story of a certain Clinton, Iowa, husband who dashed across his living room and smashed the family radio with his fists, having finally gotten fed up with the daytime serials his wife listened to hourly, only to be fined ten dollars for disturbing the peace and later sued for divorce by his indignant wife. In recent years David Susskind has been energetically throwing all kinds of criticism at the serials, saying, for example, "Soaps are all dismal and tacky. They're beneath intelligent notice. I hope they're all canceled and fade away." Even David Frost, who attempted to cash in on the popularity of the programs by presenting on his talk show six big serial stars—Eileen Fulton, Mary Stuart, Don Stewart, the late Ed Zimmermann, Ruth Warrick, and Jim Pritchett—could hide neither his ignorance nor his before-the-fact distaste for the shows. It's no understatement. The soap operas have suffered.

However, that word is most assuredly in the past tense. Suffer*ed*. Over the past few years the climate of opinion toward the shows has definitely been changing. For the first time in its entire forty-four-year history, the daytime serials have begun to be treated by the press and the non-listening public with a degree of understanding, sympathy, and even praise. Before 1968, little was written in magazines and newspapers about the soaps, and whatever did appear was both snide and condescending. Such scant treatment of a medium that was watched and evidently liked by more than twenty million people on a daily basis seemed unexplainable. Even *TV Guide,* which tries unrelentingly to like anything TV has to offer, was running superior little pieces about how soaps were earning lots of money for their producers but not adding much to cultural development.

Suddenly, within a matter of months, the tide started to change. The same formerly antiserial *TV Guide* began doing stories on how hard it was to act on a serial, how relevant the serial stories were, and how interesting and talented were their actors. Among the many *TV Guide*

profiles that appeared on the soap stars were ones on
Jonathan Frid, Joan Bennett, Jada Rowland, Laryssa
Lauret, Liz Hubbard, and Millette Alexander. Within a
year or so the friendly attitude toward the afternoon
shows had spread, and almost every magazine and newspaper began running favorable articles, often by writers
who knew little about the medium and had to do some
quick homework at their TV screens and in the TV
studios before being able to tell their readers—who probably knew the daytime stories, if they were housewives,
even better than the writers themselves—all about the
sudsy scenes. Even the supercultured *New Yorker,* which
hadn't run a piece on the serials since James Thurber did
his famous six-part study, "Soapland," back in the forties,
thought it wise to run a favorable piece by avid serial-
watcher/writer Renata Adler.

In 1969, about a year after most of these dramatic
changes in attitude took place, several monthly fan magazines devoted entirely to daytime television dramas and
their actors were launched. Their number soon grew to
five, and they are still thriving, distributing to subscribers
and magazine newsstands two million copies per month of
daytime-crammed material. Said Paul Dennis, editor of
Daytime TV: "New magazines on the soaps keep coming
out and we're so afraid that we'll all burn ourselves out.
But the strange thing is that no matter how many new
magazines come out on the newsstands, the circulations
keep going up, not down, pointing out to me that there's
really no limit to the interest people have in the subject."

In the past few years network and sponsor budgets for
afternoon fiction programing have skyrocketed beyond
all previous expectations. The viewer who started watching *As the World Turns* no more than six years ago,
and who still watches, must certainly be awed by the lavish sets the show now sports, and by the many expensive
outdoor sequences employed. All the shows have followed
similar patterns. Salaries have also soared. Where at one
time it may not have been particularly prestigious to appear on a serial, but necessary to pay the bills, it is now the
desire of almost every actor in New York. And it's not

only the promise of a yearly salary of $50,000 to $100,-000 that lures these actors (Rosemary Prinz reportedly received $750 a day on *As the World Turns*); the new star status that daytime actors have been enjoying of late helps to sweeten the pot. This new status came so swiftly, in fact, that most serial actors were unprepared for it. Eileen Fulton tells of how, after marrying her record producer, Danny Fortunato, in what she thought was a secret hilltop ceremony, an item appeared the next day in Earl Wilson's widely read news column, and then, two days later, ABC-TV's six o'clock and eleven o'clock news announced, "On a rainy, North Carolina hilltop, Eileen Fulton, *As the World Turns'* Lisa Hughes, married record man Danny Fortunato." After the announcement, Miss Fulton and her new husband sat on their living room sofa too stunned to talk.

There were many others besides the ever-popular Miss Fulton who might never have even considered fame but who suddenly had to face their new public image.

Emily McLaughlin always tells the story of how, before the tragic death of her movie-star husband, Jeff Hunter, some years ago, she and Jeff would walk down the street and it would always be she was was accosted by people calling her by her character's name, Jessie Brewer (*General Hospital*). Somehow the people either did not recognize Jeff or were too timid to talk to him. After all, as a movie star Jeff was bigger than life, but as a serial star, Emily was just one of the family. And famous.

Moreover, hardly five or six years ago, magazine interviewers meeting the actors were made to feel as if they were entering the confines of some secret society whose high priests and members all knew "the right way" but, because no one else knew it, feared persecution. Actors would confess how insecure they felt in the world in which they worked—too many of their friends considered it a second-rate way to make money. That was especially true if they had spent much time out in Hollywood, where the very mention of soap operas would cause a loud guffaw and an ironic, whimsical glance. At the same time, while being insecure, these same actors told of a real emotional involvement with the shows on which they appeared. *Another World*'s former Rachel of four years' standing, Robin Strasser, discussed how much of a challenge it was for her to go to the NBC studio every day to portray "a bitch without equal," someone as different from herself as she could imagine. "There's a part of me, though, that really is like Rachel, and acting on the show is the only way I can let her out into the open." Robin's own husband, Larry Luckinbill—an ex-daytime serial actor who now does TWA commercials—wrote a piece for the *New York Times* referring to his own work on soaps as little more than prostitution of his talents and went around telling all of his fellow actors to beware of the "easy soap money." To that common charge (but not specifically to Larry), George Reinholt, who still plays Steven Frame on Robin's old show, responded: "I love my soap, and I'm tired of defending what I do to the bigots, the people who put it all down. I work very hard, and I'm proud of the fact that millions of people believe in my character. But when I'm around most groups I don't even bother talking about it."

Almost all soap actors wish more people would understand how much closer they've felt toward their audiences since appearing on daytime television serials. It isn't all that difficult to see how a Judy Garland, who herself thrived on the love and closeness of her audiences, could feel sympathy for all such relationships and could join millions of housewives in her attachment to afternoon fare.

But the serial actors' attitudes were once secret, hidden, never confessed openly but only revealed semi-apologetically to a few reporters in the dark shadows of lavish living rooms or the exclusive temples of murky restaurants. Five or six years ago, that is—before the avalanche of magazine articles in *Life, Look, TV Guide, The New Yorker, Show, Pageant, People, After Dark,* and before the two million or so monthly issues of daytime television fan magazines were published, making people like George Reinholt and Susan Flannery major celebrities in the fan publishing world. "All the magazines want to talk to me and photograph me," George Reinholt said recently. "And I'm not even handsome! What's happened to soap operas?" What's happened is that the serials have gone *public,* even for the public that couldn't watch if it wanted to. Everyone knows about them now or has heard the names of some of the stars, if only from reading about them or seeing their names emblazoned across the covers of newsstand magazines.

Actors no longer talk about why they like being on a serial "even though . . ." Viewers no longer sound defensive in their letters, but expose their addiction openly and happily. Today viewers' curiosity about the stars of the serials, the stories of the shows before they began watching, the behind-the-scenes activities, and all kinds of *serialiana* is boundless. It is this curiosity that has produced this book, which will show the whole panorama of the world of the daytime serial—from what happens off-screen to what has happened on-screen since the shows began.

❧ II ❧

Live Tape!

ONE OF THE first things that strikes a viewer about the incredible world of afternoon serials is the absolutely Herculean feat of producing an original, half-hour dramatic show *every day*. During the Golden Age of Television, the Fabulous Fifties—when nighttime viewers watched original television plays on *Studio One, Philco Playhouse, Armstrong Circle Theater, Danger, Lights Out!, Lux Video Theater,* and myriad others—daytime viewers were also watching live TV drama on *Love of Life, Search for Tomorrow, The Guiding Light,* and *As the World Turns,* to name a few. Since all of these shows originated from New York, a number of actors shuttled between the nighttime and daytime programs. But in general, few performers who had the good fortune to work steadily in nighttime TV were willing to work on the daytime serials. Not that they were snobs, or thought themselves too talented for the soaps—it was just common knowledge that when you worked on serials your whole existence became a ceaseless uphill struggle. This was the toughest kind of television. Veteran Golden Age actress Georgann Johnson, who's now seen almost daily as Ellen Grant on *Somerset,* would never do a daytime serial before that one was offered to her several years ago. "Actors used to be terrified of them," she recalls. "You have no idea how hard one

14

has to work on a soap. I remember on *Kraft* or *Philco,* we'd have a whole week of rehearsals just to do a one-hour live show. We'd do our scenes over and over; learning lines was never a problem. On a daytime serial, you've got to do all your rehearsing and camera-blocking and polishing in one day. People don't realize how hard soap actors have to work—if only they could see how we spend our day."

In the wee morning hours of semidarkness, a dozen actors arrive at a big television studio right smack in the wilds of residential Brooklyn. Actually, the building looks like an abandoned junk warehouse, and the performers resemble sleepwalkers about to bump into one another at any second. Inside, one floor below an elaborate maze of corridors and offices, they all huddle around a big coffee urn, mumble a few words of greeting, take bites out of danishes, and fall comatose into plain wooden chairs.

Who are these sleepy people? Theoretically, they are the residents of *Another World*'s Bay City, who come into millions of homes each day at three in the afternoon, bringing with them their internecine conflicts, their strong personalities, and their untiring concern and matchless wisdom. At the moment, however, they look more like groggy displaced persons. This *couldn't* be brilliant lawyer John Randolph who, with baggy pants and tousled hair, is slouched silently in a corner reading a paper—one feels like offering poor Mike Ryan a quarter. And as Beverly Penberthy's long, lovely hair falls over her face and dangles precariously over her coffee, it's hard to see how this droopy flower will ever be transformed into John's talkative wife, Pat Randolph. Connie Ford, who plays Ada Downs, looks as if she hadn't slept all night, and Gil Dolph Sweet, her on-screen husband, looks just as tired. Victoria Wyndham, who plays troublemaker Rachel, is too foggy-eyed to cause a flea any trouble, and George Reinholt is too giddy with morning playfulness ever to be convincing as austere businessman Steven Frame.

And yet these adroit actors, untimely ripped from their beds, within hours will become those characters who are instantly recognizable to millions across the land—when, as if by magic, man-made magic, another well-planned, -produced, and -executed episode emerges from all this studio confusion.

Down in the colorless rehearsal room, aided by coffee and a clever director named Ira Cirker, the actors go through two hours of their first rehearsal—called a "dry run" because there are no props or scenery. Constance Ford has to pour Dolph Sweet an imaginary cup of coffee and go through the motions of opening phantom kitchen cupboards, like a child playing house. Mike Ryan has to ring an imaginary bell, and James Douglas, who plays Eliot Carrington, has to look toward a place on the wall that represents a bug on the bookshelf—"bug", meaning the kind the Watergate Seven first got caught trying to repair (by now at least two soaps have shown characters bugging one another). During this inhumanly early first rehearsal, most of the actors stumble over their lines or read directly from the scripts; for, despite having studied their lines the night before, the words aren't yet committed to memory. The movements and stage business with props are awkward and choppy. At this juncture it would seem that only an act of God could help the actors get all the words and motions smoothly assembled by tape time, some five hours later.

While the rehearsal is continuing in a subterranean cell without cups or sofas or bugs, the equipment lacking downstairs is being furiously hoisted about upstairs in a super-huge auditoriumlike studio. Tables and chairs and all sorts of food for the refrigerator are being carried into Ada's three-walled kitchen by technicians—the men who do all the work of physically assembling the serial homes, according to the instructions of the director and the scenic designer. The pace of carting objects, snapping up cables, and setting up booms is always hysterically quick because everyone knows that the actors must rehearse their lines again in the finished sets by 10:30 A.M., when the camera angles are first set up, a step called "camera blocking." Delays of mere minutes in setting up the scenery can cost the sponsor plenty. And so while the actors bump into each other downstairs and try to recall and repeat the words they studied the night before, the hustle of prop assemblage continues upstairs.

Although most television studios operate in this way, there's an extraspecial urgency on the set of a continuing daytime serial. There's an extra madness. To an outsider, it all looks like the superbusy and supersinister lair of a James Bond villian. The director sits in the control room staring at dozens of dancing TV screens, while in the next room a hundred henchmen are darting about, fooling with the objects of an advanced technology, deftly setting up Phase IV before the final phase . . . or is it the final act. . . ?

Back in the underground rehearsal cell, there's just been a snag. During the dry run for Act 1 (each of the five-minute segments between one-minute commercials are called "acts"), Eliot Carrington has discovered the hidden microphone and must fool it by telling John Randolph absurd things about his sister-in-law, Alice Matthews. John is furious and says upon departing: "I'd rather be naive than a dishonorable philanderer!" There's general smirking over the line. " 'Philanderer' was what my father called me when I was cheating on Pat," laughs Mike Ryan. "He said, 'I thought I brought you up better than that!' "

"It sounds like 1817," quips George Reinholt, who asks what this scene is about anyway. George has just arrived after an hour and a half on the subway. He is dressed in red mod shirt and bell-bottom trousers. Director Ira Cirker quickly explains that the show being taped today takes place eight days ahead of the one done the day before to accomodate the availability of some of the actors. There's agreement all around and Mike Ryan's line is changed to: "I'd rather be naive than dishonorable." Later, George Reinholt comments aside: "I wouldn't say a line like that, and the producers know it."

There's some more rewording of the script by the actors and director. In Act 3, Mike Ryan must remark to Bev Penberthy, concerning her request to talk about his new hostility toward Eliot Carrington: "I'm not going to spoil our lunch by discussing a man I detest!" Mike can't resist playing the line for laughs, and he starts gesturing as if he were a silent-movie hero condemning a foe. Everyone thinks it's hilarious. "So terrrrrr-ibly arch," says George. "We'll have to change that," says Ira. "How about to, 'a man I hate'?" offers Mike Ryan. "Or maybe just to, 'that man.' " Ira agrees.

All through the two-hour dry run, the actors are cutting up like mad. At the end of the scene in which John Randolph storms out of Eliot Carrington's den in a fury, Eliot (James Douglas) mimes a kiss meant for John. Later, Dolph Sweet, who has to offer to take Connie Ford to dinner, objects that with all the dining out they've been doing "the goddamn bills are running up!" But Ira solves the problem by telling Dolph that Gil and Ada go to cheap Bay City restaurants. Later, the director, not to be outdone by his clever actors, reads the whole cast a clipping he got from the Sunday *Times* about an Australian parrot who sat and watched all the soaps from his cage the whole day. He loved them all, but during *Another World* he began squalking in absolute ecstasy.

Such are the goings-on during the propless first rehearsals of the day. The attitude of the actors and the director toward the serious story material may be less than reverent—but all that cutting up is strictly on the surface. The actors are indulging in some comic relief before their professional stamina as actors on a continuing serial is strained nearly to the breaking point. Behind all the silly jokes is the fear, the absolute dread, that their performances will be less than perfect while millions of people watch—the fear that whole speeches will be forgotten, or a cue or a movement will be missed, while the videotape machine mercilessly grinds away.

The director knows that his power to guide his actors through five hours of preparation for a finished performance on the same day is strictly limited. He can set the tones for the style of scenes, correct details, tell an actor that he's overplaying something, but he cannot tell an actor *how* to learn to do a performance in a matter of hours. Besides, he has other things to worry about—so many things, in fact, that most shows have at least two directors to handle the burden. On *Another World,* the directors—Ira Cirker and Melvin Bernhardt—alternate one week apiece. But like any other director of a daytime serial, they must have the patience of a lion tamer, the endurance of an Olympic runner, the creativity of a Tom O'Horgan, and the tact of a politician.

Summed up, the director's job is to decide how scenes are to be played, what sort of props are to be used, what kind of music will be played, and the most important matters of how the actors are to move about and how the cameras are to photograph them. It all looks so simple, even ridiculously easy, when you see the televised episode. But every camera shot, and every single movement, with the corresponding words in the script, have to be drawn by the director on an elaborate map of the sets that are to be used. All this "blocking" is given to the studio technicians—the audio men, the technical director, the lighting director—as soon as the director arrives in the morning. So, in terms of homework, the director has almost as much work to do on a script as the writer.

"Every director works differently," says Ira Cirker, a wiry, aesthetic-looking man. "Some directors wait until the night before a show to do all their work. Since I alternate weeks with another director, I prefer to use my week off to work on all my scripts for the following week."

Although soap-opera directors make a great deal of money, anywhere from $50,000 a year to more than twice that amount, there are probably some who sneer at their work and laugh all the way to the bank. But truly dedicated men like Cirker do not operate that way. He says, "I like directing serials. They're like long novels. The long, drawn-out pacing makes them a great challenge." His counterpart on *Love of Life,* Larry Auerbach, who started with the show way back when it began in 1951, says, "Obviously I wouldn't be directing one show this long unless I got pleasure out of my work. There are other things a director can do to make money."

To work well with his actors, a daytime serial director like Ira Cirker tries to be sensitive to what they like or don't like about the lines they're reading, as in the scene described above. If someone objects, for example, that his recap material (dialogue meant to tell the viewers what happened on previous shows, in case any were missed) is too much like yesterday's recap, the director often allows the actor to rewrite his own lines. All soaps permit this, the reasoning being that much of the dialogue is custom-written for a particular actor's style of acting, anyway. If certain lines do not suit his own behavior patterns, why not change them for the sake of believability?

While Ira Cirker has already done a great deal of work in preparing the episode now in production, including his extensive homework and the two hours of dry rehearsal, he knows these are but skirmishes compared to the major battles yet to be fought and won. All this lackadaisical atmosphere will soon dissolve into a fearful condition-red! The director is deliberately saving his energies for the ordeal ahead.

Meanwhile, as the dry run comes all too quickly to an end—each actor has by now gone through his lines twice for the director—the quiet hysteria of men assembling equipment in the upstairs studio grows in amplitude until there is a steady roar of back-and-forth shouting. Eventually—as if by some higher plan not visible on the immediate scene—all the booms are in place, with one soundman sitting on each and another carrying it around, and all the dangerous-looking cables are properly plugged in and pushed out of the way.

Eventually—ta *tum!*—the actors arrive, looking worse than before, if that is possible. The men have a particularly lost, wrinkly-browed look—maybe because they've been napping for the last fifteen minutes in their dressing rooms on the floor above. The women appear top-heavy with huge pin-rollers in their hair. All the actors are forever looking about, waiting to be told what to do next by someone in authority. And out of this muck—this chaos of half-learned lines and movements, of crisscrossing cables and too many arms and legs—must come a finished and polished half-hour dramatic episode in a matter of hours. The weight of that reality would cause anyone's brow to wrinkle.

Finally, the three television cameras—those three Cyclops' eyes, which bring millions upon millions of soap-opera addicts into various homes in Bay City—are put into place. Each of these twentieth-century miracles is operated by a genius indecorously known as the cameraman. He should more properly be known as a *photographer ne plus ultra.* Everything the viewer sees is framed and focused by him, according to what the director tells him through his earphones. What could happen to the most ardent scenes of a Victoria Wyndham or a Jacquie Courtney without good camera-work was evidenced a few years ago when CBS cameramen went on strike, and the most poignant soap-opera scenes were wrecked by exposed booms and haywire focus.

Now comes the part of the soap opera day when everything the director planned must suddenly come together for the first time. And a first effort it seems. The director sits in the control booth, from where he watches the set on three TV screens—each one a different camera angle—while his assistant helps the actors coordinate their words and movements with camera movements. It's nip and tuck, and this is perhaps the one process that makes serial performing the roughest of all media. For not only are the actors required to commit to memory pages of dialogue in one day, but they must also immediately learn on which line, and often which *word,* they are to make specific movements—such as crossing to a refrigerator, picking up a cup, or walking around a sofa. On these particular words or lines, the cameramen are cued to come in for a close-up or to move back for a long shot; or perhaps another camera will pick up the scene from a different angle. It can ruin a scene if an actor forgets a cue line, or faces the wrong way when he says it. Should that happen, the camera might be forced to shoot out into the studio.

Incidentally, actors who are particularly good with props are always assigned lots of busy-work with them, especially in kitchens. Viewers love the idea that the characters in a story behave in a familiar way in their own kitchens. "Connie Ford has a reputation around here for being an excellent prop actress," says Virginia Dwyer, who plays Mary Matthews. "Everyone respects her for it."

At this point in the day, the actors seem to be a pack of rats on a treadmill, trying to get someplace they're never going to reach. They don't seem to know their lines *or* their movements, and in just three hours everything must be perfect! Constance Ford is tearing her hair out because she turned a fraction of an instant too soon before she said, "Look Gil . . ." Dolph Sweet slams the table in anger when he realizes that he forgot to lift his cup high enough for the camera to get a better shot of Ada pouring coffee. In the control booth, the director stops everything while the technicians try to locate the source of some unidentified foreign noise, and he later dickers with the assistant director over how to get the cameraman to make a clearer shot of the bookshelf bug that the audience is supposed to see. By now, any outside observer's head would be spinning.

Compounding the tension, each and every actor on *Another World* is nervously aware that he is rehearsing to perform on "live" tape—that is, the director is not going to order the tape stopped for a retake if a line is flubbed; if he did, the show would never get off the ground. It's just too expensive to stop tape, so an actor knows that his lousy performance, or his mistake, will be heard and seen by an audience larger than any stage actor could dream of. So the soap actor, like Avis, tries harder.

No wonder daytime serial casting directors try to hire only actors and directors skilled in this kind of roughhouse work, and no wonder actors who are on heavily for a few weeks start quietly talking about seeing psychiatrists or doing Broadway plays again. There are horror stories of countless well-known Hollywood actors, like Jan Sterling and Troy Donahue, having to give up their daytime serial roles in utter desperation.

Toward the end of camera-blocking, before run-through, Paul Rauch enters—without fanfare or drum roll. But in the adrenalin-activated minds of each actor on *Another*

World, there is a silent orchestral introduction as he enters the taping studio for the first time, for he is the unquestioned King. He is the Executive Producer. And that means that he is the one man, besides the sponsor way far away in the Never-Never Land of Cincinnati, who can say yes or no to all the pent-up requests and can deal with the urgent complaints of the actors. He'll tell Victoria Wyndham whether she can have a week off in a few months, or George Reinholt if he'll have to shorten his fashionably long hairstyle, or Jacquie Courtney if he'd be willing to junk the whole last act of the show because it'll make her character, Alice, look ridiculous. When Paul Rauch walks into the studio, he comes in with an invisible aura of authority around him. He's the Great White Father, and all the actors instantly dart their eyes in his direction.

Soap producers are exceedingly powerful, and they come in all types and with diverse natures. Many achieve their results by being harsh and demanding. Paul Rauch is the exact opposite—he is Mr. Pleasant, Mr. Tact. All the actors on *Another World* offer a chorus of praise for the sensitive way he handles them and their problems. And he is the most *unlikely*-looking person for the important job of executive producer of a daytime serial. A handsome man in his early forties, he has deliberately made himself "now"-looking with the kind of contemporary hairdo and moustache that barbers like to picture in their windows. The improbable look suits him, for he impresses everybody as having a temperament in a constant state of restlessness; the electricity he throws off attracts actors like millet attracts birds.

"Paul Rauch understands the importance of the intuitive instincts of the actor," states George Reinholt, in one of his typical professorial outbursts. "Paul treats us very fairly," says Victoria Thompson, who plays Janice Frame. "He gives us a lot of freedom to try new things out all the time." Nick Coster, who plays Robert Delaney, chimes in that Paul was once an actor himself, and it shows in the way he treats his colleagues. "And besides," says Nick, "he's just an incredible person. He drove me to work one morning and he kept rattling off all these German names of Mahler's art songs. Now how many people know the names of Mahler's art songs?"

Paul lives alone and dates actresses—"I used to be married ... but I let myself get too fat." He spends a good part of the morning at home, for he thinks more clearly there, and much of his time is spent going over script ideas with the show's gifted head writer, Harding Lemay. Pete—Harding's nickname—and Paul telephone each other constantly to discuss the script. Actually, what Paul does is what any producer of a soap does: he represents the sponsor and in so doing makes the ultimate decisions on how the program will look. All the smaller parts of putting together a show—like the writer's grinding out daily dialogue, or the director's daily struggle with camera angles and dramatic style, or the actor's rewriting of his own lines to make them more comfortable to him—do not get the producer's attention. He comes into the studio in the late morning and the first time he sees or hears the day's show is when he watches the run-through in front of the cameras. At that time, if he doesn't like something, he tells the director.

Most important, the producer sets the *style* for a soap. Paul, for example, has been encouraging Harding Lemay to develop his characters psychologically, employing long, slow looks at certain characters. Many serial producers are afraid to use this technique, however, for fear of boring their audiences with a lack of action and story devices— murders, trials, sudden amnesia, etc. Also, with Paul Rauch and Pete Lemay collaborating on the show's style, a character like Rachel, who at one point was strictly the villainess-troublemaker of Bay City, has ever-so-slowly been gaining more and more of the viewers' sympathies. The tears she sheds now are absolutely real. Viewers these days don't know whether to love her or hate her, so they simply shake their heads and feel sorry for Rachel, as well as for all the trouble she makes for other people. This was a drastic change for *Another World,* and one that only the producer and writer could have made in concert.

There are other matters that are solely Paul Rauch's

province. About two years ago, right after Pat and John Randolph were reconciled, and Steve and Rachel were about to marry, Paul decided to transfer almost half of his cast to a setting in St. Croix by using a complicated "blue-screen" method—that is, taping the actors in bathing suits against a screen that contained an on-going film of a St. Croix beach. "It was expensive as hell," says Nick Coster. "Paul could have just decided to send all the characters to New York or something. But he liked the exotic setting of a tropical beach and he asked the sponsor for permission to do it. Paul's got imagination."

Some time after, when George Reinholt and Jacquie Courtney were to do an emotion-drenched scene involving the reconciliation of Alice and Steve after a stormy separation lasting almost a year, Paul absolutely proved his mettle as a producer. Right after the run-through, Paul told the actors there would be *no dress rehearsal!* He wanted them to tape the scene immediately. Jacquie objected —she said she needed more rehearsal time. Paul knew better. He also called Cincinnati and asked Procter and Gamble if he could rearrange the commercials so that he could run the whole ten-minute meeting between the characters—for which viewers had been waiting on pins and needles for months and months—without a pause and without even a prologue. During taping, Jacquie acted her heart out. Almost every throat in the studio was choked up as Alice struggled to hold back tears. Harding Lemay had written an absolutely gorgeous scene involving emotional complexities that could be communicated only through certain key words, pauses, and looks. After the scene was carried off without dress rehearsal, Jacquie Courtney exhaled and said, smiling in her girlish way, "You were right, Paul. I could never have gotten it all up again for taping." Only the cleverest of soap producers could have figured out such a way of telling the audience that *the* electric moment in the story had arrived.

And only the most talented and dedicated of actors could have pulled off that most difficult and arduous scene a mere three hours after its first rehearsal and at exactly the moment the producer had asked for it. When Paul

Rauch first came to *Another World* a few years ago with all his new ideas—he had never produced a soap before—he was fortunate indeed to have inherited an extremely lively, sensitive, and creative cast that responded instantly to his and Pete Lemay's concept of turning the show into psychological or "inner drama." And, naturally, whenever you have real talent, you also have "temperament."

"When I started on *Another World*," admits Victoria Thompson, who recently turned up in Bay City as Steven Frame's wandering sister, Janice, "I wondered if all these little personal conflicts I saw between the members of the cast were typical of other serials. This was my first, you see. Then a few actors told me that it wasn't typical—that *Another World* was somehow different. So many of the people on our show seem to me to be high-strung. Maybe that's because they're so talented."

Temperament shows up on the show in other ways too. Jacquie Courtney has a reputation among fan-magazine editors for considering herself "too good" to give out interviews. Yet this is but a facet of her talent-temperament, for Jacquie's abilities as an actress leave one breathless. She's been portraying Alice Matthews ever since she was sixteen; but only in the last five years—because Agnes Nixon (who used to write *Another World*), decided to involve her in a major love triangle (with Steven Frame and Rachel Davis)—have viewers become aware of her uniquely compelling sensibilities as a performer. "Jacquie feels every single little thing she does right down to her toes," says her on-screen mother, Virginia Dwyer, who also admits to having been a kind of backstage mother for her ever since the show began. In real life Jacquie is as oversensitive and vulnerable as Alice and often is hurt by the inevitable backstage politics and personality clashes.

George Reinholt, on the other hand, is unique in serialland in that he *doesn't* play himself. His performances as the selfish, love-torn businessman Steven Frame are artifice, sheer acting. About this extraordinarily complicated and brilliant young man, his one-time fellow co-star on *Another World*, Val Dufour (who played Walter Curtin), recently said: "His sensitivity is well hidden, but it's there all the same. He has a low level of pain, perhaps because he had been terribly hurt at one time. He offers his trust to very few, especially to anyone who is older than he. He is utterly outspoken, and yet he is a great and receptive listener. He has a marvelous sense of humor and will laugh a very long time at a very small thing and will continue to laugh as long as it is repeated. He laughs until he cries. He can be a clown. His movements and facial expressions are very animal-like, especially when he doesn't know he's being observed—a cub, a fawn, a bear . . ."

Although Victoria Wyndham can at times be as snappy and cold as her character, Rachel—"There's something in me that understands her grasping nature. I too have often felt a desperate need for things that I knew I could never have."—her first appearance on the show, several years ago, had an incredibly positive influence on everyone. Her accomplishment in helping to breathe life into Harding Lemay's refocusing of the scripts toward psychological dilemmas cannot be overpraised.

With the exceptions of the outright villains, the actors on *Another World,* as well as on the other serials, play themselves. It's much easier for the writers and actors to produce half-hour dramas every day, year in and year out, if the actors do not have to worry about *inventing* personality and character. However, because of the sensitivity and temperament of the actors on *Another World,* some of the performers carry their roles to an extreme. For example, Victoria Thompson finds it incredible that she "relates to the other actors on the show according to how my character relates to their characters! I find, for example, that I'm drawn to George Reinholt, my brother on the show, and to Vicky Wyndham and Nick Coster, whom I'm supposed to love in the story—but not to Susan Sullivan, who plays my rival, 'Lenore'. In fact, we're a little cold toward one another."

Producer Paul Rauch has taken all the electric ego-charges and routed them into the right circuits. His way of encouraging and channeling the spontaneous creativity of his writer and his actors has brought the show's ratings up from the bottom five of the Nielsen Ratings to the very top of the mark. "I've got an ego too, you know," he remarks.

Paul goes to the monitor in his office to watch the dress rehearsal, the point at which the actors are in costume and the show actually starts to resemble a finished product. For the first time, the sound effects are put in—doorbells, telephones, radios. Miraculously, the performers now say their lines without reading from a script or asking to be given cues. When and how did they ever get it all straight? "It just happens by osmosis." says a bystander. "Suddenly you just know your lines and your movements." The cameras, too, seem to be well choreographed —no more screaming for booms to be higher or lower.

But there's still much confusion and panic over minor problems as the intensity of the mood deepens. More people join the cast of workers. In the control booth, the assistant producer, Mary Bonner, joins director Ira Cirker and aids him by taking notes while a production assistant times scenes to the second with a stopwatch. Ira's assistant sits next to him and talks to the studio crew and cameramen through microphones, while Ira listens to it all through his earphones. There's a panicky rush of jargon flowing from all directions into the control booth's microphones: *cut, fade, cue, dissolve, close-up, stretch.* Ira, ordinarily composed, suddenly appears to have an attack of apoplexy. Chris Allport, who plays Tim McGowan, is fooling around with a briefcase during a scene—obviously wrong. "Why *can't* that kid ever remember a thing he's told!" yells Ira, slamming a palm onto the control-booth counter. "Look, make a note. Tell Vicky Wyndham she's got to pause a little longer before she walks out the door—and there's that humming again! Haven't we found the cause of it yet? Tell Mike Ryan that he's still overplaying that scene!"

The atmosphere in the control booth gets heavy with outbursts of temper and displays of expertise. Hands wave wildly about in exasperation, chests exude great gobs of pent-up air. The actors in front of the cameras are no less anxious. But it's their job to keep all the anxiety beneath the surface while the merciless television cameras come in for relentless close-ups, probing eyes for the glow of character-sincerity, mouths for the changing shapes that represent a character's proper reactions to spoken words. Actors must get used to the fact that at times the camera is but a foot away from their faces. They must neither show an awareness of it nor any discomfort, and of course they must remember their lines—if they don't, they can always try to steal a glance at the teleprompter. It's this nerve-wracking nature of the whole process that, ironically, helps actors do their best work.

Right after dress, Ira Cirker meets with his actors someplace in the building—perhaps the make up room—and presents each one with his own very special present: a note, a critical remark about what an actor is doing wrong that must be corrected during taping. Chris Allport promises not to hide Dolph Sweet's face. Dolph swears that he won't throw the newspapers around so much during the breakfast scene. Victoria Wyndham says she is already aware that she was hiding Chris Allport's face during dress, and Mike Ryan had a feeling he was overplaying the scene and will tone it down. It's all quick and congenial, and no one really cares about who is standing in front of whom, anyway, just so the final performance is smooth and wondrous.

And it usually is! Suddenly, after spending a whole day at the studio, from eight in the morning until four in the afternoon, one realizes what all this has been for. Millions of people will see Rachel's tears and Ada's maternal concern, and they too will become involved—they too will delight in art and in the life that it reflects.

Soon after taping is finished, all the actors leave the studio and the technicians begin to wrap up their work and put the cameras to bed, so to speak, while the staff finishes up in their offices. The work of adding one more episode of *Another World* to the 2,342 already finished is over. Suddenly all attention shifts to the next day's show, but talk about that can wait until the following morning.

One last surge of activity takes place—this one a pleasure for the actors and their hungry egos. A band of teen-agers waits outside the NBC studio door on Avenue M: "Steve Frame?" "Yes, that's right—how are you?" "Oh, I watch you every day . . . would you sign this? My mother's going to be just wild when she sees it!" Off go the teen-agers. The actors, as they leave in taxis, limousines, autos, act as if it were midnight, not four o'clock in the afternoon with at least another seven hours left before bedtime. They head straight home to throw their tired bodies into the arms of husbands and wives, to have a bite to eat, to kiss the children—and to start all over again studying scripts for the next day's show.

⋖§ III §⋗

The Bauers—
On and Off Screen Since 1937

IN ALL THEIR thirty-five years before the American public, the Bauers never looked as happy. They were being saluted by their proud sponsor, Procter and Gamble, which had helped keep word of the Bauers' joys and heartbreaks—births, deaths, marriages, divorces, misunderstandings, terrors, and love affairs—in a surprising number of American homes since 1937. It was a gala party atop the Hilton Hotel, attended by everyone connected with the show, including the lady who credited it, Irna Phillips. Champagne bubbled, photogs clicked, food platters were passed, and the old guard and the new generation of *The Guiding Light*'s "family" happily mingled. Finally, after the cake cutting, P&G's spokesman, Richard Muma, addressed a group of about sixty, reviewing the lives of some of its oldest actors:

"... First, Theo Goetz. It's been a lot different here from that Russian concentration camp, hasn't it, Theo? Back in 1938 ..."

Theo listened at the back of the room, unassuming as usual. He was seventy-seven now, wondering in his humble way why he was even still on the show. "Every time my contract comes up for renewal I figure it's time for me

31

to retire, but they always talk me out of it. How much longer can I *last*?" Theo Goetz, who died less than a year after that celebration, has become a soap-opera legend. He was the first of the Bauers, the patriarch—"Papa Bauer"—and at the time, he had been on the show longer than any other actor. So proud of him was Procter and Gamble—he became a symbol of the endurance of *The Guiding Light*—that he was brought to Cincinnati by the sponsor and wined, dined, and interviewed until he could hardly move. He was after all, already in his seventies. To his interviewers, this beloved old man always said, "God wanted me to be Papa Bauer."

Richard Muma's voice came up again: ". . . and Charita Bauer. She auditioned for the radio show in 1950, when we were still a fifteen-minute radio show, and to our delight, she has been with us ever since."

Charita, a short, handsome woman, sporting her classic, bedimpled Bert Bauer smile, hardly looked old enough to convince anyone that she had spent the last twenty-four years learning daily scripts for a daytime serial. Soon, with the imminent death of Theo Goetz, she was to become the show's most important person—the only Bauer left from the old radio show, the only real connection remaining between the *now* and the *then*. Said Bruce Cox of Compton Advertising, P&G's producer for this show, "Charita's all we've got now . . . and we're going to take *very* good care of her."

"Now we come to Irna Phillips," Muma went on. "Where would we have been without her? She conceived the show in 1937 and wrote it for years." Irna—a neat, dignified-looking woman of sixty-eight, who was often cited as *the* most important famous serial writer before and after her death some two years later—radiated. *The Guiding Light*, after all, was her first successful daytime television serial. Had it not been for her success in transferring this soap from radio to television, she might not have gone on to create *As the World Turns,* her next TV success, or *Another World,* her third.

Richard Muma was now singling out: Lucy Rittenberg, the producer, associated with *The Guiding Light* almost since the first day it began on television, and the one person who has helped keep the Bauers "in character"— "She'd yell to high heaven," said a Comptom executive, "whenever a Bauer was called upon by a writer to do something a Bauer would *never* do.".; and Fossie Richards, the wardrobe mistress, who has been keeping all the Bauers and their Springfield friends in respectable attire for nearly two decades; and Ed Mitchell, the set designer, who would always give the show his special homey touch.

The whole cast of *The Guiding Light* was at the party. Many of them, of course, were relatively new to the show. There was Don Stewart, the singing "dazzler" who came on the program some six years ago to take over the role of Michael Bauer; but six years is only a drop in the bucket compared to the whole history of this amazing serial. And there were other "new" actors: Mart Hulswit, Caroline McWilliams, Roger Newman, Lynn Deerfield, Barbara Berjer. None of them could possibly have sensed, first hand, the nature and magnitude of *The Guiding Light*'s past; and yet they knew they were part of a tradition, a special fraternity—a kind of close-knit family of Bauer actors.

A rare tape-recording of the old radio show is played for the audience, and a few hearts travel back to the good old days, remembering hurried rehearsals and risky broadcasts in front of live radio mikes. Most in that room, however, could only try to conjure up some sort of mental image of what the show's incredibly colorful past must have been like.

Imagine Irna Phillips—aged before her death on December 23, 1973, by nearly fifty years of accomplishment in radio and television broadcasting and by just plain living—as a smart-looking, career-oriented young woman who was the creative center of a whole new form of entertainment. Imagine a swarm of actors, producers, directors, and New York advertising executives descending upon the post-Depression Chicago of 1937—all getting in on a miraculous new daytime radio product that had mysteriously developed there. Imagine dozens of radio studio rooms abuzz with twenty-five daytime soap operas: actors huddling around live microphones with scripts in hand; sound-effects men simulating doorbells and foot falls; organists sounding ominous chords; announcers waxing orgiastic over detergents, as stories were broadcast daily to twenty million old radio consoles, while housewives listened. Imagine the era of the Chicago-based soap opera; we shall never see it again.

When *The Guiding Light* began on January 25, 1937, new serials were being spawned like fish larvae. In the twelve months preceding, fifteen daytime serials began. These shows were fifteen minutes apiece. That would be equivalent to today's television networks adding seven new serials to their lineups in one year! The new shows included *Pepper Young's Family, John's Other Wife, Big Sister, Bachelor's Children,* and *Aunt Jenny's True Life Stories.* Naturally, the producers of *The Guiding Light* and of these other new shows had no way of knowing that they were all destined to become broadcasting giants.

From the very start, *The Guiding Light* was produced by the Compton Advertising Agency for Procter and Gamble, which did not then own the show but merely leased it from its creator, Irna Phillips. Listeners, who had their radios tuned to NBC Red, always knew when they were about to hear another episode of *The Guiding Light.* Those dramatic organ chords from Goetzl's "Aphrodite" were a giveaway.

When the show premiered in 1937, Miss Phillips had not yet thought of the Bauer family. They came on in the early 1940s. Originally, *The Guiding Light* was about the life of Dr. Rutledge, pastor of a church in the city of Five Points (Anywhere, U.S.A.), and the lives of the members of his family and parish. The show had a rather religious tone, with a theme that faith brings happiness. Whole episodes were frequently devoted to a single sermon by Dr. Rutledge. In fact, this minister had given so many sermons on the show that they were eventually published in a book that sold 290,000 copies! Each year on Good Friday, Dr. Rutledge would give the traditional Good Friday message, "Seven Last Words," which was repeated on the show, year after year, even after the Rutledges were gone and the Bauers had replaced them totally. In a way, *The Guiding Light* has always been "a religious" story—minister or no minister—for its core families have always displayed faith and togetherness.

The original cast on the show was as follows:

ARTHUR PETERSON (Dr. Rutledge)

RUTH BAILEY (Rose Kransky)

MERCEDES MCCAMBRIDGE (Mary Rutledge)

ED PRENTISS, later JOHN HODIAK (Ned Holden)

GLADYS HEEN (Torchy)

RAYMOND EDWARD JOHNSON (Mr. Nobody from Nowhere)

The Guiding Light of those days, like most of the radio soaps of the thirties, would strike us today as obvious and unsophisticated. There would be more organ music connected with each episode than even a band of angels could endure, plus the endless cash prize giveaways that always required the purchase and label-cutting of four or five boxes of Procter and Gamble soap. The stories themselves, although often inspirational, were hokey to say the least. Each day, the announcer would introduce the story with a long statement that would frame the characters and situations for viewers. In the late thirties, an episode of *The Guiding Light* (this one dealing with one of its many subplots), would begin thusly:

Organ Music.

ANNOUNCER: *The Guiding Light.*

More organ music.

ANNOUNCER: The country's biggest selling laundry soap brings you (*sound of a cash register*) the biggest contest in value of cash and prizes any soap has ever offered.

More organ music.

ANNOUNCER: Well, friends, here's wonderful news for you—

WOMAN: Just a minute. If you say one more word about all those people who won all that money in your contest I'll just—I'll—well, I don't know what I'll do!

ANNOUNCER: You sound as if you're jealous.

WOMAN: I'm plenty jealous. I'd like to win some of that big money myself. But I forgot all about entering . . .

ANNOUNCER: Now don't worry . . . here's good news for you. Starting today, another big P&G Soap contest gets under way. And again, a thousand-dollar bill, five five-hundred-dollar bills, and fifty Electrolux refrigerators must be won this week!

WOMAN: Wonderful!

ANNOUNCER: Now remember, just add twenty-five words or less to the statement, "I like P&G Soap because . . ."

WOMAN: I like the way P&G helps cut grease on dishes and gravy. P&G is so economical, and yet my yellowish-looking sheets and tablecloths turn out a clear, snowy white!

ANNOUNCER: Well, everyday experiences like that can win. All you have to do is finish the statement, "I like P&G Soap because . . ." and send it along with four P&G Soap wrappers to *The Guiding Light,* Cincinnati, Ohio. Entries judged for sincerity, originality, and aptness of thought. Judges' decision final.

More organ music.

ANNOUNCER: And now . . . *The Guiding Light . . .* (*announcer softens voice*) There are times in our lives when we seem to have lost all sense of direction, all sense of identity, when we as individuals seem suspended in midair . . . when living seems hopeless, without objective. It was an apathetic, listless young woman who returned to her apartment in San Francisco this morning. Not even the flowers that had been sent by Martin Kane on her arrival seemed to arouse her from a feeling of detachment. Not even during the rehearsal at the studio later in the day, or during her evening broadcast, was she aroused from the almost dead sadness that had taken possession of her.

Martin Kane, sensitive to the mood of the young woman, suggested that they go to a quiet restaurant right after the broadcast. Seated across the table from the girl whom he hopes someday to marry, he suddenly loses patience with her apparent disinterest in him, and says—

MARTIN: Snap out of it, Mona.

MONA: Is there anything to snap out of, Martin?

MARTIN: It seems to me there is . . . look here, you're not being very fair.

MONA: You don't think so?

MARTIN: No, I don't.

MONA: I told you that I preferred to go home right after my broadcast. I told you that I pouted. You insisted that I needed a little recreation. I really wanted to go home.

MARTIN: Don't you think you owe a little something to your friends?

MONA: At this moment I don't feel anything. I haven't since I got back.

MARTIN: Your divorce . . . it did that to you?

MONA: I don't want to talk about the divorce. It's over.

MARTIN: But not as far as you're concerned.

MONA: Please believe me, Martin, it's over as far as I'm concerned. As far as everyone is concerned. And I don't want to talk about it.

MARTIN: Don't you think you can rouse yourself from your own thoughts long enough to at least be . . . well, human . . . to someone who's trying to help you over a rather tough spot.

MONA: It's very nice of you to help me over what you believe is a tough spot. But that tough spot is in your imagination. Oh, Martin, I get constantly out of patience with you. You make me feel that I have to be on the alert, constantly enthusiastic . . . you want me to be something I'm not. Just because you want it to be that way . . .

If you were to actually listen to this priceless old excerpt from *The Guiding Light,* you'd hear the combination of the enthusiastic announcer, all the churchy commentary from the organist, that wordy opening statement that set the mood, and the actors' reading of the sudsy dialogue—and it would all have an overwhelming effect on you. Despite yourself, as you first began to hear this episode of *The Guiding Light*, aired nearly four decades ago, you'd soon find yourself actually *listening*. Martin and Mona are talking about very little, and yet the quiet, intimate, hushed way they talk mysteriously takes hold of your imagination. You feel like you're eavesdropping. It's astonishing, but one understands instantly how twenty million housewives could have gotten so involved in a radio show that seemed to have so little polish.

A few years after *The Guiding Light* began, it was moved to Hollywood and then in 1949, to New York, as were many other radio serials. Once in New York, the whole show was revamped, and the Rutledge family was replaced by the Bauer clan. They included Papa and Mama Bauer, their son Bill (called "Willie"), and daughters Trudy and Meta. The Bauer's were first- and second-generation German-Americans who managed to stay together despite many adversities. They believed in the old-fashioned virtues of love and marriage and of doing whatever was best for one's children. In effect, Dr. Rutledge's religious beliefs were being tested on an everyday basis by the Bauer family.

When the Bauers came on, the show's locale was moved from Five Points to Selby Flats, a mythical suburb of Los Angeles (inspired by the show's move from Chicago to Hollywood). In fact, that's how Cedars Hospital—where Ed Bauer, Stephen Jackson, and all their doctor-friends in Springfield now practice medicine—came into being. Cedars Hospital was supposed to remind people of the famous Cedars of Lebanon Hospital in Los Angeles, and it was later miraculously relocated in Springfield (Anywhere, U.S.A.), where the characters in the story moved before the show made the transition to television.

All these moves were effected by the writers and producers for one reason alone: to give the characters bigger, more urban settings to move around in. Ten years after the premiere, listeners still heard the announcer proclaim the same serial title, but everything else about the show—with the exception of its underlying theme of family togetherness, which has always been the same—had changed. The organ music was shortened to a few brief chords; there were no more big-money prizes, only a curt message from the sponsor; and the plots were now rather "adult," dealing with insanity, morbid deaths, drawn-out tragedies, disastrous love affairs, and unwanted pregnancies.

The Bauer saga has been going on for more than twenty-seven years, and there have been hundreds of subplots centering about the family. However, in all that time there has been only a handful of major stories involving the family. At the start, PAPA BAUER (Theo Goetz) and MAMA BAUER (Addie Klein) had come over from the old country and settled in Selby Flats, California, a seaport town. Their three American-born children—BILL BAUER (Lyle Sudrow, and later Ed Bryce on television), META BAUER (Jone Allison, and later Ellen Demming on television), and TRUDY BAUER (Charlotte Holland)—were all young adults when the Bauer story began.

Bill Bauer married BERT (played the first year on the New York show by Ann Shepherd and for the next twenty-six years—up to the present—by Charita Bauer) shortly before Mama Bauer died, leaving Papa Bauer as the sole family head. Bill was a hard-working young man. But Bert, who is today a sympathetic character as head of the Bauer family, was then selfish and unsympathetic as his materialistic young wife. There were many marital conflicts. One of them, for example, centered around Bert's constant obsession with getting Bill to buy a house even though they couldn't afford it.

Trudy Bauer married a man named Clyde and eventually waltzed off with him to find a life in New York City. Although the character was important to the story during the early radio era, Trudy lasted only briefly on television (played then by Lisa Howard) and is never talked about by the Bauer family these days.

Meta was the most colorful member of the Bauer family for many years, as well as being a pivotal character on both radio and television. Meta had burst out of the tightly knit family, running away to the big city to become a model. She soon got involved with the reprehensible TED WHITE, became pregnant by him and married him. After their son CHUCKIE (Sarah Fussell) was born, Meta and Ted White were divorced, and Ted won partial custody of their son. He was an overbearing father, however, insisting that his timid son become tough and learn to box. Meta kept objecting to his unreasonable treatment of Chuckie. One day, while Chuckie was being forced to box, he had a freak accident and was killed. Meta went out of her mind and shot and killed Ted. While she was on trial for the murder of her ex-husband, a newspaperman named JOE ROBERTS (Herb Nelson) fell in love with her, believing she had killed her ex-husband only as a result of temporary insanity. After he helped gain her acquittal, they were married. Shortly after, however, he died of cancer. Then Meta and KATHY ROBERTS (Susan Douglas)—Joe Roberts' daughter by a previous marriage and therefore Meta's stepdaughter—both fell in love with the same man (Whit Connor) and became enemies. Eventually, Meta settled and married DR. BRUCE BANNING (originally Les Damon, then for many years Barney Hughes, later Sidney Walker, and currently Bill Roerick).

Kathy married BOB LANG and had a daughter by the name of ROBIN (played as an older child by Zina Bethune, then Nancy Malone, and Gillian Spencer) who married DR. PAUL FLETCHER (originally played by Michael Caine, then Bernie Grant). One day Robin, who was confined to a wheelchair, was killed by a truck that had swerved to avoid hitting a child. Paul Fletcher's son by a previous marriage—JOHNNY FLETCHER (Don Scardino, later Erik Howell), a young medical student—fell in love with teen-ager PEGGY DILLMAN (Fran Myers), who was on trial for the murder of her husband, Marty.

Much of the above, of course, took place on television as well as radio. Bert and Bill Bauer, on radio, had two sons, MICHAEL (see the list of actors who played this role on page 47) and EDWARD BAUER (played as an adult by Bob Gentry and Mart Hulswit), who grew up to become a lawyer and a doctor respectively. Over the years Bert and Bill's characters seem to reverse—Bert became a paragon as a wife and mother, teaming up with Papa Bauer to settle family crises, and Bill became the weakling. For a long time he cheated on Bert with Peggy Dillman's mother, which threatened to break up his marriage, and he later became an alcoholic. Bert had to contend with his drinking problem for years. Eventually Bill turned over a new leaf—just in time, in fact, to help his son, Ed, get over *his* newly acquired battle with alcoholism. But Bill Bauer was ultimately killed in a crash of a chartered airplane heading toward Alaska, and the tragedy of his father's death only aggravated Ed's drinking problem all the more. (*Note*: for the more recent plot of *The Guiding Light*, see page 278.)

Whether on radio or television, the continuing story of *The Guiding Light* always had a powerful effect on viewers, primarily because its tragedies and love entanglements were always presented within the context of unbreakable family ties. Many people who were listeners of the old radio show still remember, for example, the sting of little Chuckie's death, which caused the Bauers so much grief but also made them huddle together for mutual solace. (One listener who reacted strongly to Chuckie's death was the mother of the Minnesota Vikings halfback, William "Chuck" Forman. An item in the sports section of the New York *Post* recently revealed how the noted football player got his nickname: "Mrs. Forman decided, wiping a tear from her eye, that the world should have a 'Chuck' to take the place of the dead little boy. So Walter Forman, for as long as he can remember, has been called Chuck.")

As steady viewers of the show well knew, no matter how unsympathetic an individual in the Bauer family became, the family always closed ranks and rallied to his or her support. Brothers might clash over love of the same woman, the father might cheat on his wife and come home soaked in gin, but no calamity or personal conflict on earth could turn Bauer against Bauer. This has always been the secret of their happiness as a family—and the formula for family solidarity that radio listeners and television viewers of *The Guiding Light* have been following for more than thirty-seven years.

Mark Hulswit, a relative newcomer to the TV show as Ed Bauer, says the one thing that struck him from the very start was the strong emphasis on the togetherness of the Bauers. One day he even gave Theo Goetz a T-shirt emblazoned with the words BAUER POWER. The whole cast cracked up when they saw it, for the message was so true.

The head of the Bauer Clan—Theo Goetz as Papa Bauer—came on the radio show in 1949, and stayed Papa Bauer until his death late in 1972. When Theo Goetz came to this country from Vienna in 1938, escaping Hitler's scourge, the middle-aged actor didn't have a dime in his pocket and couldn't speak a word of English. Once, in Germany, he had been a worldly and well-known actor; but here in New York, a refugee, he slept in a one-room walk-up on the upper West Side, living on coffee and doughnuts for lunch and a sandwich for supper.

Mr. Goetz, in an interview shortly before his death, recalled, "In my neighborhood uptown I remember there was a movie theater which impoverished actors like me used to go to. I would sit there and listen to those movies and little by little I'd teach myself English. I kept wondering: *how am I going to get a job?* An actor is nobody here, especially one who hardly knew the language. And I was afraid to talk to people, afraid that I wouldn't know what they were saying to me. And I was lonesome. But I think that at 'that moment God must have seen my condition and decided that he was going to start his special plan."

Theo had picked up enough English to get a CBS radio audition. The network's Earl McGill liked the charming gentleman so much that he offered him the role of a doctor on *Young Doctor Malone,* the title role being played by Allan Bunce. Theo could get through his own lines well enough—his special brand of heavily accented English was loved immediately for its warm quality—but he had trouble knowing what the other actors were saying from one moment to the next.

A few years later, Irna Phillips was holding auditions for her Bauer family on *The Guiding Light*. "After I did the audition for Papa Bauer, I saw Irna Phillips applauding me when I looked toward the booth behind a glass partition. 'You will hear from us,' she said. But I didn't hear another word for two months. Then I got a call from some secretary who said, 'You have to make a record for our client, Procter and Gamble . . . What? You mean no one called to tell you you got the part as Papa Bauer?' I didn't know then that I had gotten a lifetime job."

Incidentally, Theo once told how, just after he got his famous twenty-four-year-running part, the producer asked one of the show's actresses to "help Mr. Goetz with his German accent for the role of Papa Bauer."

Over the years Theo Goetz received many rewards from his role as Papa Bauer, not to mention the steady paycheck. He liked the feeling of being loved by so many people—any actor who has ever played a Bauer has felt this. Theo was especially gratified when the show went on television in 1952 and millions saw what he looked like for the first time. He'd walk into a butcher shop or a grocery store, and complete strangers would greet him as warmly as if they had known him for years. All this was unheard of for a respectable German actor who had spent most of his life playing before select and small (compared with television, anyway) paying audiences. He admitted that he actually cried at the sight of twenty-two sacks of presents and thirty-nine thousand congratulatory letters and telegrams sent by viewers when *The Guiding Light* announced on the air that Papa Bauer had reached his sixty-fifth birthday and suggested that viewers send birthday cards. One ninety-five-year-old man and his ninety-three-year-old wife sent him an affectionate poem, and he received marriage proposals from women all over the country—even though he was already happily married to Rhea Brown, a painter.

"When I went up to that CBS mailroom and saw all those letters pouring in, I became choked up. In the beginning, you know, I was worried that I wouldn't pass the sponsor's popularity test—that I wouldn't get enough letters. I even asked all my friends to write me letters, just to make me look good. But then I saw all those letters for me! So many people! Whole villages and factories wrote in. I said to myself, 'This is unbelievable!' I came over to this country an unknown nobody who didn't know the language. And now all of those people were paying me this honor."

It was an important moment for Theo for several reasons. His early experiences in a Russian concentration camp, his later struggle to survive in Nazi Germany, and his coming to this country as a refugee—cut off from all family and friends—had left him emotionally insecure, unsure of the regard others had for him. Papa Bauer was a perfect part for Theo. The interest in him of millions of viewers reassured Theo that he was indeed highly regarded. However, it may not have been enough. "I don't think that Theo Goetz knew how really loved he was," Charita Bauer said sadly, shortly after the actor's death, when she had had a chance to talk with Theo's widow. "And I don't think any of us had any idea that Theo didn't feel loved."

By the time Charita Bauer came on the radio show in 1950, she had already had a vast radio and stage career. She played every conceivable kind of heroine and heavy on radio soaps like *Young Widder Brown, Just Plain Bill, Rose of My Dreams,* and *Ma Perkins.* "There were so many shows I couldn't remember them all. I remember that I used to love to play sexy gunmolls and criminals. It was more fun to be mean." As she sits in her New York living room discussing her years on *The Guiding Light,* she displays a perky smile—the same one that she must have had when she was a child actress on the stage. Moments later the expression changes to mature interest.

"When I first came on *The Guiding Light,* the show had just moved to New York from Hollywood, like so many of the other ones. Our show was fun in those days. It seems to me it was more colorful. We were on radio, and so you used your imagination more when you heard the show than you do today. Our writers weren't confined to specific sets, and actors didn't have to look their parts. Today it seems that more happened on the old radio program —but then I don't know. The past always seems to be more interesting than the present, somehow." Of course Charita, playing a young wife in her early days with the show, got involved in more complex and dramatic entanglements than she does today, playing essentially a "recap" character: Bert Bauer, the middle-aged head of the Bauer family, who now can only sympathize when her relatives and friends get into trouble.

"I was only on a few years before the producer told us that we'd be going on television. Our first day was June 30, 1952. We were all so happy and excited. For the first time people would see what we looked like—instead of just hearing our voices—and we were going to make more money since we would still be doing the radio show at the same time. In the morning I'd go over to Liederkrantz Hall to do the live TV show, and later, at a quarter to two, I'd rush across town to read the same script for the live radio show. For four years we did this! If you missed a show on television, you could catch it the same day on radio.

"Naturally television was a lot more work. In radio, you just read your script in front of a microphone after a few hours of rehearsal. In television you had to memorize all your lines, and to do just one show on the air took a whole half day. When the show went to television, we were directed by Ted Corday, and most of the radio cast came right onto TV. On TV we were produced by Dave Lesan (our producer now, Lucy Ferri Rittenberg, was then the associate producer). Jone Allison left after six months and was replaced by Ellen Demming as Meta; and after a few years on television Ed Bryce replaced Lyle Sudrow as Bill. But of course Theo Goetz was still Papa Bauer. We really were a tightly knit little group then— much more than today. We used to help each other out in so many ways. Now there are just too many actors on the show for your relationship with them to be that close. But there's always been a good feeling among the actors."

In 1956 the radio segment was discontinued, four years before the last radio soaps faded into oblivion. "I was sad when the radio show stopped. It was the end of an era—and besides, we were going to lose that extra forty dollars a show!" Now, only the relatively new medium of television could keep that light guiding the footsteps of the Bauer family.

Little Michael Bauer was born shortly before the show went to television. While Charita was still playing the pregnant Bert Bauer, she went to Irna Phillips and asked her if the child was to be a boy or a girl. The show's writer said it was to be a boy. Then Charita asked if Miss Phillips wouldn't make life a whole lot simpler for Charita by naming the new arrival Michael. Her own son, Michael, had just been born, and Charita was afraid of becoming confused over the names of her two children! So that's how Michael Bauer became Michael Bauer. (Incidentally, as long as we're on names, Charita explains that her own son is Michael Crawford, not Michael Bauer, since he takes the name of his father. Her own last name was not a model for the name of the family on the show. "Nearly everyone asks me that," she comments. "It was mere coincidence.")

Charita now shuts her eyes, thinks back, and a warm smile comes to her lips as she remembers one story in particular concerning her two sons. "Glenn Walken played the first Michael on the TV show. He was only seven years old, and my Michael was six. Now my Michael had seen Glenn on television, and he knew that the little boy had the same name in the story and how he'd gotten the name, and it didn't seem to bother him much. One day I took my son on a shopping trip to Best and Company and we ran into little Glenn Walken and his mother. We stopped and talked for a while, and then I started home with Michael. He suddenly grew very quiet. 'What's the matter, dear?' I said. Then he said, 'Mommy, who do you love more—the real Michael or the make-believe Michael?' I was stunned. 'You, darling! Of course I love you more!' I've never forgotten that; I was just so touched. I guess finally seeing Glenn Walken in person suddenly made the other Michael seem real."

Michael Crawford, who today is a young executive in his mid-twenties, has watched his mother's show ever since he was little and, of course, having a special stake in her fictional son, has followed Michael's phenomenally fast aging process through six different actors. According to Michael Crawford's memory: after Glenn Walken played the child, Michael Allen played the teenager, and then Paul Prokop played the young adult attending law school (the character by then was ten years older than the real Michael), then Gary Pillar, Bob Pickering, and finally—and currently—Don Stewart. Michael Bauer is now close to forty and nearly twice as old as his one-time little shadow in real life.

Soap acting is hard work, yet backstage the Bauers and their friends have always had time for a laugh or two. Charita remembers a few funny stories. "One Thanksgiving we were supposed to be at Meta's, and we were all sitting around the dining table. Ted Corday, our director, wanted the camera to pan around Theo Goetz's head, but there was just no way of doing it without Theo coming into the camera lens. Ted told Theo, 'Could you slip under the table and then come back after the camera pans.' Ellen Demming was convulsed, but Ted, who didn't always have such a great sense of humor, didn't think it was funny. I remember Theo would roll his eyes when he went under the table ... And then there was the time when Susan Douglas was pregnant, but her character, Kathy, wasn't. She had to be shot from the shoulders up or while seated. But invariably the director would decide to take her in full profile, and he'd ask her, 'Could you hold your tummy in?' ... I remember once Ted Corday, who died five years ago, went wild because he kept hearing some strange clock ticking all the way through a scene during dress rehearsal. It turned out that the crew was just playing a joke on Ted. Ted didn't laugh."

Once Charita herself was the object of a joke. The show was on the air at 12:48—live—and Charita was having a scene with Theo Goetz. Walter Gorman, who had replaced

Ted Corday, was directing then. Suddenly his voice came over the loudspeaker: "More voice, Charita!" Charita, stunned that the director was mistaking air for dress, didn't bat an eyelid but kept on doing the scene with Theo. "Come on, Charita, you can do better than that!" came the director's voice again, for millions across the land to hear. Finally Charita looked into the camera and said in a soft voice, "Walter, are you putting me on?" After the scene was over, Charita stormed furiously into the control booth, only to confront the hysterical laughter of Walter Gorman and his henchmen. She breathed a sigh of relief when she discovered it was all a big joke. They were not on air at all; the show had been preempted.

Like the Bauers on-screen, the actors themselves off-screen—some who have been playing their roles for years and years—behave uncannily like a family. As Charita revealed, when the show had a smaller cast with fewer incidental characters and ran only fifteen minutes, there was more of a sense of closeness among the acting "family." Yet essentially the Bauer-feeling—or "Bauer Power," as Mart Hulswit calls it—has always been there. Theo Goetz was always the patriarch, both among his fellow performers and in the story. Ed Bryce, while on the show, had had personal problems about which the other Bauer actors worried, just as in the story the real Bauers worried about Bill's problems.

Fran Myers had grown up on the show with a second family of older actors, while in the story her Peggy Dillman was growing up right before viewers' eyes, and under the perpetual care and concern of the Bauer clan: "I came on the show when I was fourteen. *The Guiding Light* has been like a real family to me—especially Lucy Rittenberg, the producer. All these years she's been almost a mother figure. And I've always been close to Charita. The funny thing is that I never let my *real* mother come to the show."

Ed Bauer is the ever-faithful son in the story, a man all the other family members can rely on in a pinch. Mart Hulswit, who plays Ed, has precisely the same role with his fellow actors. He's a warm, reliable human being who, like any good son, holds frequent get-togethers at his apartment—which his lovely wife, Maria, hosts—for the other Bauer actors. Charita praises him to the rafters, as if she were praising her own flesh and blood.

The backstage Bauers are also like any close family in that the group has an especially strong reaction to any member who thinks he's a "star"—the son who wants to be a great novelist, or the daughter who thinks she'll become another Barbra Streisand. When Don Stewart came on *The Guiding Light* as the new Michael Bauer, the other clan members were aware of a new sort of performer-animal in their midst. Don had a press agent who got his name in newspaper columns (Charita: "Oh, my god, we've *never* had an actor with a press agent before!") and a manager who got him singing jobs in nightclubs. There Don would leap onto the stage in tight-fitting, sexy white jumpsuits. Lots of stories appeared in all the fan magazines about how no woman was good enough for him. It wasn't long before they began calling him by his nickname backstage: "The Dazzler!" Don—who loves pet names anyway—used to answer his telephone with: "Don Stewart, World's Greatest Lover!" He has a fabulous sense of humor about the name and loves being kidded for his star-aspirations by the other "Bauers." Of course, they are Don's kin, and deep down they all want him to succeed. Anyway, his personal publicity, his singing appearances on all the talk shows (Mike Douglas, David Frost, Dr. Joyce Brothers), and the superstar image he brings to the public when he's performing as a singer (not as Michael Bauer) have helped the Nielsen Ratings of *The Guiding Light* enormously. And why not? Off-screen or on-screen, Bauer helps Bauer.

And Bauer weeps for Bauer!

The rash of recent off-stage tragedies that has ravaged the show left all of the actors in a state of shock. "It'll take a long time before any of us really gets over it," says Charita.

What Charita was talking about were the sudden deaths of three important people on the show within a period of six months. It was like the rush of sadness that soap writers sometimes inject into their stories for greater realism—only no one was writing, and the tears were real indeed. On July 6, 1972, an important actor on the show, Ed Zimmermann, who had played the part of Dr. Joe Werner since 1967, collapsed in York, Maine, of a heart attack, just as he was about to appear with Arlene Francis in the play *Who Killed Santa Claus?* Hours later he was dead, at the age of thirty-nine.

Death is always sad, but it is devastating when it strikes a young person, even more so when that person is as talented as Ed Zimmermann was. Death had taken not only a fine actor, but an excellent writer. Only months before his untimely passing, the Bobbs-Merrill Publishing Company brought out Ed's first novel, *Love in the Afternoon.* It was a finely written comic tale of an actor, like Ed himself, who plays the role of a villainous young doctor on a daytime serial—like *The Guiding Light.* Ironically, the character in his book, Steven Prince, was forever complaining about his heart beating too fast and about his tired, bedraggled condition after playing a long stint on the serial. After Ed's death, other actors on his show remembered him complaining about heart palpitations quite often. However, he was not known to have had a diagnosed heart condition. Ed was a shy, talented, handsome man, who left a widow and a pretty fifteen-year-old daughter.

One of the first members of *The Guiding Light* to learn the news about Ed was Charita Bauer, who was in tears, when she called several other actors on the show to let them know. Each of the Bauers, and their friends in turn, expressed their grief, privately or openly. On July 10th services were held for Ed at Frank E. Campbell's funeral parlor in New York City. Almost everyone in any way connected with the show came to say their last good-byes. It seemed somehow natural for Mart Hulswit—the good Bauer son in the story, and one of the most dutiful and sympathetic members of the "family" backstage—to be the one to read Ed Zimmermann's eulogy at the services, just as it would seem natural for him to read Papa Bauer's eulogy some months later in a chapel service on television.

Said Ed, "It seems out of place to be unhappy at anything having to do with Ed Zimmermann. His career was blossoming with success after success, and he was on the threshold of greatness. Now, only we who have shared his path for a while can know of his great performances, his great writings, that have been denied future audiences and future readers. We are all better men and women for having known Ed, and are all emptier at his loss."

In Ed Zimmermann's book, *Love in the Afternoon,* there's a passage in the beginning that goes:

> A director friend of mine—a tough man named O'Brian—once confessed to me over a second highball, "Actors are daredevils. I'd never be able to do it." Coming from O'Brian, it was the nicest thing I'd ever heard said about the profession. This wasn't some actor's agent with a lisp and a Cardin suit, or one of those literary ladies with three names who like to talk about art or get their names on patrons' lists—this was O'Brian talking. A guy who played lacrosse at Dartmouth, fought in World War II, and went to football games in the snow.

That was actually a thinly disguised description of Walter Gorman, who directed *The Guiding Light* for more than ten years and who was sincerely loved by everyone who worked with him. Only weeks after Ed Zimmermann died, Walter Gorman also died of a heart attack. It was a second savage blow, especially for Bauer actors who had been on the show for years. Said Charita, "I was even more upset by his death than Ed Zimmermann's. I had known Walter for more than twenty years. The man had been so good to everyone. Ed adored him. He would talk all the time about Walter Gorman. That's how I knew as soon as I read his book that it was Walter he was describing."

Six months later, on December 29, 1929, Theo Goetz passed away in his sleep at the age of seventy-eight. When Rhea, his widow, called the production office that morning to tell them, it was as if someone had called to say that a part—a big part—of *The Guiding Light* had just died. Theo Goetz, the first Bauer, was gone. Once again, the end of something, the death of someone, marked the fade-out of an era. In life, sadness never stops, for, just as in soap opera, there are but long interruptions of happiness—and then only if we are lucky.

At least Theo, unlike Ed Zimmermann, had lived a long life. If there was great sadness at his passing, there was also a feeling of contentment on the part of all the long-time Bauer actors that Theo Goetz and *The Guiding Light* had had such a happy relationship together for so many years. Until the very end, Theo was of sound mind as well as sound body, and he could still do two or three shows a week—although, as Mart Hulswit recalls, six months before his death he began to have trouble remembering his lines. "I remember when he couldn't remember his lines, he'd mumble these little curse words to himself, barely audible to other people. It was so cute—no one ever took offense ... And if he didn't like a script—and you know how he was always complaining about the scripts—he'd say, 'It's sheet!' and throw it down on the floor ... One time I remember they put Papa Bauer in the hospital with gallbladder trouble. And Theo loved it! 'I have something to do!' he said, because usually he just sat around and talked about other people."

Bruce Cox, in charge of daytime programming at Compton Advertising Agency, and therefore, theoretically, Papa Bauer's boss, remembers how Theo would come regularly, every three weeks, all the way from the studio at 221 West 26th Street to the agency at Madison and 59th to say hello to everyone. "It was just his way. He was an old-world gentleman and he was showing us European politeness. He'd stick his head in every door with a greeting, and then proceed to tell me all these beautiful stories about the old days on radio. Oh, I loved them! And how he shattered my illusions! When I was a boy I listened to the radio soaps and thought the actors worked so hard, and here he was telling me that they just came in and read their scripts and left. I could have listened to him talk for days at a time."

It was fitting that Bruce Cox, as Theo's boss and good friend, should have read the eulogy at Campbell's when the services were held for Theo Goetz on January 2. All of the Springfield players listened, quietly:

"Theophile Antonius Menu was born in Marseilles, France, on December 14, 1894—seventy-eight years ago. Seventy-eight years of living—and over half a century working as an artist. That's quite an accomplishment. His mother wanted him to be a banker. The theater was an uncertain way of life. Fortunately for us, he didn't follow her advice and for more than fifty years Theo Goetz worked successfully, honorably, and happily at his chosen craft.

"He was a major figure with the Vienna State Theatre, touring all of Europe—playing leading roles in the great classical and contemporary drama. In 1938, this first career—and half a lifetime—came to halt when, as president of the Austrian Actors' Union, he was forced by Nazism to escape from his homeland with so many thousands of others to the United States of America. Theo made this country his own, and in his own way loved it fiercely and possessively. In mid-life he learned and mastered a new language; he married an American painter, built a fine new reputation, and enchanted audiences for another thirty years: Broadway, the famous radio programs of the forties—and then, in 1949, he made Papa Bauer and *The Guiding Light* his very artistic own.

"Just two weeks ago, on his seventy-eighth birthday, Procter and Gamble sent him a telegram which moved him to tears. I would like to read their message because it expresses so well what we all feel about Theo:

A very happy birthday, Theo, on this your seventy-eighth. Few actors ever achieve what you achieve with your characterization of Papa—or play their roles with greater dedication. Thank you—for your artistry, your talent, and the endearing humanity you have brought to *The Guiding Light* for so many years.

"Farewell, dear Theo—"

Real life and the life that goes on inside serial storie have a way of imitating one another. The boundaries be tween this kind of fiction and the life that inspires it hav a way of dissolving easily. A month later, when the writ ers and producers had Papa Bauer die on the show— would have been *inconceivable* to replace Theo Goet with another actor—it was as if all the events surroundin Theo Goetz's death were being repeated in fiction. Th reactions of the characters—Bert's saying to everyone, " can still hardly believe it!"; people calling one another an exchanging stories about Papa Bauer and how wonderfu he was and what an inspiration to the family; Ed's fon way of talking about him—was precisely what had hap pened off-screen when news of Theo's death hit the actors Serial fiction has a way of not being just an imitation c real life. Often actors act out stories that they themselve have helped to create in the course of their own lives.

Daytime serial actors are loathe to admit to this becaus they feel that, if it is true, they appear foolish—that the are not actors at all, but mere pawns. For example, Char ita Bauer, like any other actress, wants to feel that she i just doing a job, and is neither "living" a character whe serves as a model for a story that millions of people see nor being molded by the story she acts out. "Oh, I woul hate to think," says Charita, "of a soap actor getting con fused with his role." Yet the grief that Miss Bauer dis played off-screen at the passing of her co-worker was pre cisely the same grief that she showed millions of viewer as Bert Bauer when Papa Bauer died on the show. Some how, Charita and Bert had come to feel the same way about certain things and certain people. Perhaps one car also reflect here that many serial actors, like Theo Goetz *need* their longevity as characters. It helps them feel more secure, more needed. But don't ever ask a serial actor tc admit this, for it is a feeling that is regarded by actors as a sign of weakness. "I entertain people by playing Bert Bauer," says Miss Bauer, with the typical serial actor's protestation, "and what I get in return is satisfaction and my paycheck. It's as simple as that and it stops there."

It wasn't surprising that Don Stewart was chosen to sing "I'll Walk With God" during the TV funeral. The producers had heard Don sing the same hymn at Campbell's and felt that nearly everything there should be repeated in that little chapel in Springfield where Papa was eulogized. When millions of *The Guiding Light*'s watchers heard Don sing, and Mart Hulswit, as Dr. Ed Bauer, read Papa's eulogy, they could just as easily have been at Campbell's listening to Bruce Cox talk of Theo Goetz. Here's an excerpt from the script with Papa's eulogy, aired Tuesday, February 27, episode number 6,569. As you read it, you may begin to suspect that this is *not* fiction:

(*Ed rises from his aisle seat and crosses to the lectern. The minister moves to a chair and sits down. Ed looks over the people in the room, then down at the family in front of him. All of them, including Leslie, look toward him, waiting. There is almost a serene expression on their faces.*)

ED: (*Almost as if he were talking to only one person at a time here.*) Papa had great faith, so he rarely was afraid. He said it wasn't always that way. When he was a young man, it was different. The faith was there, but it hadn't had time to grow strong. I think we all share that faith—to one degree or another. The littlest Bauer, Frederick, Papa's great-grandson, doesn't know what it is yet, but he will—someday. (*He looks toward Hope*) Papa Bauer's lovely young great-granddaughter—she has faith, and a lot of it came to her from Papa. (*Beat*) Papa came to this country from another land, another country. When he was young he loved his native land, but soon some terrible things began to happen there. And so he found his way to *this* country. And a pas-

sionate love for this, his adopted country, began t
grow in him. He made it *his* country; its history, hi
history. He would never let us call him a wise man. H
would only say that if you live a long time, you liv
through so much that you begin to have an understand
ing of human events—but no more than that. He be
lieved in people, in the basic goodness of people. Some
times we'd argue with him. We'd say, "the basic good
ness of *some* people, Papa." But he'd shake his hea
and say, "It's there, God put it there in all of us. Bu
sometimes—in some of us—it never has a chance t
bloom, not even to sprout a little."

(*He pauses a second or two, looks about*) We all share
Papa. He meant one thing to one person, somethin
else to another. We all carry part of him in our heart
and in our minds. My brother has a daughter wh
knew him well, and I know that someday she will tel
her children—and maybe her grandchildren—abou
Papa Bauer. I have a son—who won't remember wha
Papa looked like—but his mother loved Papa (*He look
toward Leslie*) just as the rest of us do—so there wil
be something of Papa in my son's life, too, and in hi
children's lives.

(*A warm look comes into his face*) So he's still here in the
love we have for him, in the memories we have of him
He is here with us, and he'll always be with us. I know
that. (*He pauses, looks toward Mike*) There was a song
my grandfather loved, that Papa Bauer loved. My
brother is going to sing it for him—for all of us."

(*Ed remains standing as Mike rises and crosses to the are
where the organ is located. This will then give time fo
Ed to take his seat. During Mike's song, we should pan
over the faces in the room.*)

(*Mike sings "I'll Walk With God." At the completion o
the song, Mike bows his head as the minister rises and
goes to the lectern.*)

MINISTER: Those of you who wish to do so, please join me
in "The Lord's Prayer."

(Everyone rises, bows his head as the minister softly re-cites "The Lord's Prayer" with the group responding.)

Fade out

Music bridge

6th Commercial

⋖§ IV §⋗

How Did the Serials Start?

HELEN TRENT—remember that wonderful lady? Remember the twenty-seven years she spent on radio setting out "to prove that a woman can have romance at thirty-five—and even beyond!"? Helen, in all the years from 1933 until television finally wiped out all the radio serials, never really aged a day past that magic thirty-five mark. Well, maybe she did get a few gray hairs once. One afternoon in 1948 (according to Mary Jane Higby in her book *Tune In Tomorrow,* highly recommended reading for all old-time daytime radio buffs), what seemed an ordinary broadcast of *The Romance of Helen Trent* turned into an hilarious, unforgettable disaster. On that day, as usual, her constant suitor and sometime fiancé, Gil Whitney, once again begged for the tender but unattainable love of the woman he worshipped, our own Helen. His voice purred like a kitten but Helen only responded with bewildered "no"s and reluctant sighs. "Ah, for chrissakes, lay the dame and get it over with," came another voice right on the air. A man—perhaps some unwitting technician?—began giving specific advice to Gil on exactly what he should do to Helen, no graphic terms spared, and millions heard it all! CBS control-booth personnel were struck dumb with shock. They frantically began trying to track down from which of the hundreds and hundreds of network interceptor points—on what was then the complicated Round Robin system—the frank advice-giver's voice was coming. The search for the voice was hopeless and the outrageous expletives continued.

That was what radio was like in the old days—just plain risky. Appearing on a fifteen-minute afternoon soap was rather like a game of roulette because it was live, it happened *every* day, and an actor—to make ends meet—often had roles on several serials which were aired from studios too far from one another for comfort.

Don MacLaughlin, who for twenty-five years played radio leads such as David Harding on *Counterspy* and Dr. Jim Brent on *The Road of Life*—"Dr. Brent, call *sur-ger-ee!*"—before taking on his long run as Chris Hughes on TV's *As the World Turns,* talks about the frantic day of the typical radio-serial actor of the thirties and forties. "We'd all rush from studio to studio in those days with a briefcase full of scripts, doing four or five shows a day—and that was the most difficult part. The thing that terrified us most, I remember, were fluffs. With so much acting every day they were hard to prevent." Bess Johnson came on *Counterspy* one day and said, on the air, "Operator, get me Spounterskies." Craig MacDonald once tried to say "poppycock," but it came out—"That's a lot of poppy-cak—poppy—COCK!"

Naturally, all the rushing around to different studios and the hectic way in which the soaps were produced invariably caused near-disasters. The late, great James Thurber recounted dozens of such "panic-button" stories of the old radio serial world in his mid-forties magazine series, "Soapland," written for the *New Yorker*. He tells, for instance, of a young actress on *The Story of Mary Marlin* who one day simply walked out of the radio studio just before air time, mistakenly believing that the dress rehearsal she had just done in front of a microphone was the actual broadcast. The show had already started, with a minute left before the actress's cue, and a near-deranged assistant director just walked out into the halls and dragged in the first actress he saw to play the role. On *Just Plain Bill,* a whole week's supply of scripts was destroyed in an air crash, and the writer, Charles Andrews, had to dictate that day's episode over the telephone while the show was in progress. The audience, no doubt, wondered why the actors kept pausing so long between words.

For eighteen years Mary Jane Higby starred as Joan Davis on *When a Girl Marries*. In her book, *Tune In Tomorrow*, Miss Higby was careful to point out that actors on radio soaps were terribly professional and always played it cool whenever fluffs and mishaps occurred on the air. But occasionally they didn't and couldn't. For example, in her book she told another story that seems completely unbelievable, at least by today's standards of daytime broadcasting. Once, on her show, the entire cast cracked up on the air while trying to act out a script overstuffed with tragedy. Instead of sounding worried over such miseries as crop failure, nervous breakdown, and the burning down of a house, they laughed hysterically for minutes, trying desperately at least to get the words out, but they simply couldn't stop. The director in the control booth finally gave up and his head fell limply into his arms. There seemed to be endless crises like this in front of the sudsy mikes, for, of course, broadcasting was still in its infancy, and daytime programs were low-budgeted and quickly produced.

Many, many actors from the old radio days managed to make the transition to television serials, despite the vast differences in acting abilities that the two media required. Those who are still around today on television seem unanimously agreed that although radio soaps were cruder, they were more fun to work on. Teri Keane, who now plays a policeman's wife—Martha Marceau on *The Edge of Night* —had radio roles as Chichi, the heroine on *Life Can Be Beautiful;* Hope, a heavy on *Big Sister;* Jocelyn on *Road of Life;* and Terry Burton on *The Second Mrs. Burton,* among many others. "I had wonderful times on radio," says Miss Keane, "You had to work hard, but the actors were all so much closer than on television. Also, there were more opportunities. At nighttime I might be playing a heavy, and in the daytime I'd be playing a heroine on a serial."

Mandel Kramer, who of course is known by daytime-serial lovers as Miss Keane's husband, Police Chief Bill Marceau on *The Edge of Night,* was, back in the old radio days, even better known as the most frequently heard villain's voice on almost every cops-and-robbers nighttime show of the time, including *The FBI in Peace and War* and *Gangbusters.* On daytime radio he was best known as Lt. Tragg, Perry's ominous rival on *Perry Mason.* Mr. Kramer spent the years between 1940 and 1955 building up a certain mystique on radio with his voice—a mystique that was shattered when he finally had to shift his career to television, where his basically gentle looks appeared incongruous with his criminal roles. Before that, in his more than fifteen years as radio bad guys, he estimates that he must have been sentenced to about fifty thousand years in jail, hanged about twelve times, and left for dead on the street "more times than I can remember." He says, "Of course, I had to start playing good-guy roles on TV because people could now see what I looked like. You know, in radio it was all imagination. Today I guess it's hard for the young people to know how enjoyable radio used to be—radio is nothing but disk jockies now. But then you'd hear a show and you'd see everything in your mind's eye. When I first started on radio I think I was successful because I knew the trick was to suggest, not be too specific. Most actors who played criminals went out of their way to *sound* like gunmen, or at least their idea of one. You know, you can sound so much more menacing if you keep your voice down and say quietly, 'I'm going to put a bullet in your head at the count of three.' I think that's why my criminal type succeeded. I understood how to suggest, and in radio suggestion was everything."

Incidentally, since voice and suggestion were everything on radio, listeners developed the kind of voice sensitivity that blind people usually have. Even today many people are stunned by the sudden reminder of a soap opera voice of twenty or thirty years ago. Says Teri Keane, "I was once in a department store and I told the saleslady I wanted to see a hat, and right away the sales manager comes running out and tells me, 'As soon as I heard that voice I knew it was Teri Keane!' "

Don MacLaughlin adds: "Oh, those days in radio were wonderful. I look back and I miss all the fun I had—all the many roles I got a chance to play, all the friendships I made. It was a terribly exciting and unique experience. You grow older and an experience like that one can never be recaptured. Today we veterans are always getting together. Ginny, Teri, Charita Bauer, and myself go out to Mandy Kramer's and retell all the old stories. I guess to an outsider we'd sound a little crazy."

"Ginny" is Virginia Dwyer, *Another World*'s Mary Matthews, who played Chrystal Shields on *Joyce Jordan, Girl Interne,* Sally on *Front Page Farrell,* and other ingenues on shows like *Mary Noble—Backstage Wife* and *Houseboat Hanna.* Like Teri Keane, she played opposite Don MacLaughlin as Jocelyn on *The Road of Life.* Virginia, who is a far more urbane, worldly woman in real life than any of the heroines she has ever played on the soaps, remembers how she got the role of Jocelyn. "My husband, Walter Gorman, was directing *The Road of Life* at the time—that was in the fifties. Walter and I had an unofficial agreement that we would never work together. We believed in keeping marriage and work separate. But I wanted the part of Jocelyn and everyone else connected with the show kept telling me how right I was for it. Walter wouldn't hear of it. I actually had to threaten to leave home before he let me have the part." Jocelyn, who originally came from Samoa, where she was raised on beautiful beaches by an old man, finally came to civilization, where she began dying of something called "rubimortis." "Then Chuck Gussman, the writer, gave me Meniere's syndrome—a lot of people in soaps in those days got that." *The Road of Life,* just in case you're not old enough to remember, is remembered today as one of the more important daytime radio shows.

For many a young daytime viewer, the soaps began when Procter and Gamble and producer Roy Winsor presented Mary Stuart in a New York–based serial called *Search for Tomorrow* in 1951. But the hard-working, tal-

ented performers who pioneered in the early radio days
know better. They know that the daytime television serials
really started in another era, another city, and another
medium. Soap opera is a form that began rather casually
at first, then grew at an incredibly quick pace in the midst
of the Depression in Chicago.

Why did this multimillion-dollar broadcasting form
choose Chicago for its founding instead of New York,
where all the big money and radio resources were, or Hollywood, where all the nation's fantasy tales originated?
Probably because those two giant centers of culture would
have laughed at such a home-spun, "folksy" art as the
woman's soap opera. In those days, only the networks in
and around Chicago seemed to be open to the needs of
the Iowa or Ohio housewife. Money also played a part. As
Virginia Dwyer, who worked in radio in Chicago, notes,
"The daytime serial started in Chicago because there was
immense freedom there to experiment with different
forms. Economics did not require that you concentrate in
any one area." Only in the late thirties, when it was becoming increasingly obvious that big profits were to be
had in daytime radio dramas, did the soaps move from
Chicago to New York, for that was where all the big ra-
dio-producing ad agencies were.

How did the old radio serials start? Which one was the
first? It may seem hard to believe, but most historians feel
that the first real inspiration for the several hundred fifteen-minute daytime radio serials that were to be broadcast for thirty years was—are you ready?—*Amos 'n'
Andy*. That analysis may seem even more strange when
one realizes that the ancestors of today's modern daytime
television dramas were daytime radio dramas, which
therefore makes *Amos 'n' Andy* the real grandpappy of
As the World Turns, Another World, and all the others
on TV. Historians point out that after 1926, when
Freeman Gosden and Charles Correll introduced their two
lovable Negro characters on a Chicago radio station and
made a huge success of the continuing series, all sorts of
radio stations were looking to achieve successes with episodic stories centering around the personal problems of

one set of characters. The public soon took to other nighttime radio serials: *The Goldbergs, Clara Lu 'n' Em, Myrt
and Marge.* At this time, daytime radio was a wasteland.
If a housewife turned her radio on in the daytime, all she
heard were *Live Stock Reports, Our Daily Food,* and
Mouth Hygiene; so of course she didn't bother very often.

It wasn't long before the nighttime *Amos 'n' Andy*-
type serials were modified and adapted for women in the
daytime. In 1930 an Ohio schoolteacher by the name of
Irna Phillips was hired by Chicago's WGN (a strictly local, nonnetwork station) to write the first daytime serial
drama for women: *Painted Dreams.* Soon a few other
daytime dramas were experimented with locally. By 1933
the soaps were hitting the networks, and housewives all
over the country were listening to shows like *Betty and
Bob, Marie—The Little French Princess, Today's Children, Just Plain Bill, The Romance of Helen Trent,* and
Ma Perkins. The daytime serial was born, and so was, in
a way, daytime broadcasting.

During the next few years the daylight hours hummed
with dozens of fifteen-minute continuing stories of family
troubles, romance, heroine-ism, and personal dilemmas.
Eventually the audience swelled to more than twenty million listeners. Many of the titles of those shows are still
memorable. In 1935, listeners first heard *The Story of
Mary Marlin* and *Mary Noble—Backstage Wife;* in 1936,
David Harum, Girl Alone, John's Other Wife, Big Sister,
and *Bachelor's Children;* in 1937, *Aunt Jennie's True
Life Stories, The Guiding Light, Our Gal Sunday, The
Couple Next Door, Lorenzo Jones,* and *The Road of
Life;* in 1938, *Woman in White, Joyce Jordan—Girl In-
terne, Valiant Lady, Young Widder Brown, Stella Dallas,
Life Can be Beautiful,* and *Houseboat Hanna;* in 1939,
*When a Girl Marries, The Right to Happiness, Against
the Storm,* and *Young Doctor Malone.*

The growth of the new daytime radio serial was unbelievable. The Depression had been a sad time for the average American, and there was a great need for this kind of
entertainment. Daytime dramas of the period affirmed the
belief that life was but a series of misfortunes intermingled

with periods of happiness, and that this happiness was only found in love and marriage. The serials also afforded the housewife escape from the drudgery of her own life into the romantic worlds of heroines like Sunday, Stella Dallas, Helen Trent, and Mary Noble. The fictional characters were just ordinary women when they started out, but they soon proved to every housewife that romance and adventure were possible even for women chained to dustmops. Millions of housewives yearned to live like Helen Trent, and so did it vicariously.

Irna Phillips was one of the earliest creators of the daytime serial. Her astonishingly successful career of more than forty years, which included both radio and television writing—she was the *only* important serial writer to become successful in both media—came about by accident. She had been teaching school in Dayton, Ohio, for five years when one day, so the story goes, while on a visit to her native Chicago, she took a tour of one of the radio studios. Some harried director mistook her for an actress, handed her a script, and shoved her in front of a mike to do an audition. She was so good that the surprised director offered her a job. She refused then, but that summer (1930) reconsidered and took an unpaid radio job with WMAQ in Chicago, extemporizing *Thoughts for the Day.* In the fall she quit teaching and began writing *Painted Dreams,* the very first serial, for the Chicago *Tribune*'s local station, WGN. And, until her recent death, she had never stopped writing daytime serials since. In a way, a mere accident changed the face of radio and television for the next four decades.

In her radio creations—the most famous: *Painted Dreams, Today's Children, The Guiding Light, Woman in White, Road of Life,* and *Right to Happiness*—Irna Phillips established a pattern of pace, development, and "core" material that would be imitated by other serials all the way up to present-day television. In Miss Phillips's work, the endurance and sanctity of the family was the most important element, and her plot situations always grew naturally out of the strong characters she created. The problems that beset the Moynihans of *Painted*

Dreams, the Bauers of *The Guiding Light,* and the Kransky's of *The Right to Happiness*—developed from a subplot of *The Guiding Light*—were problems that would continually plague other families of other serials by other writers. She was also the first writer to use organ music as a way of setting a mood and bridging breaks in the narrative, and the first one to employ doctors, nurses, schoolteachers, and ministers as her main characters. (Can you think of a single daytime television drama today that does not have at least *one* doctor as a main character? You can thank Irna Phillips for that fact.) It is said that she was also the very first writer to have won the label "soap opera" for one of her creations, sponsored by Procter and Gamble, a soap company which was thereafter to sponsor innumerable other daytime serials.

In the beginning of her radio career, Irna Phillips wrote all of her own dialogue—some sixty thousand words, or the equivalent of an average-size novel, each week—and even acted in one of her early creations; she played the part of Mother Moran in *Today's Children.* Later she hired writers to help with dialogue—Agnes Nixon became one of her protégés—and started dictating her own dialogue, acting out all the various parts in different voices, to a secretary. Eventually her income soared to over a quarter of a million dollars a year (with the exception of Anne Hummert, she may well have become the richest woman in serial-land), and she recently estimated that her lifetime word-output is the equal of twenty-five hundred average-size novels.

People have always asked her how a woman who has never been married nor ever had a family of her own (she has two adopted children, however) could have portrayed family life and romantic problems so well in her creations. "Well, all of these problems couldn't be mine," she once answered. "I have lived the kind of life that most have lived and have had to adjust to experiences in it. Any tragedy that I have had has not been romantic, but I have been in love." At another time Miss Phillips admitted that she wrote from observations of other people. So curious was she about people that often she would chat at great length with the milkman, or newspaper boy—or whomever she'd meet that day—about their problems.

Only two other people have had a greater impact on the daytime radio serial than Irna Phillips. They were Frank and Anne Hummert. While Irna Phillips was writing the first radio soap opera, these two Chicago advertising people decided to set up their own radio production company. Their aim from the start was to fill the void in daytime radio broadcasting with serial fiction aimed at housewives. Years later, in a letter to Raymond William Stedman, published in his book, *The Serials,* Frank Hummert admitted that his idea that this kind of program would succeed was simply a guess, a "shot in the dark," based on the observation that newspaper comic-book serials went over very well. From that first guess, however, was to come almost all of the long-lived radio soaps that the public was to take to its heart. They introduced (in chronological order) *Just Plain Bill, The Romance of Helen Trent, Ma Perkins, David Harum, John's Other Wife, Our Gal Sunday, The Couple Next Door, Lorenzo Jones, Valiant Lady, Young Widder Brown, Stella Dallas, Houseboat Hanna, The Light of the World,* and *Front Page Farrell.*

The Hummerts did not actually write the scripts, but they originated the general theme of each show, along with a brief outline for its first six months or so. From that point on they operated what could only be termed a kind of General Motors of the daytime serial world—a script-writing factory. In essence, they had a number of story writers and dialoguers who never dealt directly with the bosses but had to go through supervisors or script editors. The system worked extremely well, and made for the Hummerts a king's ransom in income, although it did not especially inspire creativity. Some of their writers, however, managed to become famous despite the corporate structure. Charles Robert Andrews, for example, single-handedly wrote *Just Plain Bill* for more than ten years, and he gave *Ma Perkins* its unforgettable folksy flavor, until Orin Tovrov eventually took over.

And then there is Elaine Sterne Carrington, who was already a successful magazine writer when she began writing *Red Adams* for nighttime radio in 1932. The show was to be renamed *Pepper Young's Family,* and rebroadcast in the daytime. By the mid-thirties the name of Elaine Carrington was almost a household word. Among her other daytime successes were *Rosemary* and *When a Girl Marries*. It's generally conceded that Mrs. Carrington was one of the most literate of all radio soap writers.

People who grew up in the age of television may find it hard to believe that today's elaborate, expensive, and highly sophisticated daytime dramas really grew out of those old cornball—and they've been called far worse names—radio soaps. It may be easier to believe that only the *idea* of the daytime serials came from radio, rather than the content and the mystique. Nevertheless, television really did little more than refine and urbanize the old radio product. Essentially it was still the same, and we should be thankful for that. It was a good product, and it was loved. The millions of avid viewers who followed the adventures of Joanne Tate of *Search for Tomorrow* had the same spirit of devotion as the millions of listeners who were delighted for years by the many human involvements of Ma Perkins, Helen Trent, and all the other grand ladies of the afternoon.

If anything, listeners were even more fanatically devoted to their favorite heroines in the days of NBC Red and NBC Blue. According to James Thurber's "Soapland," listeners took their serials extremely seriously. For instance, once on *Just Plain Bill* the characters of Mr. and Mrs. Kerry Donovan (played by James Meighan and Ruth Russell) were expecting their first child, and the fictional couple received hundreds of baby gifts from their at-home admirers: "bonnets, dresses, booties, and even complete layettes." And several years later, when the same child that drew all those presents was killed in an automobile accident in the story, thousands of sympathy cards poured into the studios. In those days the severely embarrassed networks had a hush-hush policy about such identity-confusions on the audience fringe. Today, although similar things still happen, the audience is more sophisticated and is more likely to write kind or angry letters to the producers of a show for doing "this bad thing" or "that good thing" to characters.

As they do today, radio listeners of thirty or forty years ago became deeply upset when favorite actors playing familiar characters were replaced by other actors—for many of the same reasons you hear about now: a sudden Hollywood offer, a money dispute, or sheer boredom. James Thurber gave a wonderful example of this: On *Pepper Young's Family,* Elaine Carrington had a husband and wife talking in bed, episode after episode. According to Thurber, the man playing the husband eventually quit and was replaced by another actor, who continued in the same bedroom scenes. Many outraged women then wrote to the station, "protesting against these immoral goings on." Also, since actors often played on several serials simultaneously (unlike today), some women found it outrageous that a man married to one woman on one show could be married to another woman on another show.

Thurber also tells another wonderful radio story. Lucille Wall, who is now nicely settled into her role as the good-hearted senior nurse on *General Hospital,* was famous for many years as the bold lawyer-heroine, Portia, on *Portia Faces Life.* Once she had been critically hurt in a fall (in real life) and for many weeks had to be replaced on the show by Anne Seymour. At that time there weren't so many fan magazines spreading the news of stars' personal lives, but Miss Wall's fans found out about her illness and deluged her with letters and flowers. Miss Wall was moved to tears by the interest of so many people in her condition. So, at the end of one episode of *Portia,* from a microphone set up at bedside, she thanked the audience for their kindnesses and assured them she'd be back to work soon. In fact she was back on the show hardly four months after her accident. The doctors had predicted that she'd probably be out of work an entire year; there's little doubt that the demonstrated concern of her thousands of followers gave her the spirit to recover in a third of the time. Similarly, years later, Marjorie Gateson, who played Grace Tyrell on *The Secret Storm,* suffered a stroke and

was replaced by Eleanor Phelps. Telegrams and letter
poured in from all over the country wishing Miss Gateso
a speedy recovery. Although at this writing Miss Gateso
is still not fully recovered, she says how very grateful sh
was for all the kind thoughts and how much better the
made her feel.

On the surface, the radio soaps were very different from
today's half-hour shows. For a starter, many of them be
gan with those familiar opening thematic statements, o
"epigraphs", which had been almost the trademark of the
radio soaps. Just in case you've forgotten: after a few
strains of the tune of "Red River Valley," you were treated
to the opener: *"Our Gal Sunday*—the story of an orphan
girl named Sunday from the little mining town of Silve
Creek, Colorado, who in young womanhood married Eng
land's richest, most handsome lord, Lord Henry Brin
thrope. The story asks the question: Can this girl from a
mining town in the West find happiness as the wife of a
wealthy and titled Englishman?" Or, after "How Can
Leave Thee?" you might have heard: "And now *Stella
Dallas,* the true-to-life sequel—as written by us—to the
world famous drama of mother-love and sacrifice." And, o
course, along with "Juanita" you heard: "The Romance of
Helen Trent—the story of a woman who sets out to prove
what so many other women long to prove in their own
lives, that romance can live on at thirty-five and even be
yond." Or, after delighting to a bit of "Polly-Wolly
Doodle" played on harmonica and banjo, we heard: *"Just
Plain Bill*—the real-life story of a man who might be your
next-door neighbor . . . a story of people we all know."

These were wordy radio openers; but then words, not
visual images, were what made the radio serial work for
listeners. Today's TV serial listener learns the events of
yesterday's episode (which she may have missed) through
a sophisticated device in which characters discuss what
has happened recently in the story—but for the radio lis
tener of yesterday, the announcer did the recapitulation of
the story. So, with the epigraph and the announcer's re
cap—and a lot of theme music—the audience always had
to wait some time before the actual story began. (Today,

not only does the story begin almost immediately after the title announcement and commercial, but at least one show—*The Guiding Light*—begins the story *before* the title, as many movies do. This is meant as an enticement to keep viewers of *As the World Turns,* the previous show, from turning the dial.)

For instance, hear how one radio episode of *Mary Noble—Backstage Wife* started out: "*Mary Noble—Backstage Wife!*—the story of Mary Noble, a little Iowa girl who married Larry Noble, handsome matinee idol, dream sweetheart of a million other women, and her struggle to keep his love in the complicated atmosphere of backstage life." . . . Commercial . . . "And now, *Mary Noble—Backstage Wife! . . .* Mary has been the victim of a false friend, Armand Delubeck, who took her diamond engagement ring with the promise of having it repaired. But instead Armand pawned the ring and tried to blackmail Mary and Larry. And when Marsha Maring tried to make it appear that Mary was in love with Armand and had given the ring to him, she turned Larry violently against her. And thereupon Marsha conspired with Armand to get even with Mary and Larry. When Mary and Larry later discover that the ring has disappeared from the shop, Mary is heartbroken, and Larry is determined to notify the police."

By today's standards the epigraph was an obvious device, but it served its purpose well. It told listeners exactly what a show was all about; it was a boon to new serial listeners, and a good reminder to the old ones. Even the earliest daytime television serials used epigraphs, albeit much shorter (*Another World* and *Love of Life* did, and *Days of Our Lives* still does). In a way, it's a shame that epigraphs aren't still being used before the beginning of each episode as a way of conveying the theme. If they were, some shows that have gone astray, losing both their original themes *and* their ratings, might not have been so willing to change horses midstream. With an epigraph, *The Secret Storm,* for example, might not be just another memory, but as popular today as it was in the early sixties

when it was still dealing with the anguish and strife of the
Ames family.

Of course, there were many outrageously silly things
connected with the old radio soaps. None were sillier than
the jewelry giveaways that were awkwardly worked into
stories and then offered to listeners at the end of the program by some terribly embarrassed actor in the show. Listeners were required to send in a boxtop or two and at
least a quarter for a piece of costume jewelry "worth many
times that amount." Other sorts of premiums were offered,
but jewelry was chosen most often because it could be
worked more easily into the script—some brooch that Ma
Perkins was especially fond of, or some pin "with real sim-
ulated-gold flashing" that Lolly-baby had been given by
her wealthy husband. Actors always dreaded the incursion
of saccharine phrases that surrounded the introduction of
a piece of jewelry in a story, for this invariably meant
they'd be forced to sell the cheap, horrible thing to the audience at the end of the show. James Thurber heard a
young actress give this rehearsal dialogue reading: "I am
happy to meet you, Mrs. Nelson, and where in the world
did you get that perfectly stunning orchid clip? Why, it
gleams like virgin gold, and just look at those gorgeous
colors—exactly like a rainbow and sunset coming together
in a resplendent display of almost unimaginable beauty.
For heaven's sake, do I have to read this glop?" The director assured her that if she didn't they'd both be out of
a job.

Apart from such atrocities committed against the audience's intelligence, daytime radio drama was filled with
great imagination—perhaps more so than today's daytime television drama because writers and listeners weren't
restricted by the boundaries and limitations imposed
by visual sets and real faces and forms. Consequently,
Stella Dallas, in her continual fight to protect her daughter,
Laurel, from the vicissitudes of life, became a sort of
cross between Jane, girl of the jungle, and a concerned,
sedate mother like Joanne Tate. How wonderful it was
in one episode to hear of Stella's fight for survival in
the African jungles—especially grand for sound-effects

men, who had a field day—and in the next to "witness"
her dangling by a single thread from a tall building and
escape by sheer dint of her wits. Other heroines, too, were
far more colorful than today's TV breed. Mary Marlin, an
ordinary woman, made it all the way to the Senate; Mary
Noble, a simple girl from Iowa, not only got a chance to
marry dreamboat Larry Noble, a handsome matinee idol,
but eventually reached the stage herself and surpassed him
in acting ability. Pygmalion-like Sunday got a chance to
mingle with English hoity-toity, and Portia took on the
whole male-dominated legal profession by becoming a
lawyer herself and beating most of her male colleagues in
the courtroom. Helen Trent not only found what all other
women longed to find, but also became a top Hollywood
fashion designer to boot. This indeed was imagination, *ne
plus ultra!*

What these radio heroines lacked, however, was sex.
Some were married, but the closest any came to showing
any sort of carnal desires was the eternally long, breathy
sigh, or else the soundman simulated a quick mouth-to-
mouth kiss, and that didn't happen too frequently. There
were some divorces as the radio serials progressed, but never any illegitimate births. That phenomenon was to come
years later on television, along with abortion, illicit sex, sex
"bitches," and all the other shockers that daytime television scored with. What would Helen Trent and her
at-home admirers have thought if they had heard a recent
episode of *The Young and the Restless* in which Snapper
Foster and his mother have an outright discussion about
his sexual relations with one girl, and his confession that
another girl refused to go to bed with him after being
raped? Helen, who was still a virgin when she went off the
air in 1960, would be turning in her sudsy grave right
now.

In seeking out the graduates of radio serials who now
play roles on daytime television, one is not surprised to
find that they all seem to have one thing in common: longevity. Don MacLaughlin has been playing Chris Hughes
for over eighteen years on *As the World Turns;* Virginia

Dwyer has been playing Mary Matthews for more than ten years on *Another World;* Mandel Kramer and Teri Keane have played the Marceaus on *The Edge of Night* for just as long; Charita Bauer has played Bert Bauer on *The Guiding Light* for more than twenty-four years; Lucille Wall has been Lucille Weeks on *General Hospital* since the show started in 1963. It is not surprising that these people have managed to hang on to their television roles for so long. They were radio actors, and radio actors were a different breed from today's TV-born actors. A radio actor seldom turned up his nose at the security of a long-running part on a soap. Says Don MacLaughlin, "We in radio became businessmen, in the early days especially. Oh, other actors sneered at us, considered it beneath their dignity to appear on a radio soap, or any other radio program for that matter. Radio was too new—it didn't have much prestige. You'd hear people say about you, 'Oh, my God, he's over there doing a radio show.' But a certain group of people did it, prestige or no prestige, and made a lot of money at the same time. They always said that Gertrude Warner made more money in radio than Helen Hayes ever made in the theater. Of course, you only made good money if you worked hard. Actors started out in the morning on their way to the studios with briefcases filled with scripts, just like executives on Wall Street. I had more financial security in radio than theater actors. An actor in radio could buy a home in the country—my kids went to college."

The radio serial actor, therefore, didn't have to worry about fighting for glory—that came from the listeners, not from the critics or his colleagues. And so he became as persistent and consistent as any business executive. Many actors stayed with their roles for incredibly long periods of time—like Virginia Payne as Ma Perkins for twenty-seven years, or Mary Jane Higby as Joan Davis on *When a Girl Marries* for eighteen years, and Virginia Clark and Julie Stevens splitting twenty-seven years as Helen Trent. Those who chose to continue their roles on daytime television serials, after the death of radio soaps in the early to late fifties, carried along with them the same desire for longevity in a role.

When radio serials were vanishing in the fifties, many actors chose not to switch to television, however. Vivian Smolen, whose voice will never be forgotten as that of the soft-spoken Sunday, is today retired and living in a Manhattan apartment with her businessman-husband, Henry Kline, and their two poodles, Trudi and Trinket. Ann Elstner, whose deep voice was that of Stella Dallas between 1938 and 1955, runs a restaurant in Lambertville, New Jersey. Occasionally, if she takes a shine to a customer, she'll create shivers of nostalgia by reciting once again, "Lolly-baby, I ain't got time for nothing but trouble." Mary Jane Higby of *When a Girl Marries* turned author a few years back with her book, *Tune In Tomorrow,* and she spends a lot of time these days with her old friends.

It was Friday, November 25, 1960, that the last four remaining daytime radio serials faded away. *Ma Perkins* stopped baking her apple pies; the Braden Family stopped searching for their *Right to Happiness; Young Dr. Malone* had to retire of old age; *The Second Mrs. Burton* had to move from her second place to no place at all. It was a sad time indeed. The villain, TV, had slowly been usurping the radio soaps' right to live—for how could the sexless radio serial, which continued to hold on to the policy of only sighs and back-of-hand kissing, compete with the visual mouth-to-mouth kissing and love-clinches of TV's daytime stories? Radio soaps, for many, had become hopelessly old-fashioned. Audiences no longer wanted to see their heroines stay virgins for thirty years. But still, when the prudery of radio soaps died, so did their endless imaginative quality. Many were deeply saddened when the inevitable end came. When those last four shows faded out of existence, even some of the most hardened critics of the radio soaps shed a tear of remorse for the demise of that once seemingly eternal breed of heroines and heroes who were heard and loved, but never ever seen.

❧ V ❧

Television Takes Over

IN THE EARLY 1950s—when daytime TV was first threatening the established radio serials—there was a panicky movement on the part of radio actors to try to quash this new and terrible incursion of the video monster on their lifeblood.

It didn't help. For ten years radio and TV shared serial listeners, until, in 1960, the last serial heroines were killed by the stiff competition, and radio soaps became just a memory, its history merely a subject for memoirs.

However, it did take ten years, and no one was really sure who would win the war for the favors of listeners (and viewers) of daytime serials. For a while there was so much soap opera going on in both media that housewives were like happy children, gleefully lost in a candy store, not knowing which confection to select. In 1956, for example, the housewife could choose from at least ten visual serials, and many more radio serials. There were even three serials—*The Guiding Light, The Brighter Day,* and *The Road of Life*—that were aired on both media, for a while, anyway, so if a viewer missed the radio show, she could watch it later in the afternoon on TV. Soap lovers never had it so good.

Many soap actors, directors, and producers were delighted to have the opportunity to work in both TV and radio. Naturally, television chose most of its daytime stars from its radio serials because of the actors' experience and reliability in a continuing story format. But just as many radio actors were terrified of having to make the transition. They had had it so good for so many years, doing little more on the serials than a few quick rehearsals and then reading parts directly from scripts they held in front of the mikes. The new TV serials required a lot more: memorizing lines—what radio actors dreaded most, especially on a daily basis—hours and hours of rehearsing, moving about in front of hot lights, camera-blocking. "You didn't have to be very good on radio," says Don MacLaughlin, "just very fast. And because you just read your script, you got into the bad habit of settling into your one little niche. When the radio serials showed signs of disappearing because of television in the 1950s, there were many radio actors who became sad cases at a certain point. There was such discouraging talk, and a lot of insecure feeling about learning lines. I must admit I wasn't very confident myself before I started on *As the World Turns*."

The early TV serials were grueling work indeed for radio actors who turned to this brave new world. Stefan Schnabel, who for the last nine years has played Dr. Stephen Jackson on *The Guiding Light*, remembers a short stint he did on that TV show back in the old Liederkrantz Hall when it first began in 1952. Television itself was only a few years old at that time. "I remember you always needed so much light to work in front of the cameras. The temperature was 120 degrees, and you tried your best not to look worn out during the live broadcast. You had to wipe your brow a lot. There were three batteries of forty-eight 3,000-watt bulbs to make the system work properly. It's absolutely nothing like that now in the studios." For a long time actors on the TV serials didn't even have teleprompters in case they forgot lines.

Officially, the first televised soap opera was a one-day experiment with the broadcasting of the radio serial *Big Sister* in 1946. But it is Irna Phillips who claims responsibility for the very first continuing televised daytime serial, called *These are Our Children*, launched on a Chicago TV station shortly after the *Big Sister* one-day experiment. About the same time, 1947, the first New York local television soap opera was sent over the airwaves. It was called *A Woman to Remember* and was televised from the old Dumont studios at Wanamaker's department store. *A Woman to Remember* starred John Raby—who was then also costarring with Mary Jane Higby on radio's *When A Girl Marries*—Patricia Wheel, Ruth McDevitt, and Frank Thomas, Jr.

This serial didn't last long, and some of the actors who appeared in it went back to their radio cohorts with such horror stories of daily working conditions, adding to the already spreading fear and panic over the new TV demon. Mary Jane Higby in *Tune In Tomorrow* remembers how her costar, John Raby, came back to their radio show after his debut on *A Woman to Remember* and "shook slightly" when he picked up his script; he was "pale and pensive." He told Mary Jane that during the TV show he played a scene with an actress who simply panicked and tried to run off the set. He had to grab her, push her into a chair, and say her lines as well as his own. After the show he threw up. For all his heroic efforts, he was making a wopping hundred dollars a week on *A Woman to Remember*.

Despite that disaster, CBS was willing to give a daytime serial a try in 1950. That first nationwide network serial was called *The First Hundred Years;* it dealt with the problems of newlyweds, one of whom was played by James Lydon. Nat Polen, who is now Dr. James Craig on *One Life to Live*, was also in the show. Compared to *A Woman to Remember*, this effort was a big success. It lasted one whole year. One would wonder, with this kind of dismal record, how any of the radio heroines could have worried a whit about their right to life and happiness on the airwaves. To observers, TV serials seemed doomed from the start.

NBC was the next to try two network daytime serials after CBS: *Miss Susan* featured Susan Peters in the title role of a young, crippled girl, and *Hawkins Falls*, was a

kind of sexless *Peyton Place,* patterned after an actual
town—Woodstock, New York. The show was expensive,
with all the outdoor scenes filmed on location at Woodstock, and it lasted for four years.

The early daytime television serial had many things
against it. Radio serials, for one, were still going strong,
and for another, they were much cheaper to produce.
(*Ma Perkins,* only cost $1300 per week to produce, and
the average weekly cost of a daytime television serial was
more than five times that amount; today, they cost from
$40,000 to $60,000 per week to produce, or more than
six times the original cost of television serials, and more
than thirty to forty times those of radio!) Major actors on
TV serials had to be paid $300 a week or more (Mary
Stuart was paid an astonishing $500 per week when she
began), whereas on radio, A.F.T.R.A. permitted producers to pay serial actors a minimum of only $152.50
per week. Why would a sponsor want to buy time on the
shaky new daytime serials when he could spend less
money, for a larger share of the audience, on radio? One
reason is that CBS-TV was absolutely enthusiastic about
the potential of daytime TV serials. In fact, in the beginning it was mostly CBS's pioneering spirit and indefatiga-
ble belief that what housewives wanted—and would always want—was soap operas, that gave television daytime
dramas their initial boost.

NBC did not share the same faith, much to the disad-
vantage of its new daytime programming. So lukewarm
and undecided was this network about what it wanted
women to watch in the daytime that it followed a self-de-
feating pattern of scheduling and canceling serials on its
TV network; and in 1955, NBC even killed four of the
best-known soaps on its radio network: *Just Plain Bill,*
Lorenzo Jones, Stella Dallas, and *Young Widder Brown.*
Then the tears of radio addicts started to flow! NBC replaced these radio shows with a multi-program, "up-to-
date" conglomerate called *Newsweek,* a dismal and monu-
mental failure that embarrassed the network.

CBS, the broadcasting "guiding light" of the soaps,
gave the go-ahead to producer Roy Winsor for his new

TV serial, *Search for Tomorrow,* which premiered on the historic date of September 3, 1951. One says "historic" because that show, along with the ones that followed shortly afterward, proved how absolutely right was CBS's faith in the soaps in those days. Today, *Search for Tomorrow* is the longest-running daytime serial—longest-running television show of any type, in fact—and Mary Stuart, the star, is today *the* most celebrated serial heroine. Needless to say, *Search* made considerable money for its sponsor, Procter and Gamble, then, as it does now.

CBS was developing a daytime windfall. On September 24, 1951, a mere three weeks after *Search for Tomorrow* premiered, CBS started *Love of Life,* which is now TV's second oldest serial. Like *Search, Love of Life* was conceived and produced by Roy Winsor, working through the now defunct Biow ad agency for its client, American Home Products.

Love of Life, like all TV serials then, was a fifteen-minute, black-and-white, studio-created show. All the scenes took place in the simple, simulated homes of Barrowsville, a fictional town—later on, all the action moved to Rosehill, New York, to give the characters a more urban background. From the first day, the show was directed by Larry Auerbach, who—one could say he's sort of the Mary Stuart of daytime serial directors—is still with the show. He says, "In the early days everything was very simple. We had free-standing doors and we used black velour for walls. The characters worked almost in an abstract set. We didn't have to worry about having props in color then."

Unlike today, *Love of Life* had a very clear-cut theme when it began in 1951, and the theme stayed that way for nearly ten years. It was primarily the story of two sisters: Vanessa Dale, played by Peggy McCay, and Meg Dale Harper, played by Jean McBride. Van was good, and believed in everyone's essential right to dignity, but her sister, Meg, wasn't. "Van," says Roy Winsor, thinking back on the show, "was a *real* person living in a world of hypocrites." Reminiscent of the radio serials, this show had an epigraph. *"Love of Life*—Vanessa Dale's search for human dignity."

It was, in its own way, a televised radio serial; for all the daytime radio soaps also had clear-cut themes and at least one heroine who fought for the right-to-happiness of those around her. Viewers, like radio listeners, knew exactly what they were watching and what the point, or moral, of the whole story was. But, in another way, *Love of Life* was already more advanced than the radio soaps, which were still being aired at the time this show premiered. During the first episodes, Meg was already suing her husband—played by Paul Potter—for a divorce and was playing around with other men. Sex was no longer a forbidden subject, but had become essential to the story. No attempt was made to keep Van different from other housewives—as was done, say, with Mary Noble or Sunday. Although unmarried, Van was most concerned with the welfare of her nephew, Beanie; so she was therefore also a kind of mother. Later, unlike untouchables such as Helen Trent, Van married, just like any other woman. TV, from the very start, brought sex to the soap. Serial historian Raymond William Stedman, in his book *The Serials,* makes the observation, "On the same day that Helen Trent was resisting the advances of Kurt Bonine, Vicky Harcourt [the character], on TV's *Love of Life,* was teasing a producer into giving her a part by touching the top button of her blouse and laughingly threatening to 'call for help and say you were molesting me.' " Audiences who heard both serials that day must have thought Helen an absolute nun by comparison!

So CBS, and Roy Winsor particularly, must have been thinking right. Almost all the folksiness of shows like *Just Plain Bill* and *Lorenzo Jones* had disappeared, and the unreal storybook quality of the super-heroines like Helen, Stella, Sunday, and Mary Noble became the practical, everyday attractiveness of housewives like Joanne Tate, Vanessa Dale Raven, Bert Bauer, and all the rest. Women at home could now see *themselves*—at their very best—in their serial stories, for they were growing up and they wanted their serial heroines to grow up, too.

Of course, there were those who, when the TV soaps first began and were having trouble gaining an audience, declared that television could never duplicate the incredible imagination of the afternoon shows. How could you possibly show characters running in the rain, on trains, caught in earthquakes, going on safaris? And where would casting directors ever find actresses who would remain the great beauties that radio heroines were supposed to be? Well, they couldn't and didn't; and it turned out that simple conversations and indoor sets were as effective in capturing audience involvement as anything the radio soaps had offered—and, when all was said and done, most of the action in radio daytime serials happened indoors anyway. In any case, when TV serials first started, housewives seemed to use them the way they used radio—they *listened,* and while they listened they would move away from the TV set and do all their chores: ironing, cleaning, cooking, etc. Now, of course, twenty-four years after the premiere of *Search for Tomorrow* and *Love of Life,* the point is no longer moot. With spectacular color productions, and characters shown rushing in and out of doors, getting hit by cars, wandering through open woods, and wearing beautiful clothes (Mary Stuart now wears dresses worth five hundred to a thousand dollars each), few people are still willing to settle for just listening.

On June 30, 1952, the network made another happy decision when it premiered Procter and Gamble's *The Guiding Light,* simply continuing the story from radio (where it also stayed until 1956). It was still being expertly written by Irna Phillips, still had its familiar organ music, and was now, on television, deeply concerned with the exploits of Meta, one of the three Bauer children. Ted Corday directed the show. Most of the radio actors did the TV show while still doing the radio version later on in the day.

While CBS-TV was doing all the right things in establishing popular, long-lived daytime serials, NBC-TV was doing all the wrong things. The network officials simply had no concept of what viewers wanted, and whenever they did hit upon a good serial—like *First Love*—they were too insecure to keep it going. All their efforts, unlike CBS's entries, appeared and disappeared rapidly, usually within a year. *The House in the Garden* (also called *Fairmeadows, U.S.A.*), about marital troubles, began late in 1952 and lasted only three months. The next serial, *The Bennetts,* was based on a similar theme of marital discord and lasted only six months—from July 6, 1953 to January 8, 1954. It starred Don Gibson, Paul Houston, Jerry Harvey, and Ray Westfall. Then NBC started a group of serials about "the woman alone," a kind of TV answer to Helen Trent and all those movies of the forties about attractive women who prefer loneliness to unhappiness with the wrong man. This was not what the modern housewife wanted—she simply couldn't identify with these stoics who loved to wallow in romantic indecision. Among these failed serials was *Follow Your Heart* (it ran from 1953 to 1954), written by Elaine Carrington, who had previously made a success on radio with the young-girl-in-love theme of her *When a Girl Marries.* In the serial, Julie Fielding (Sally Brophy) and her mother (Nancy Sheridan) were Philadelphia society ladies who disagreed about who Julie and her sisters should marry. In the next one, *Three Steps to Heaven* (nearly the same dates as *Follow Your Heart*), Poco (Kathleen McGuire) was a New York model with romantic troubles. Other actors in this serial were Phillis Hill, Lori March (of *Secret Storm* fame), Laurie Vendig (as Alice), Ginger McManus (as Angela), and Mark Roberts (as Bill). Next in 1954, was a story about a girl reporter, called *A Time to Live,* and it starred Pat Sully and Larry Kerr. Then a soap about a widowed physician, *The Greatest Gift,* started in 1954 and lasted a year; it starred Anne Burr as Dr. Eve Allen and Phillip Foster as Dr. Phil Stone. There was also one about an aspiring singer, *Golden Windows* (same dates), which starred Leila Martin and Herb Patterson. *First Love* followed, lasting for two years, and then came *Concerning Miss Marlowe,* which lasted for one year.

These last two serials were outstanding efforts and certainly deserved to be aired longer than they were. *Concerning Miss Marlowe,* about the problems of a fortyish

actress still searching for love, was well written and ha
the considerable talents of Louise Albritton, John Raby
and Efrem Zimbalist as the romantic leads. *First Lov*
was an engrossing and tempestuous tale of two newl
married people deeply in love—Zach James and his wife
played with charisma by Val Dufour and Patricia Barry.

Val played the role for two years with Miss Barry (nov
Addie on *Days of Our Lives*) and has since gone on to
number of other daytime roles, including a heavy, Andr
Lazar, on *The Edge of Night;* a district attorney, Walte
Curtin, on *Another World* (a role he had for eight years)
and his present role on *Search for Tomorrow,* attorne
John Wyatt. He says today that he thinks *First Love* wa
a fine show and probably could have succeeded as
long-term soap. "But NBC was so erratic in those days
They just didn't know what they wanted. They woul
confuse audiences by starting and canceling shows to
quickly. Now, you know that for one show to catch on i
the daytime, there should be good ones before it and afte
it. NBC's policies at that time prevented this, so *Firs
Love* was forced to leave the air, even though our charac
terizations had caught on with a lot of people."

In those days, Val had to travel four hours a day to do
the program live in Philadelphia. He lived in New Yor
City. When he got up in the morning, it wasn't even ligh
out, and he didn't get home until evening. For all his ef
forts, he was paid only a fraction of what he earns now o
Search for Tomorrow.

While poor NBC struggled along, forever canceling an
starting again—ABC-TV wasn't concerned yet with tele
vised soap operas—CBS continued adding to its successfu
afternoon lineup. *The Secret Storm* was first seen o
February 1, 1954. It was an instant success—exactly wha
daytime TV audiences were waiting for: complex drama
passion, good characterizations, the story of a big family
Unlike many serials that had soapy-sounding workin
titles, *The Secret Storm* lived up to the promise of its title
Under Roy Winsor's expert "packaging," the serial reall
did offer viewers a unique "secret storm" of desperate in
ner conflicts and hidden desires—all outwardly manifeste

by the continuing melodrama of the family of Peter Ames.

And this *was* melodrama! On Winsor's program there were more shocking deaths, sudden bouts with insanity, illnesses, and embattled love affairs than on any other daytime drama. Viewers became familiar with and interested in the Ames family from the very first episodes. The serial, for example, opened up with a death so devastating in its effect that it left the Ameses in a state of confused bewilderment that not even tears could express. Hence: their "secret storm."

"There were two aspects to the story of *The Secret Storm*," says Roy Winsor. "On the one hand, you had a story of Peter Ames, a man trying to show his family that how they coped with their problems at home was in a way symbolic of how successful they were in dealing with the whole world. On the other hand, you had a kind of tale like that of O'Neill's play *Strange Interlude*—with all the members of one family withdrawing into their own secret worlds of despair." Winsor laughs, "I remember we were originally going to call the show *The Inner Storm,* but Bisodol was going to be one of our sponsors, and we didn't want any unfortunate imagery in the title. So we went from 'Inner' to 'Secret'!"

Once again Roy Winsor exhibited genius with his invention of *The Secret Storm* theme. Six years after the show started, few daytime devotees dared spend a weekday without peeking in to find out what new tragedies and entanglements were befalling the long-suffering and fascinating Ames family.

CBS, however, wasn't always to remain a leader in originating and maintaining the excellence of daytime television dramas, and the network's later bungling of this fine serial became a tragedy for millions of daytime soap lovers. *The Secret Storm* lasted exactly twenty years and one week—then CBS finally canceled the show.

Storm was Roy Winsor's third successful daytime television serial in a row. When no one else seemed to know what kind of soaps housewives wanted to watch, if any, Winsor came up with one creative idea after another, determining what daytime television would be like for the next twenty years. "You might almost call me the 'Father of Daytime TV Serials,' " he says, timidly adding, "I guess I'm proud of that."

Winsor had written and produced many of the old radio serials that originated in Chicago and, in the early fifties, was vice-president in charge of radio and television for the Milton H. Biow advertising agency. "Television was new and expensive compared to radio, but Procter and Gamble thought it could make a success of daytime television serials as it had with radio. They approached the Biow agency, and I came up with the theme and story for *Search for Tomorrow*." Winsor says that it didn't take long before he, the sponsor, and the agency knew that *Search* was a ratings success. Soon afterward, American Home Products approached the same agency for a similar deal, and Winsor created the themes of *The Secret Storm* and *Love of Life* for them. What was Winsor's success formula? "I had no formula, I just came up with good solid themes. The audience could always follow what we were doing in the stories. I'm not so sure that they can today. Viewers usually don't know *what* they're watching when they see a daytime serial today. The themes of shows aren't clear anymore." In those days, Winsor seemed to have that rare ability both to originate the idea and to carry it through as a producer. Today, of course, producers just *produce*—they don't come up with the themes or stories of serials. (Just recently, Roy Winsor became head writer for *Somerset*.)

The Secret Storm began in 1954, and although it gave CBS its fourth strong daytime serial, the network still only had four fifteen-minute shows, or exactly one hour's worth of afternoon television. NBC was still floundering about trying to find the right sort of format for daytime shows. All the "woman alone" type serials had collapsed, and so had their two updated versions of *Ma Perkins*: *Hawkins Falls* and *The World of Mr. Sweeney*. The latter was a series of self-contained stories which first began on *The Kate Smith Show* and starred Charles Ruggles as Cicero P. Sweeney, the widowed owner of a general store. Helen Wagner, known to millions since 1956 as Nancy Hughes on *As the World Turns,* made her daytime TV debut here. By 1955, *Hawkins Falls* and *Mr. Sweeney* were both gone.

Radio, on the other hand, still had nearly twenty daytime serials of long-standing popularity—many more hours of daytime drama than television had. In the mid-fifties, radio soaps seemed more popular than ever. Naturally, then, a few network executives put their heads together and wondered why daytime television couldn't do just as well as radio by offering *exactly* the same thing. After all, *The Guiding Light* was now doing fine in both media. The outcome of this logic was the introduction of a whole series of radio soaps on CBS-TV; NBC-TV more timidly tried out only one. CBS started the back-to-the-old-radio-serial ball rolling by introducing, in 1953, a new edition of the defunct Hummert soap opera, *Valiant Lady:* "The story of a brave woman and her brilliant but unstable husband—the story of her struggle to keep his feet planted firmly on the pathway to success." Flora Campbell had the lead. CBS, in 1954, also brought forth the old *Portia Faces Life,* which had originally starred Lucille Wall as the brilliant lady lawyer but now featured Fran Carlon; *The Brighter Day*—now starring Mary Beller and Lois Nettleton—the story of the people of Three Rivers; and *The Road of Life,* all about the trials and tribulations of Dr. Jim Brent and company and still starring Don MacLaughlin. Meanwhile, NBC came up with *One Man's Family,* which, incidentally, had been a night-time radio show until a year after it premiered on daytime television; then the show went onto daytime radio in 1955, where it fared much better. That was a switch! NBC assembled an incredible cast for this serial: Eva Marie Saint (and later Anne Whitfield) as Claudia, Tony Randall, James Lee, William Schaaf, Russell Thorson (as Paul), Marjorie Gateson (who soon after took on the role of Grace Tyrell on *The Secret Storm* and remained in that part for many years), Arthur Casell, and Theodore von Eltz—later replaced by Bert Lytell—and Mary Adams (as Father Barbour and Mother Barbour). Carlton E.

Morse, who had written the radio version, also wrote the television script.

Radio and television serials were obviously not incompatible; but the fact that only *The Guiding Light* on CBS, of all the ones relocated, was to become a permanent part of the daytime scene (*The Brighter Day* did last as long as four years), seemed to prove that radio soaps were rather old-fashioned for modern television audiences. Yet millions still listened to them on radio. (*The Road of Life, The Brighter Day,* and *The Guiding Light* could be heard simultaneously on television and radio.) In other words, television executives still had to keep looking for their own daytime thing.

And CBS continued to do just that. In 1956 a historic decision was reached. The network premiered both *As the World Turns* and *The Edge of Night* as the first half-hour daytime TV serials. It was a phenomenally successful experiment that made CBS the daytime broadcasting titan of its day.

As the World Turns really came about because of a disagreement. Irna Phillips, who had been writing *The Guiding Light* for Procter and Gamble, told the soap company that she thought the show would do well as a half-hour venture. It was a matter of sheer economics: one thirty-minute show would cost less than two fifteen-minute shows, and therefore would produce greater profits for the sponsor. But *The Guiding Light* had been doing well for nineteen years as a fifteen-minute show and P & G was afraid to jostle the format. Miss Phillips, always the strong-minded innovator, then proposed a new half-hour soap—the very first ever—to prove her point. So *As the World Turns* was custom-tailored by its creator for a new longer format. The network and the sponsor bought it and again a milestone in the history of daytime television serials was achieved.

Miss Phillips presented not more story with her extra fifteen minutes, as one would have expected with another writer, but more elaboration—closer looks at the things she knew people especially liked about daytime serials. Viewers now saw a soap couple, Nancy and Chris

Hughes, having longer conversations, going into greater detail than did couples on other shows. The Lowell family, too, was seen pondering their problems and working out their interrelationships for longer than they would have on a fifteen-minute show. The result was that the world of *As the World Turns* turned ever-so-slowly indeed, and the audience instantly fell in love with the style. *This* was what the networks were looking for. *This* was the form that was completely right for afternoon TV. Viewers could not follow *As the World Turns* the same way they listened to a radio serial—while looking after the ironing or cooking—there were just too many long pauses, slow turns, quiet looks, and nuances of expressions. Irna Phillips had once again invented a form—the daytime television serial.

There was probably no greater threat to the rights-to-happiness of the radio heroines than the arrival of *As the World Turns* on television—for the show soon became terribly popular. To a handful of radio actors, however, the show was a boon. Ted Corday, the show's new producer, and Walter Gorman, the director, had both been radio directors for many years. They knew how reliable and talented radio actors were, and so lifted almost the entire original cast of *As the World Turns* right off the radio. William Johnstone—Grandfather "Judge" Lowell—had been *The Shadow* for many years. (Oh, those poor souls who never heard Mr. Johnstone intone: "Who knowsss—what *eee*vil—lurrrrks—in the hearts of men? The shadow knows!") Mr. Johnstone's sidekick on that ever-popular nighttime radio thriller, Commissioner Weston, was Santos Ortega, who now played Grandpa Hughes. Anne Burr, radio's *Big Sister,* was hired as Claire Lowell; and Les Damon, the old *Thin Man,* played her unfaithful husband, Jim Lowell. Their daughter on *World,* Ellen, was played by Wendy Drew, once heard by listeners as "Young Widder Brown" herself. Of course Chris Hughes has always been played by Don MacLaughlin, who was still playing Dr. Jim Brent on *The Road of Life* and rushing off to *sur-gerr-eeeee* when Ted Corday hired him for *World.*

The Road of Life, however, was both the TV *and* the radio version—so Don did have some experience on daytime television. But Walter Gorman, the director, had practically to force him into doing the TV *Road* in 1954, so nervous had Don been about his first television show. By the time of *As the World Turns,* however, actors felt lucky to get good parts on afternoon television.

A few of the first *World* actors didn't come from radio. Helen Wagner (Nancy Hughes) had only recently made her television debut on *The World of Mr. Sweeney.* Ruth Warrick, playing Edith Hughes, had once been a big movie star. Rosemary Prinz (playing Penny Hughes) had only just come from playing a minor role on NBC's *First Love,* with Val Dufour and Patricia Barry. However, by the time she finished her twelve years as Penny, Rosemary had become so famous that she could practically write her own ticket. Daytime TV producers were promising this one-time obscure young actress *anything*—a king's ransom in salary, her own say in the story line—if she would only agree to star in another soap. *As the World Turns* really made phenomenal stars out of *all* of its long-time actors simply because it was a phenomenal show. Ted Corday couldn't have made a better decision than to hire radio actors for a show such as this, which required absolutely precise pacing and good character delineation, for radio taught those skills. Ted Corday, Walter Gorman, and Irna Phillips (now all dead) were radio products themselves. In so many ways, radio created *As the World Turns.*

Within a few years of its debut, it was estimated that twenty million viewers heard, every day, the familiar announcer's voice: "And now—live!—for the next thirty minutes! *As the World Turns!*" Some polls even claimed that fifty million different viewers would, in one week's time, watch the show, which for years was to occupy place number one in the Nielsen ratings.

The Edge of Night, which began on the same day as *As the World Turns*—April 2, 1956—was another milestone (aside from the fact that it also ran thirty minutes) in that it was the very first non-soap-opera daytime serial. *Edge* was primarily an imitation of the old radio *Perry Mason*

and concerned the exploits of Assistant District Attorney
Mike Karr, played by John Larkin, who was one of the
old Perrys on radio. Other actors in the original cast were
Teal Ames, as Sarah Lane (later Mike's wife, Sarah Karr),
and Don Hastings as her brother, Jack Lane. Walter
Greasea played Winston Grimsley until his death recently.
Don Hastings was practically born on television, while
television itself was being born. He played the Video
Ranger on *Captain Video*—and what thirty-year-old today doesn't remember *that* brilliant series?—while still in
his teens with radio actor Al Hodge (*The Green Hornet*)
and Nat Polen as Agent Carter. (Says Nat, "We received
just thirty dollars a show for *Captain Video!*") A few
years later Don found a permanent daytime television
home for himself playing Bob Hughes on *Edge*'s twin, *As
the World Turns*.

CBS now had six successful serials, and NBC only had
The Brighter Day, which lasted eight years, from 1954
until 1962 (it left radio in 1956). But that was to be it for
a long while. From 1956 until the early sixties NBC kept
up its seemingly useless struggle to build a competitive
daytime serial lineup. NBC had already recently failed
with two shows, *The Way of the World* (with Anne Burr
and Addison Powell) and *Date With Life,* about schoolteacher Jennifer (June Dayton), who couldn't decide
whether she should marry her boyfriend, David (played
by Dean Harens, Miss Dayton's real-life husband). Viewers, however, had already made up their minds about the
conflict. Then CBS came up with some valiant follow-ups
to their successful half-hour shows: *Hotel Cosmopolitan*
and the experimental *The Verdict is Yours.* The latter was
a well conceived simulated courtroom drama, with Jim
McCay playing the part of reporter-narrator. Neither
show got a good ratings verdict, but at least the network
was showing the same fine spirit of experimentation that
had won them their initial lead on daytime. NBC then revived two radio serials: *Kitty Foyle,* with Kathleen Murray as Kitty and Judy Lewis (later, Susan Ames on *The
Secret Storm*) as Molly; and *Young Dr. Malone,* with
William Prince playing the old Allan Bunce radio role of

Dr. Jerry Malone, John Connell in the old Bill Lipton role of Dr. David Malone, and Augusta Dabney (Mr. Prince's on- and off-screen wife) as Tracey Malone. The radio and TV shows ran simultaneously until 1960, when it was discontinued on radio. The television show ended in 1963.

In 1958, NBC also tried two other daytime serials: *Today is Ours,* about the problems of a young mother, played sympathetically by Pat Benoit, and *From These Roots* (premiered June 30, 1968), which ran only four years but will probably be remembered by all longtime daytime watchers for its fine story and exceptionally bright cast. *Roots* was a good title for this soap, for there had probably never before been a daytime drama with so many actors who were later to become famous on other, more successful serials. Try this for a start: Ann Flood played Liz Fraser Allen (Ann is now Nancy Karr on *The Edge of Night*); Bob Mandan played her playwright husband, David Allen (Bob became Joanne Tate's fiancé, Sam Reynolds, on *Search for Tomorrow*); Billie Lou Watt played Maggie Weaver (she's now Ellie Harper on *Search*); Audra Lindley played Laura Tompkins (Audra became Liz Matthews on *Another World* and later went to Hollywood to star in *Bridget Loves Bernie* with David Birney, another ex-daytime star); Barbara Berjer played Lynn (Barbara played Claire Cassen on *As the World Turns* and is currently Barbara Norris on *The Guiding Light*); Millette Alexander played Gloria Saxon (she's now Dr. Sarah McIntire on *The Guiding Light*); and Craig Huebing played Tom Jennings (he's now out in Hollywood in a *General Hospital* lead as Dr. Peter Taylor). Also, Henderson Forsythe, *As the World Turns'* Dr. David Stewart, was seen for a while as a heavy. *From These Roots*—an apt title, wouldn't you say?

The story dealt with the problems of the Fraser family, who lived in the New England town of Strathfield and was headed by Ben Fraser (Joseph Macauley), editor of the local paper, *The Record.* Why this excellent serial lasted only four years is a mystery. Was it a brief ratings problem? Or was it NBC's "cancellation fever" hitting again?

If 1958 was a bad year for daytime television, it was a simply dreadful one for radio serials. NBC had heartlessly killed several within a few years, and now even CBS radio was giving up on them. Poor Mary Noble, Sunday, Jocelyn, and Nora Drake—all left out in the cold when, in December of 1958, CBS canceled *Mary Noble—Backstage Wife, Our Gal Sunday, The Road of Life,* and *This is Nora Drake.* For the housewives who preferred their television tubes in the daytime, this was no great tragedy. But for many people who had spent years listening to these serials, it was as if someone had told them that some of their favorite friends had not survived the winter. Daytime radio lovers were heartbroken.

Meanwhile, back on the TV tube the tragedies were compounded by some stillbirths. In 1959, NBC tried a socially conscious series about juvenile delinquency called *The House on High Street.* Like its *Modern Romances,* which faded a few years before, the format was episodic. It featured Phillip Abbott and Leona Dana, and the show didn't last long. During the same year CBS started *For Better or Worse,* which turned out to be the latter. Even the presence of pre-movie star Dyan Cannon, as the newly wedded wife, playing opposite Ronald Foster as her husband, couldn't spell success. That was also the case with *Full Circle* and *The Clear Horizon,* both premiering in 1960. *The Clear Horizon* was a marvelous story, about the first Cape Canaveral astronauts and their courageous wives; the fine cast was headed by Phyllis Avery and Ed Kemmer, who is now Ben Grant on *Somerset.* CBS was never cancellation prone, so one must conclude that *The Clear Horizon* would probably have succeeded if it had been on nighttime television with a higher percentage of males in the audience.

In 1960, several important things happened—not especially *on* daytime television, but mostly *because* of daytime television. The last four radio serials—*The Right to Happiness, Ma Perkins, Young Dr. Malone,* and *The Second Mrs. Burton*—signed off on November 25, 1960. This was the same year that the so-called Golden Age of Television was on its way out. The term "Golden Age" usually refers to the era of Sid Caesar and live nighttime television dramas like *Philco Playhouse, Armstrong Circle Theater,* and *Playhouse 90* (recently revived!). The success of daytime television dramas and the large amounts of money that sponsors were able to make from these continuing serials slowly began to influence nighttime television producers. The trend actually started in the fifties with more and more continuing stories—distinguished by the fact that, like daytime soaps, they had the same set of characters each week—like *I Remember Mama* and *Father Knows Best*; culminated in the sixties with soap imitations such as *Peyton Place*; and continued into the seventies with more depressing and morbid police-crime-murder series than one would imagine the average family could take. The point is, daytime television, and its profitable economics, caused nighttime television to do a little imitating of its own, and in doing so pushed all those great, live nighttime TV dramas off the networks. However, by no stretch of the imagination could the daytime serials be blamed for the wasteland that nighttime TV eventually became. On the contrary, as this Golden Age of Television was drawing to a close, the daytime serials were becoming the last strongholds of *personal,* in-studio drama written especially for television—the last holdover of the best that the Golden Age had to offer.

In the next few years, until about 1963, daytime television remained fairly static. CBS held most of the action with its six shows, with its share of the audience increasing rapidly each year, while NBC was left totally empty-handed when it tried, and failed, to launch a serial called *Our Five Daughters.* That network had gone to the trouble of importing Hollywood's Esther Ralston to play the part of the mother, whose five daughters included Patricia Allison, Iris Joyce, Nuella Dierking, Wynne Miller, and Jacquie Courtney (now Alice on *Another World*—she was hardly sixteen at the time). Michael Keen played the father. ABC-TV, which had never before attempted to compete with the other two networks for daytime audiences, tried two serials of their own: *Road to Reality* in 1960 and *Dr. Hudson's Secret Journal* in 1962. Neither show made it, but at least ABC was getting into the act. Both NBC and ABC were becoming increasingly irritated with their lack of daytime power. Something vague was beginning to appear—something in the air—a spirit of war, perhaps. CBS was bragging too much, flexing its daytime muscles too broadly. Surely there would be a battle soon. And somehow the waters would part for the two exiled networks to march across.

⊷§ VI §⊷

The War of the Daytime Networks

IT WAS ALL-OUT war! Starting in 1963, a daytime ratings battle among the three major networks began that was so fierce as to make the War of the Roses look like childish Mayday games. At stake were the favors of not just a few imperiled princesses, but those of all twenty million viewing housewives in the land. At last ABC and NBC had found their proper weapons—no more the bows and arrows of the "lonely-woman" or the "marriage-in-jeopardy" themes, but the viewer-grabbing, cannonball power of The Hospital! As if their armies were in collaboration, NBC and ABC introduced their hospital-centered serials on precisely the same day: April 1, 1963. While John Beradino as Dr. Steve Hardy and Emily McLaughlin as Nurse Jessie Brewer wrinkled their brows over the terminal patients on the Seventh Floor, Internal Medicine Division of *General Hospital* on ABC, James Pritchett as Dr. Matt Powers, head of Hope Memorial Hospital, comforted—and courted—Ann Williams as the troubled Dr. Maggie Fielding; they were just two of *The Doctors* on NBC.

CBS was surprised by the sneak attack on its audience-hold, but not nearly so much as when NBC, a year later, crept into the enemy camp and stole Irna Phillips away long enough for her to create another *As the World Turns* for NBC. Was it just a sense of humor that made her call the serial *Another World?*

NBC's stealing Irna Phillips to pull that little trick is akin to our stealing the top Russian missile expert and prodding him to develop an anti-missile missile custom tailored to protect us against the Russian missiles. *As the World Turns* was of course CBS's prime missile, and *Another World* was designed so similarly as to entice the millions of lovers of the old serial to watch the new one. Miss Phillips took the wealthy Lowells and the poorer Hugheses of *As the World Turns* and turned them into the two branches of the Matthews family of *Another World,* one rich and one middle class. In both cases the poorer families were the happier ones.

However, there was one important difference between the two serials. Miss Phillips had imparted to *Another World* a tenser dramatic atmosphere, reminiscent of *The Secret Storm,* with all the members of one family struggling to control their turbulent inner feelings. In the very first scene of the serial's premiere—May 4, 1964— viewers saw Liz Matthews crying on her bed. Her husband, William Matthews, had just died. The drama immediately set out to trace the impact of the tragedy on the lives of the families of the two brothers: William's, which included his widow, Liz (Liza Chapman), and her two grown children—Susan (Fran Sharon) and Bill (Joe Gallison); and Jim's (originally John Beal), which included his wife, Mary (Virginia Dwyer) and their three grown children—Pat (Susan Trustman), Alice (Jacquie Courtney), and Russ (Joey Trent). Soon after William's death, Pat became pregnant and in a rage killed the boy who caused the pregnancy. A murder trial ensued, and the whole family was drawn into the conflict. Meanwhile, Aunt Liz, the wealthy widow, was parading about in mink coats and throwing her higher social status in the face of good, plain Mary Matthews, her sister-in-law. *Another World* raged with drama, and viewers loved it.

The new psychological tone that Miss Phillips gave to this offspring of *As the World Turns* (once again, owned by Procter and Gamble) was summed up in the "epigraph" that viewers heard before each episode: "We do not live in this world alone, but in a thousand other worlds. The events of our lives represent only the surface, and in our minds and feelings we live in many other worlds."

So much faith did everyone have in Miss Phillips's ability to make this serial a stunning success that it had an advertising "advance sellout" six weeks before the show even began. The network and Procter and Gamble had lined up more sponsors for the show than could be accommodated. Certainly the network's great success with *The Doctors,* which went on the air thirteen months before, also had something to do with these great expectations. The show was produced by Allen Potter, who later produced *The Doctors* and the same network's newest serial, *How to Survive a Marriage.* The show was directed by Norman Hall (eventually transferred to *The Doctors*). Irna Phillips was assisted with script writing by William Bell, who presently writes *Days of Our Lives.*

Bolstered by two successful sabotagings of CBS's daytime television stronghold, NBC wasn't about to stop with just *The Doctors* and *Another World.* On September 27, 1965, it premiered two daytime dramas: *Morning Star* and *Paradise Bay. Morning Star* was about young fashion designer Katy Elliott, played by Elizabeth Perry, and her romantic troubles. The people around her were played by Adriane Ellis, as Jan, Nina Roman, as Liz, Olive Dunbar, and Edward Mallory, who later scored a big success as Bill Horton on *Days of Our Lives. Paradise Bay* had an exotic theme and setting, with sultry Keith Andes playing Jeff Morgan, the manager of a radio station in "a picturesque town between Hollywood and the Mexican border," so the press release for this one said. It went on: "The serial's episodes will explore the problems confronting the two worlds among the town's mushrooming population—the anxious world of adults and the frantic, frustrating world of youth." The show starred, along with Keith Andes, Marion Ross (as his wife), Heather North, Walter Brooke, Charlotte Baxter, June Dayton, and Debbie Cole. These two seemingly colorful serials weren't at all what viewers wanted and both went off the air on July 1, 1966. The network also experimented with a serial produced in Toronto, Canada, called *Moment of Truth*. The show was first seen on January 4, 1965, with a cast headed by Douglas Watson, Louise King, Barbara Pierce, and Michael Dodds. Its moment of truth came about a year later.

ABC, after its dynamite debut of *General Hospital,* wasn't sitting around with its hands folded, either. It now tried launching three serials. *The Nurses,* about you-know-what, starred Mary Fickett, Nick Pryor, Melinda Plank, Judson Laire, Valeria French, Lee Patterson, and Nat Polen; *Flame in the Wind,* a romance, featured Maggie Hayes, Lenka Peterson, Beverly Hayes, Joanna Miles, Tom Field, Ray Poole, and Terry Logan; and *Never Too Young,* another romance, included in its cast Patricia Wymore, Michael Blodgett, Cindy Carol, Tony Dow, Robin Grace, and Tommy Rettig. All three efforts lasted hardly more than a year, though ABC tried to salvage *Flame in the Wind* by changing its name to the soapier *A Time for Us,* but even that maneuver didn't delay the ax. Only the network's *The Young Marrieds* seemed to put up a brave ratings battle. That show began October 5, 1964 and wasn't canceled until the spring of 1966. Its exciting cast had Peggy McCay (unforgettable as the first Van on *Love of Life*), Paul Picerni, Mike Mikler, Scott Graham, Roger Hogan, and Brenda Benet.

All these cancellations cost both networks plenty. You may be asking: Why did they even bother?

Networks, from about 1963 to the present, have been hotly fighting each other for the favors of daytime viewers. They all keep trying and trying, even though millions of dollars are poured down the drain when daytime serials fail. Why, exactly?

First, there are the Nielsen reports to consider. A. C. Nielsen is not a man or a woman, but a company—a terrible, fire-breathing dragon of a company that has the awful job of telling networks and their sponsors how many people are actually watching their $40,000-to-$60,000-a-week daytime soaps from week to week—and whether it's even worth the trouble. A. C. Nielsen puts machines on 1200 television sets (the machines, if anyone cares, are called audimeters) in a random sampling of "typical" American homes; the company also entices another 2400 families to fill out "diaries" of daily viewing habits and send them to Nielsen headquarters weekly. The families are reimbursed modestly for their troubles, and in return all the networks and sponsors find out what they've been waiting to hear all week: are their soaps selling soap?

Second, by the mid-1960s, each minute of advertising on a serial cost a sponsor anywhere from $4,000 to triple that amount. That's a lot of money for just a minute. Since there are always five minutes of advertising on each serial, each show started taking in from $100,000 to $300,000 per week in advertising. In the fifties, daytime serials took in only a fraction of that much advertising revenue, but of course production costs were much lower, too. By the sixties, much more was at stake, and the vast difference in advertising revenue from show to show, believe it or not, depended almost entirely on those dreaded Nielsen weekly reports, based on the viewing habits of a mere 3600 different families each week. The sponsor would hear the good or bad news, as the case might be, in two different ways from A. C. Nielsen: in terms of "ratings points," that is the percentage of *all homes with television sets* that are tuned into his serial; and in terms of "shares," or the percentage of *all the sets that are on at a certain hour* and tuned in to his serial. For years, *As the World Turns* has had a rating of 10 (meaning 10 percent of all TV sets in the country are tuned in to *As the World Turns,* or roughly ten million viewers) and a share of well over 37 (meaning, of all the viewers watching television at 1:30 EST, 37 percent of them are tuned in to *As the World Turns*). *The Secret Storm,* when it was canceled by CBS, had a share of hardly 16.

Starting around the mid-sixties, hundreds of thousands of dollars could be made in advertising profits by a soap with a weekly "A" report card from Art Nielsen. An "F" on the other hand, could kill a show, for in the years we are talking about production costs had risen too much for networks to hang on to serials that weren't paying their way in advertising revenue, especially when there was so much money that could be made by just one daytime serial success such as *Another World*. So, can you blame NBC and ABC for trying so desperately at this time to cut in on CBS's hold on daytime viewers?

The trouble is, once a serial has been on the air for a few years and is liked by viewers, another network has to fight doubly hard to create a serial that will snatch viewers away from it. If the already running serial is a good one, such as *As the World Turns,* other networks are afraid to schedule an expensive serial at that time—hence, for years *As the World Turns* has had almost no competition in its 1:30 EST time slot. Instead, networks like to counterprogram serials—that is, run a soap at a time when it will at least have a chance of stealing the audience from another network's soap running simultaneously. This technique of counterprograming was primarily responsible for the death of *Return to Peyton Place.* Also, because of warlike counterprograming tactics, viewers have to suffer the irritation of having their favorite serials moved to different time slots in the afternoon—occasionally opposite another serial which is also a favorite, forcing them into an incredibly difficult choice.

Anyone who watches daytime television serials is a pretty important person, at least to the networks. Serials are launched not because some network executive likes the idea, but because he thinks somebody else will like it. A daytime television viewer is courted and romanced; each network spends millions of dollars annually trying to win viewers' tears, affections, and attention. Ph.D's working in marketing departments of advertising agencies would give their all just to find out how to please this special viewer. Letters to the networks are poured over and digested one by one. And the soaps are then created with the prospective viewer in mind.

Take, for instance, the case of *Days of Our Lives.* Before it premiered on November 8, 1965, NBC had poured all its energies into creating a second family-story serial success, like *Another World*. Again Irna Phillips was called in to help create it, along with Ted Corday (who for years had been associated with other great daytime successes like *The Guiding Light* and *As the World Turns*) and Alan Chase. If these established talents couldn't put together a winner, who could?

To insure the soap's success, the producers hired movie star Macdonald Carey to play the lead. He had made over fifty movies in Hollywood. Compared to daytime TV dramas, movies are almost a vacation; but the rigorous pace of a daytime serial was nothing new to him. Mr. Carey's career started way back on the Chicago radio serials, when his voice was known to housewives as that of Dr. Markham on Irna Phillips's *Woman in White,* and now he had come full circle, again playing on an Irna Phillips-created serial.

"Mac," as he is known to his friends and coworkers, didn't see his joining *Days of Our Lives* as a come-down, but rather as another way of channeling his creative energies. A typically humble Mac Carey remark about his work on the show: "I learn something new every day. A daytime serial is an artisan's work."

Like *As the World Turns* and *Another World,* this soap was the story of a large family, the Hortons of Salem (Anywhere, U.S.A.), with lots of doctors and lawyers. The head of the family was Dr. Tom Horton (Macdonald Carey), whose wife was Alice (Frances Reid). Their five grown children were: Mickey (John Clarke), Addie (Pat Huston), Tommy (missing in action in Korea when the story opened), Marie (Marie Cheatham), and Bill (Edward Mallory). Julie Olson (Charla Doherty) was Addie's daughter and Tom and Alice's first granddaughter.

Besides the fact that prestigious, experienced people had put this serial together and that a top Hollywood actor led the cast, there was one other reason why *Days of Our Lives* seemed fated for instant success—it was produced in Hollywood by Screen Gems and could take advantage of all the lavish studio facilities and resources. Anyway, viewers love to look at Hollywood actors. They ook so much more healthy, handsome, and alive than do New York actors—the California sun does it. So the serial was premiered, and the show's heads and sponsors sat back calmly, waiting for Art Nielsen to tell them how rich they could all expect to get.

But the daytime viewers weren't to be won over so easily. Wealthy the producers didn't get—neither that year, nor the following year. Not only did viewers just not seem enthusiastic about *Days,* but one might say that they were repelled by it. What went wrong? Out of a possible thirty-our daytime programs, Ted Corday's baby was third from the bottom in popularity! This wasn't just a case of poor ratings; it was a disease. Naturally, with at-home viewers telling A. C. Nielsen that *Days* was a daytime no-no, there were those who wanted to cancel the show. The producers, however, hung on by sheer faith. The ratings budged a little after a year; a year later they soared. Currently the show wavers from week to week from the first to third top place.

This of course was a great lesson to the networks, especially to NBC—the all-time "loser" in daytime serials for more than ten years. The lesson was twofold: (1) Don't expect a show to succeed instantly just because other shows like it have done so in the past, and (2) Don't get cancellation fever when a show doesn't catch on. Daytime viewers are capricious. Their loyalty cannot be bought; they must be patiently won—and it takes time to change viewing habits.

Eight months after the premiere of *Days,* viewers saw what was perhaps the most unlikely, daring, and imaginative experiment ever to be attempted on daytime television: a Gothic serial! Who would have thought any network would have had the guts to initiate such an expensive endeavor in the afternoon, when for the previous fifteen years only family dramas seemed to succeed. The idea for the show came to producer Dan Curtis, so Mr. Curtis said, in a cryptic dream. He called his wild nightmare serial—which included vampires, bats, astrologers, and a haunted family—*Dark Shadows* and introduced it on ABC-TV on June 27, 1966.

This was a bizarre show indeed. There were so many weirdo characters and science-fiction-like switches in time on *Dark Shadows* that eventually not even the actors themselves knew where they were in the plot mosaic. Essentially, the pell-mell tale dealt with the Collins family, who lived in a brooding, bedungeoned manor—Collins House—somewhere on the coast of Maine. In the first episodes, a young governess by the name of Victoria Winters (Alexandra von Moltke) came to Collins House to meet with the moody mistress, Flora Collins (played by Joan Bennett) and her brother, Daniel Collins (Louis Edmunds). Little by little, all the family horrors were revealed to the governess. The most impressive horror of all was cousin Barnabas Collins, who was uncloaked to be a two-century-old vampire.

Soon the show was filled with every device ever used in horror-supernatural movies since the old *Phantom of the Opera*. There were live burials, living corpses, strange bedeviled young men, unknown ailments, nutty conjurers, witches—and always, the vampire stalking and puncturing the lily-white neck of the beautiful ingenue. The show's sexual implications were fairly obvious. And who did the ABC network execs expect would be grabbed by this potpourri of studio-made chills? They didn't know, but they soon found out: young housewives, teen-agers home from school, "camp" lovers everywhere, and even a great many old-fashioned but daring soap lovers who were willing to give this new experiment a whirl. Jackie Onassis herself was supposed to have watched. The network execs also discovered that they had a new daytime star on their hands, as big—maybe even bigger—in popularity than Rosemary Prinz or Mary Stuart: a one-time little-known Shakespearean actor, Jonathan Frid.

Frid, many believed, may have even been directly responsible for the instant popularity of *Dark Shadows,* for his vampire, Barnabas, had an incredible charisma. He was soon receiving more than a thousand fan letters a day, mostly from delighted teen-agers. After a year or so on the show, the forty-five-year-old actor would go on tour, and people would turn out by the thousands to greet him.

Invariably he'd be asked to don his fangs for a moment or so—and Jon always did it, just for the heck of it. ABC spent two hundred dollars for two custom-designed vampire fangs for him to wear on these occasions.

However, his popularity, and the popularity of the whole show, may have been caused by a mere accident. A quiet, soft-spoken man, Frid revealed what must certainly be the most bizarre story of accidental success on record. The *New York Times* had already run an article about *Dark Shadows'* popularity, saying at one point that there was a certain mysteriousness about the way Frid turned on millions of fans to his vampire character. The piece went on to say, facetiously, that the character had a kind of lost and forlorn look, almost as if the actor couldn't remember his lines and was trying to find them on the teleprompter. "I loved that," laughed Frid, "because, you know, that was just about true. I really do have trouble remembering my lines. And I think that's how it all started. People got turned on to a strange hesitancy in my character, which was real, in the beginning, because I was never quite sure about what to say next. In fact, I was convinced that I would be fired because I kept blowing my speeches." One day, he recalled, he had a scene and his mind went completely blank. He practically had a breakdown in front of the camera. After the show, he was distraught and convinced that he would be fired—not even realizing why he was now being applauded by cameramen and technicians on the set. "I thought they were making fun of me." Later, when he saw the taped show on television, he was struck dumb with the kind of performance he had given. "The man on the screen had an other-worldly look—terribly frightened—oh, it made chills run up and down me." For all the four years that Mr. Frid played Barnabas, his character maintained that same mystery and magnetism for viewers.

Dark Shadows was probably the first pretend, "camp" vampire television show, and it had an amazing impact on audiences. Not only did Frid become a celebrated daytime star, but a number of novels were published based on the show's plots, and even a cookbook—with such chapter titles as "Carolyn's Fiendish Fish," "Quentin's Ghoulish Goulash and Karate Chops," and "Barnabas' Bloody Mary and Other Beastly Beverages" (called *The Dark Shadows Cookbook* and published by Ace Books). Later, after the show's cancellation, Dan Curtis produced a film based on his serial called *The House of Dark Shadows,* and then even a sequel to that.

This was TV fun-horror, and even the actors thought *Dark Shadows* was a gas. David Selby, the show's Quentin, remarked: "We laugh and fool around a lot on the set. Many times when the camera cues in on us for a look of absolute horror on our faces before the commercial, we open our eyes wide with horror—and then completely crack up when the little red light on the camera goes off!" At the *Dark Shadows* taping studio there used to be a big blowup of a young girl with a horrible smile, a fang protruding eerily beyond her lips and drops of blood trickling down her neck.

Joan Bennett was the second major Hollywood celebrity to agree to star on a daytime serial. However, at first Miss Bennett was dubious, not knowing what to expect. She notes in her autobiography, *The Bennett Playbill* (coauthored with fellow daytime star and pal Lois Kibbee and published by Holt, Rinehart and Winston): "At first I shuddered at the idea of a daytime soap opera, never realizing that I'd be shuddering for the next four years in a far different way than I imagined. I'd never seen a daytime soap opera and had no idea of what went on in its sudsy world, except that the actors had to cry a lot because everything was intensely sad. Furthermore, I had some vague notion that the actors who worked on them were second-raters." Miss Bennett soon realized that daytime actors were as good, if not better, than Hollywood ones; she also learned to respect the incredible endurance of daytime performers. She notes that in Hollywood it would take a week to get on film what they were taping in a day on *Dark Shadows!* "After the first thirteen weeks, I thought I'd have to take a rest cure."

Now, with its once all-powerful afternoon "block" of serials shattered by the intrusion of at least five successful daytime serials on other networks, CBS had to act quickly. The answer it came up with was to make its own block of serials more attractive by adding a new one. (It turns out that a great many viewers stay with a block of serials on the same network, without once changing the channel, if they are programed right after one another: hence the importance of a serial block.) *Love is a Many Splendored Thing* premiered on September 18, 1967, and was a good attempt by CBS to follow the new trend started on the other networks toward slightly offbeat serials.

Thematically based on the 1955 movie of the same name (starring William Holden as the American correspondent who falls in love with a Eurasian woman, Jennifer Jones), *Splendored Thing* began as a serial about young inter-racial love, with Irna Phillips once again as head writer. For the first few months the story dealt with the love affair between an Asian girl and an American man. It included in its original cast Robert Burr, Donna Mills, Robert Milli, and Judson Laire. After a short while, however, CBS chickened out and told Irna Phillips to change her story lines to more conventional ones. In other words, the interracial love had to go. Instead of giving in, the gritty Miss Phillips just quit the show, which soon became a soap about *ordinary* young love. Its growing popularity seemed to rest totally on the audience-pull of its three talented young stars: Donna Mills as Laura Donnelly, Leslie Charleson as her sister Iris, and David Birney as Laura's sweetheart and later husband, David Elliot. Although CBS wasn't brave enough to stick with the interracial theme long enough to find out whether it would work in a serial over the long haul, it did soon learn from *Love Is a Many Splendored Thing* that extremely young stars could be as compelling for daytime television audiences as the older ones who usually headed up the daytime dramas.

The very next year ABC, now wanting to compete with the other two networks' family-centered serials (like *Another World, The Secret Storm,* etc.), asked Agnes Nixon to create a story about families. Mrs. Nixon, of course, was the next best thing to Irna Phillips, the queen of family-story serial writers, for Mrs. Nixon had been Miss Phillips's protégé for years. Mrs. Nixon's brainchild was called *One Life to Live,* and it premiered on July 15, 1968. The serial was at once totally familiar and totally new. Although it had the by-now tried-and-true soap formula of a wealthy family set up against a poorer family, it also presented most of its families as non-WASPS. On Mrs. Nixon's serial, characters talked about the fact that they were Jews, Polish-Americans, Negroes, and Irish. For example, Meredith Lord (Lynn Benesch), a wealthy WASP girl, fell in love with Larry Wolek (James Storm), a poor Polish-American with strong family ties to his brother and sister. In the beginning there were lots of questions in the serial, such as "Can a wealthy WASP Lord find happiness with a poor Pole Wolek?" Or "Can an Irish girl find happiness with a Jewish boy?" The success of this serial was another blow to the Establishment network execs who felt that daytime serials could *only* be about mid-western and middle-class typical families.

On June 30, 1968, NBC made the fatal mistake of premiering its well-conceived *Hidden Faces* at 1:30 EST. Running in the same time period as *As the World Turns,* still the top-rated show, it lasted a mere six months. It featured Conrad Fowkes (as lawyer Arthur Adams), Gretchen Walther (as Katherine Walker, a former surgeon in love with him), Nat Polen (as a corrupt businessman), Rita Gam (as the wife of a senator), and Tony LoBianco —of *French Connection* fame.

Afternoon serial blocks now became an issue of tremendous importance. On September 15, 1969, CBS premiered *Where the Heart Is,* about the romantic entanglements of the Hathaways and the Prescotts. In its cast were James Mitchell and Gregory Abels as the father and son who lusted after the same woman, and Ron Harper and Diana van der Vlis as the star-crossed lovers who finally found happiness. NBC countered with its Hollywood-based *Bright Promise* just two weeks later. It was a vehicle for movie-star Dana Andrews, who played college dean Thomas Boswell, surrounded by the problems of youth.

Also included in the cast were Susan Brown in the role of Martha Furguson, Dabney Coleman as Dr. Tracey Brown, Gail Kobe as Ann Boyd, and Peter Ratray as Stuart Pierce.

Only months later, on January 15, 1970, ABC again came up with another Agnes Nixon serial, *All My Children,* this time with Rosemary Prinz taken out of her self-imposed exile from daytime TV to play the lead of Amy Tyler, a woman with a shady past that included an illegitimate birth. Her present was filled with the desire to go off on peace marches, work for the environment, and other such contemporary activities. Miss Prinz, supported by a good story and other fine actors—such as Richard Hatch, Karen Gorney, Ruth Warrick, and Mary Fickett—made the serial another great success for ABC.

Less than three months later an historic daytime TV event occurred: *three* daytime serials were premiered simultaneously! The date was March 30, 1970, and the serials were: ABC's *The Best of Everything,* based on the novel about career girls trying to make it in New York (Susan Sullivan and famous star Geraldine Fitzgerald were in the cast); the same network's *A World Apart,* with William Prince and Augusta Dabney again playing a married couple (as they had in *Young Dr. Malone* years earlier on NBC) facing troubles in the affluent world around them; and NBC's *Another World—Somerset,* a spin-off of the parent show *Another World* (but really a crime melodrama, written by *The Edge of Night*'s Henry Slesar), starring Jordan Charney and Ann Wedgeworth as Sam and Lahoma Lucas.

The networks were by now glutted with afternoon serials. For a while during this period there were twenty—or ten hours of daytime viewing every day. Viewers were confused by the hodge-podge assortment, each network's afternoon serial block being destroyed by the incursions of the other two networks—and ratings and advertising revenues began to dive-bomb. Besides, the writers of these twenty serials were suffering from an understandable slump in creativity. After two decades, what could they possibly come up with in their stories that audiences hadn't already seen in other daytime serials?

It was a time of sheer catastrophy in serial-land. Irna Phillips, called back into action by the sudden dip in ratings of that once most popular of all soaps, *As the World Turns,* told a reporter from the *New York Daily News* at the time: "The daytime serial has been destroying itself. The people responsible for the shows have lost sight of the most important element in them—their humanness. NBC recently got a call from a viewer who wanted them to know that one of the CBS serials was stealing their plots. It wasn't theft. It was just lack of imagination. Why, at one point last year, CBS had murder trials going on all four of its house-produced serials. No wonder they can't keep an audience."

When the stakes grow too high, with millions of dollars of ad revenues at stake—as was happening on the afternoon shows around this time—imaginations become inhibited. Talent either dries up or hides momentarily in a corner. The desperate inability to make soap-story talent flow from one set of human minds, through the color tube, and into eyes and hearts of millions of people by the sheer naked power of the Ratings Game was seen most dramatically on CBS serials a short while ago. Roy Winsor, who had been producing *The Secret Storm* and *Love of Life* until 1969, notes: "I had been working on a fixed budget from American Home Products to do *The Secret Storm* and *Love of Life.* I got their money, and they got their show, and for a long time both shows were very popular. I always worked on sound principles of theme and story, the same principles that dictate great novels, and they worked for my shows. Then, when the ratings competition got heavy, CBS kept pressuring me for fancier sets, better trimmings, and with the money spent there we had to lower our acting budget and the story suffered." After CBS took over the producing of both shows in 1969, Winsor says, all his principles of good story and theme were thrown out the window. With *The Secret Storm,* the Ames family was all but gotten rid of—something akin to chucking out the Hugheses of *As the World Turns* or the Matthewses of *Another World*—something good producers of family-story daytime serials would never have dreamed of doing. Naturally, *Storm*'s ratings began to sink faster than the *Titanic*.

Similar situations began to happen all over serial-land. Some shows were just dropped immediately by the networks—like ABC's three swift cancellations in 1969 of *Dark Shadows, A World Apart,* and *The Best of Everything*. But the big cancellation panic didn't really happen until 1973. Instead, networks and producers began a system of what could only be justifiably described as writer-torture. The writers now had to respond to each little up-and-down change in the ratings. "It got to a point," says Roy Winsor, "that if a show had slipped half a point in the ratings shares, the poor writer would be given orders to make someone pregnant to push the ratings back up." If a show really got in a bind, an important character might be killed off to give a boost to the ratings. The assumption of producers—and they are partly correct—is that people become more interested in a serial when there is sudden sadness.

For example, when the ratings of *As the World Turns* were severely ailing in 1972, Irna Phillips was called in to try to write the show back up to where it had been. She did it, but in the process had to "kill off" Paul Stewart (Dean Santoro) and Elizabeth Stewart (Judith McGilligan), severely injure Dr. Dan Stewart's (John Colenback) operating hand, and bring about a complicated divorce between Susan Stewart (Marie Masters) and her husband in a record-breaking two episodes. But the show's new high ratings were only a fleeting mirage, for shortly thereafter many infuriated viewers stopped watching the show.

One striking feature of this period in the history of daytime television serials is the absolute insensitivity on the part of many producers to what viewers really wanted to see. From the success of shows like *One Life to Live, All My Children, Dark Shadows,* and *Love Is a Many Splendored Thing* they sensed that daytime audiences had changed a great deal from those of twenty years ago, but these producers were afraid to follow through on what they sensed. The new trick was now to inject "relevance" into stories, since that seemed to work for ABC's new serials and might therefore give an appearance of new vigor to some pretty worn-out plots. It was now *de riguer* for every serial to have a black neurosurgeon, or kids addicted to drugs (on *Love of Life* these young drug-takers were running all over the place for a few years), or abortions, or frank talk about sex, or deliberately controversial subjects such as a priest leaving the Church to marry (*The Secret Storm*), artificial insemination, or Women's Lib involvements.

But as Roy Winsor and Paul Rauch, the new producer of *Another World,* say, in almost exactly the same words: "On daytime serials, you can't replace good story with relevance." When Paul Rauch still worked at CBS as a daytime programing executive, *Love Is a Many Splendored Thing, Where the Heart Is,* and *The Secret Storm* were already in deep trouble with the viewers. "I suggested that we cancel them all. I knew that with the kind of old-fashioned leadership there the shows would never get new life put into them." The real trouble with these shows was, to use Irna Phillips's words, their lack of "humanness" and their lack of good themes, despite all the money that was spent on their production. For example, *Love Is a Many Splendored Thing* was a gorgeous show while it starred youthful David Birney, Leslie Charleson, and Donna Mills as the primary love interests. The network did have a chance to hold on to these actors (talented Birney quit over CBS's denial of his request for a higher salary) but instead let them go and then hired and fired so many replacements that many viewers gave up on the program in desperation. No longer able to focus the show on young love, CBS changed the story to a political intrigue between two rival candidates. But *Splendored Thing's* viewers—those who were left—weren't very interested in political cliffhanging.

In one fell swoop, CBS got rid of two of its house-produced "mistakes" when it canceled both *Splendored Thing* and *Where the Heart Is* on March 23, 1972. On February 8, 1974, *The Secret Storm* was also axed, leaving CBS with *Love of Life* as its only house-produced show. What finally made CBS concede its failures? Said an inside source at the network, "It was a matter of pride; CBS didn't like being third in the ratings. So, rather than struggle to improve the quality of these shows, it just canceled them. All the other shows it has are independently owned and could only be canceled by their owners."

The network did a terrible disservice to long-time, faithful viewers when it canceled *The Secret Storm.* Although the show was no longer faithful to its original theme or its original story of the Ames family, the network still had a duty to viewers to reinstate those story qualities that had enabled this popular soap to last for more than twenty years, instead of just giving up. The cancellation of *The Secret Storm* was the most tragic blow ever to hit daytime television.

NBC also canceled its *Bright Promise,* for many of the same reasons that CBS had terminated its soaps. On March 3, 1972, NBC replaced that show with another that had been a wildfire success on nighttime television, and was certain—so NBC surmised—to work just as well on daytime. The show was even called *Return to Peyton Place* as a reminder to viewers that the situations left unresolved in the old *Peyton Place* nighttime series would be continued and further developed in the daytime. Even some of the original actors in the prior series remained for the daytime version. The show was filled with talent: Warren Stevens as Eliot Carson, Julie Parrish as Betty Harrington, Joe Gallison as Steven Cord, Guy Stockwell as Michael Rossi, Mary K. Wells as Hannah Cord, and Susan Brown as Constance MacKenzie.

But talent and a good story weren't enough. *Return to Peyton Place* went off the air on January 4, 1974, killed by NBC's poor judgment in trying to get an instant success by transplanting a serial originally intended for another kind of audience. Said Gail Kobe, the show's assistant producer and one-time actress on *Bright Promise,* "Of course it was the ratings. We were counterprogramed against *One Life to Live*, which was a story about family relationships, while ours was about 'that dirty little town.' Viewers would have bought us if we had been more a story of interrelationships within families. Instead of just canceling, I think NBC should have allowed us the opportunity to change our format."

But daytime network executives are too high-pressured with Nielsen panic these days to sit around waiting. NBC immediately followed with a new show, for the third straight time in that seemingly dangerous 3:30 time slot, called *How to Survive a Marriage*. It premiered Monday, January 7. Essentially it is the story of a divorced woman who must face life as a single woman again after twelve years of marriage. It's certainly the most Women's Lib-type theme yet thought up for daytime television. And Rosemary Prinz was hired to star in the show for six months as Dr. Julie Franklin; it was hoped that Rosemary's short-term presence would help *Marriage* quickly build ratings.

CBS has also come into the "contemporary-serial" field with its *The Young and the Restless*, which premiered on March 23, 1973. Generally speaking, it is about young people, but more precisely, it concerns the sex lives of young adults and their relationships with their families. On *The Young and the Restless*, viewers have heard the most explicit sex talk ever heard on a daytime soap; it is probably the first "X-rated" daytime serial. Lavishly produced and well acted, it is the most contemporary of CBS's afternoon soaps.

Only ABC has outdone its two rival networks in recent innovations. With only three serials left in its afternoon block—*General Hospital, One Life to Live*, and *All My Children*—it decided to fill up the other hours with frequent, ninety-minute special "soap opera" dramas. These aren't serials, but dramas that begin and end on the same day, many of them dealing with contemporary issues. In one called *I Never Said Goodbye*, a woman doctor (played by June Lockhart) is sued for the mercy killing of a woman by the woman's husband (Jack Stauffer). There is a powerful dramatic conclusion in front of a woman judge. Other contemporary ninety-minute soaps on ABC deal with such themes as an old maid who becomes pregnant and insists on having her child out of wedlock (the doctor in this one was played by Pat O'Brien); a woman who sets out to prove that her husband didn't commit suicide, as alleged; an unmarried, pregnant woman who searches for her mother; and a woman who falls in love with a handsome writer who is out to use her. One can only say to this whole idea: Bravo! The stories are well done, appealing to women (especially), and incorporate many thoughtful ideas. Let's hope daytime viewers give ABC a break with this admirable attempt.

Although the rash of recent cancellations—especially that of *The Secret Storm*—has been depressing for daytime devotees, and although for the last several years the producers of daytime shows seemed to have been somewhat less than daring and imaginative—in fact, often seemed to be going backward instead of forward in their thinking—one is left with the impression that somehow the air has been cleared, that the networks have finally found a way to offer something fresh to afternoon TV lovers. In the past six months or so there has been less reliance on "relevance" and more on just plain good drama. If the Watergate hearings, for instance, inspired all the hullabaloo recently in an *Another World* story-line that included illegal bugging and wire-tapping, that's interesting; but the important thing is that the story itself was grand—the reference to topical, headline events was just the icing on the cake. Let's keep up Roy Winsor's old standards for stories; let's not forsake good stories about families just because families are not as "in" as they used to be; and let's keep writers, producers, and networks remembering that the most important thing a daytime serial has to offer is emotional communication and identification. As long as they do that, the networks will make heaps of advertising money and will be happy; and viewers will feel emotionally involved, and will be happy too.

⋄§ VII §⋄

Viewers

MANY PEOPLE ARE ashamed to admit that they're hooked on daytime television serials. There's an old stigma attached to anyone who becomes involved with the soaps. If those intimidated viewers knew of the excellent company they keep perhaps they wouldn't feel so cowed. The late Tallulah Bankhead—slave to *The Edge of Night* for years—once angrily called the producers after a show in which a wife was menaced by her husband. She demanded: "Listen, *dahlings*, why the hell doesn't she shoot the bastard?" There's another marvelous Tallulah tale about *her* being nervous about meeting Haila Stoddard, whom she adored as Aunt Pauline on *The Secret Storm.* Bette Davis once confessed to Val Dufour at a party that she and her friend-secretary-confidant, Vic Greenfield, were card-carrying soap lovers; so much so that whenever she misses an episode of *Another World,* her favorite show, she calls serial-buddy Fran Allison, to find out what happened. "Bette was watching the week that I died," says Val, who played the ill-fated Walter Curtin on *World* for eight years, "and then she called me and told me how sorry she was to see me go. She said, 'Your last days were just beautiful, Val!' " Once, when Lena Horne had been taping the old *Kraft Music Hall* at *Another World*'s Brooklyn studio, she admonished Val: "You stop being so mean to Lenore!" Another well-known performer, Harry Belafonte, carries his TV set with him wherever he is scheduled to perform—he's *that* afraid of missing his favorite soaps.

Many celebrated writers confess to the same addiction. There's the chestnut about P. G. Wodehouse, who abruptly interrupted an interviewer so that he wouldn't have to miss an episode of *The Edge of Night*. Renata Adler, who used to review movies for the *New York Times*, not only confessed to a long-term suds addiction but even wrote a probing, in depth piece for the *New Yorker* on what the serials meant to her.

Alec Waugh (*Island in the Sun*), upon returning to New York after a long absence abroad, told an interviewer for the *Times* that he was beginning to feel depressed to find that everything in the city had changed: the buildings, the people, the mood. Then he turned on his TV set in his hotel room. "I saw that the soaps hadn't changed," said Mr. Waugh. "They were exactly the same as before I had left the city. I felt so much better." Even musical celebrities Van Cliburn and Renata Tebaldi don't mind admitting that they watch and hate it when work keeps them from seeing important episodes.

Of course, most serial viewers aren't famous. The majority of the twenty million daily—(and fifty million weekly)—soap watchers are known to be housewives, young mothers, teen-agers, men who are self-employed or have irregular working hours, grandmothers, and shut-ins. Now, fifty million weekly viewers is a staggering number of people; yet what always amazes those associated with making the serials, or people who simply find out about them, is not so much the number of soap lovers but their absolute loyalty and involvement. Nighttime television producers are especially overwhelmed by the popularity of soaps and are even jealous that they have to spend ten to fifteen times more money than is spent on daytime serials, and they don't get a fraction of the mail response or audience involvement. James Lipton, currently writing *The Doctors,* in an article in *TV Guide* told how—while playing Dr. Grant on *The Guiding Light*—he made a trip to Hollywood and was having lunch in the Warner Brothers commissary with a lot of famous film and TV actors. A waitress happened to spill some soup on him and then a "familiar, glazed look" came into her eyes. "My God, you're not . . . Dr. Grant . . . !" When he said yes, the tray she was holding fell to the floor with a crash. Soon *all* the commissary waitresses, who wouldn't have batted an eyelid at a nighttime TV star, were lined up for autographs. Said Mr. Lipton, "Glittering film and TV stars flung down their napkins and stalked out of the room to sulk like Achilles in their trailers for the rest of the lunch hour."

A few years ago I was shown a letter written by a viewer on behalf of herself and six neighbors. She said they were all angry because they had prepared a wedding party at her house, huge wedding cake and all, to celebrate the marriage of Steve and Alice on *Another World*—and suddenly the wedding was called off. How could the writers of the show be so unpredictable? she asked. James Lipton, in the article referred to above, noted the case of a woman who called a serial producer's office one day to complain desperately that she and a number of her friends had planned to watch a certain wedding on the serial together—with a good deal of money invested in a catered luncheon meant to celebrate the happy TV event. The wedding never took place. Now what was she supposed to do with all that food? she asked of the surprised secretary who took the call.

Preparations for soap weddings go on for months and sometimes even for several years—as in the case of Steve and Alice on *Another World*, or Van and Bruce on *Love of Life*, or Adam and Nicole on *The Edge of Night*, or Joanne and Tony on *Search for Tomorrow*. These are such vastly important events for steady watchers that neighborhood wedding parties are not uncommon. Can you imagine nighttime TV viewers getting half so involved in, say, the marriage of *Medical Center*'s Joe Gannon and one of his pretty nurses?

But the annoyance caused by a canceled wedding is a minor ripple compared to the groundswell of sadness caused by a death on a serial. Some years ago, millions of viewers of *As the World Turns* became deeply upset when Jim Lowell, played by Les Damon, was accidentally killed while on a business trip in Florida. The calls and telegrams expressing unhappiness over the character's death poured into *World Turns'* office—so many, in fact, that Irna Phillips, then writing the show, decided to console all those people by sending them back her own poignant message about life and death. Part of the letter went: ". . . As the world turns, we know the bleakness of winter, the promise of spring, the fullness of summer, and the harvest of autumn . . . the cycle of life is completed. . . . What is true of the world, nature, is also true of man. He too has his cycle."

Countless deaths have occurred on daytime serials, but some stand apart from the others in the minds of producers as having provoked an especially strong response from the audience, as having been particularly unbearable. There was probably no sweeter, no more lovable a character than Sarah Lane Karr on *The Edge of Night* some years back. After several years of playing the character, Teal Ames told the producers that she wanted to leave the show to go to Hollywood. The producers were now faced with a typical problem that occurs when actors want to leave their serial parts. Miss Ames couldn't be replaced because the audience loved her too much as Sarah; and Sarah and Mike couldn't divorce because their characters were too much in love. All the producers could do, then, was to kill off Sarah. Her death came when she saved her daughter, Laurie Ann Karr, from the wheels of an on-rushing auto and was struck herself. Within minutes, CBS lines were tied up with calls of misery and grief from viewers. While the show was still on air, 260 telegrams arrived, and later more than nine thousand letters came into *Edge*'s offices, complaining of the death. The producers became worried for, from the sound of the calls and the telegrams, it was obvious that a great many people were convinced that a *real* person had died. So at the end of the next day's program, John Larkin, who played Mike Karr, and Teal Ames made an appearance together and assured viewers that Miss Ames was quite alive—they both had reassuring smiles on their faces—and that she was leaving the show to work in Hollywood.

Serial viewers have an uncanny instinctive ability to know what is real and what is unreal on their shows, and to know when writers are being too casual about killing off a character. For example, although the death of Sarah Karr on *The Edge of Night* was particularly upsetting for the audience, it was still accepted without malice toward the show or the writers. Explained Don Wallace, who was producing the show at the time, "Mothers do give their lives to save the life of a child," and that is the way viewers saw the death. But when Jill and Hugh Clayborne—played by audience favorites Barbara Rodell and Peter McLean—were suddenly killed in an aircrash on *The Secret Storm* a few years back, the audience was not as forgiving. The show, by that point, had been much too prone to kill off or send away characters the audience loved; and so viewers, rightly sensing the producers and writers were behaving like "murderers," threatened en masse to stop watching the show. Producers generally know that such threats are seldom followed through—in fact, ratings, if anything, go up shortly after a death, for word gets out among friends that the tears are beginning to flow. Yet in the long run such brutal tactics as those on *The Secret Storm* always succeed in turning off its viewers.

Daytime audience instinct for what is "right" is virtually infallible. When *As the World Turns* cavalierly killed off or otherwise sent away nearly half of the Stewart family, as mentioned in the previous chapter, ratings only went up temporarily. The producers quickly took their cue from the thousands of viewer letters that said the numerous departures were foolish, that there was no real story-cause for the deaths of Elizabeth and Paul Stewart. A shake-up behind the scenes at *As the World Turns* was the result of all those viewer complaints, and totally new story tactics were devised to try to gain back the lost confidence of the audience. Irna Phillips herself, who was responsible for killing off Elizabeth, felt compelled to try to justify the death by telling the show's followers, in a magazine piece, that she knew of other freak accidents just like Elizabeth's—the character ruptured her liver while rushing up the stairs! It's doubtful whether Miss Phillips's readers really bought the explanation.

Although heads of shows can be God-like in the way they kill off people in their stories, or simply send them out of town, or cause long, drawn-out tragedies, they usually heed their mail response and act accordingly if possible. Viewers, by their pleading letters, have saved the lives of countless characters through the years. When Marla Adams first came on *The Secret Storm* as Belle Clements, she was only meant to play a bitch who caused a lot of trouble for a short while before a just, untimely end. When it came time for her demise—Belle was dying of nephritis and expiring rapidly—viewers simply wouldn't have it. After being swamped with letters to "save Belle's life," the producers wisely did just that, and the actress went on to become the show's star. Dagne Crane, as model Sandy Hughes, was twice brought back to *As the World Turns* because of audience demands for her—each time being paid much higher salaries than before. Doe Lang was also returned to *World Turns* after hundreds of her followers signed a single petition and brought it to the producer. Beverlee McKinsey first came onto *Another World* to make a brief cameo as Steven Frame's yokel barnyard sister; she made a splash with the serial's followers, and so was brought back to the show—but this time as glamorous, spoiled, rich-bitch Iris Carrington! "And now that we know that the audience loves her," explains writer Pete Lemay, "we're not going to let her go. We intend to keep her in the story indefinitely. She may even become another Rachel."

The audience has an influence over serial stories in many other ways as well. On *The Guiding Light* Leslie (played at different times by Barbara Rodell and Lynne Adams) was on trial for murdering her husband, Stanley Norris. "We intended the trial to go on for months," says Bruce Cox, the show's representative at the Compton ad agency, "but then viewers began to write in how boring it was all becoming, and that they had seen other long murder trials before on serials. We realized, from all these letters, that it would be death for us to keep Leslie on trial, so we quickly wrapped the whole thing up, with Mike proving that Leslie didn't kill Stanley." On *The Guiding Light,* by the way, all viewer letters are tabulated by the producers according to pro and con responses to a particular story or actor; the most intelligent ones are read individually by the producer herself, Lucy Rittenberg. As Bruce Cox explains, sometimes it's impossible for producers to know *what* they're doing with their serials unless viewers write in to express opinions.

Perhaps show heads like Cox feel this way because experience is a good teacher. *Love Is a Many Splendored Thing* had had excellent ratings until David Birney, who played Mark Elliott, quit the show after being refused a higher salary by a new CBS executive. When viewers saw that Birney was replaced by Michael Hawkins, a storm of viewer protest occurred. It is generally agreed that CBS's disregarding of those protests and its refusal to pay Birney the higher salary he probably deserved—he had been getting a mere forty thousand per—was the beginning of the end for *Splendored Thing*. Only a rare and unwise producer these days does not move, and move quickly, to make amends with a dissatisfied audience.

Although the great majority of daytime viewers are fiercely loyal, one-hundred-percent believers in the reality of the stories, they accomplish this by *willingly* suspending disbelief; in other words, they are certainly able to distinguish fact from fiction. However, there is that small "fringe" audience who somehow get the idea that their sets are secret audio-visual devices that, in the afternoon, tune into the homes of real people. They think the characters are real people and that the actors who play them have no separate lives of their own. There is no telling how many people are on this daytime fringe; all we know of them comes from their letters and their bizarre deeds, but there are certainly enough of both to convince one that they are a large minority group.

Robin Strasser, while she played Rachel on *Another*

World, was at first only slightly irritated by the hate mail she'd receive and the phone calls made to her home in the middle of the night. At the time she was married to Russ on the show and cuckolding him with Steve. Then Robin and her husband, Larry Luckinbill, became concerned when she became pregnant in real life and was also playing a pregnant Rachel. Some of this fringe knew this, and they began making terrible threats when, in the story, Rachel talked about not wanting her unborn baby. She even voiced fear about walking the streets and about the welfare of her baby. "You know, a man was shot on *The Secret Storm.* Some viewer put a bullet right through his person!" Shortly thereafter, Larry and Robin gave up their apartment and fled to Brooklyn—with unlisted phone numbers.

There was nothing amusing about the fear that was instilled in Miss Strasser by some misguided viewers, but there was something funny about what happened to Marla Adams. As trouble-maker Belle on *The Secret Storm,* she had gotten used to her share of hate mail, which by then was an occupational hazard. However, one day she came home to find her housekeeper walking out on her. "I can't work for a woman like you! To treat your husband the way you do! You ought to be ashamed of yourself!" It was no use explaining. The housekeeper had been watching the show, and refused to believe that Marla wasn't Belle. It didn't seem to matter that Marla and her *own* husband were a terribly happy couple with two lovely children. Fiction won out.

Almost every daytime actor—current and otherwise—has his own favorite stories about fans who take soap plots too seriously. There's a whole group of tales about people who frantically dial long-distance to television studios to "warn" their favorite star of a new peril in the story: who's out to get him, who really committed the murder, or watch out for what's-her-name with the painted smile who's looking to steal you away from your wife. John Beradino, who plays Steve Hardy on *General Hospital,* told of a woman who called all the way from the Midwest to tell him the name of the man in the story who killed one of his patients. "She was so serious about the warning," said John, "that I didn't even bother to remind her that it was just a show. I assured her that we already knew who the killer was but were just pretending not to know." On *The Edge of Night* Larry Hugo, who played crook-catcher Mike Karr for more than eight years, received not just one, but *regular* long distance telephone calls from a fine southern gentleman informing him of all the plots and schemes devised against him by his enemies in the story. Larry's repeated attempts to explain to the gentleman that it was all just make believe were in vain, and finally Larry simply thanked the man and said that he was turning over this "new evidence" to the authorities.

Another group of viewers sincerely believes that daytime actors are the professionals they play. All the actors on *The Doctors,* for example, are flooded with requests from fans asking for surefire lumbago cures or wanting to know if that lump on a daughter's leg means cancer and could the actor come out to Someplace, Ohio, to take a look at it. Gerald Gordon—who plays neurosurgeon Nick Bellini, the one character on the show who is constantly being called "brilliant," "infallible," a "doctor with a special gift for healing"—gets the lion's share of these requests. He's always pleading, often in vain, that he's not a real doctor. His on-screen love interest, Elizabeth Hubbard, plays doctor Althea Davis and says that when she gets similar requests, she kindly advises the viewer to "consult your own physician, as he is better able to handle the problem."

Years ago, while Don MacLaughlin was playing the title role on *Chaplain Jim, U.S.A.* on radio, he received a harried, long distance phone call from a farmer, who said he had a problem. His son had deserted the Army, and he was hiding him in the coal bin, and he wanted Don's advice on what to do next. Don tried to tell the farmer that he wasn't a chaplain, just a hard-working actor, but then, hearing the real desperation in the man's voice, he tried to comfort him by assuring, "I'm sure they won't execute your son—" and then asked him to talk to his own priest.

Whenever stable marriages are threatened in the stories,

it is as if the very well-being and happiness of the viewers were being threatened. Once, when *The Doctors*' Matt Powers was tempted by a seductress, thousands of women wrote in to warn Lydia Bruce, who played his wife, Maggie Powers, that her "marriage" was in jeopardy. Another time, a writer made the merest suggestion in an *As the World Turns* script that another woman had her eyes on Chris Hughes. Viewers not only wrote in their usual warning letters, but indulged in such an outpouring of venom toward the producers and writers for even *daring* to suggest that another woman would have the audacity to come between Chris and Nancy that the audience teaser was never tried again.

"There are just some couples in the serials," says Don MacLaughlin, who plays Chris Hughes, "that have to be happily married, as a sort of continuing marital ideal for the viewers. When everyone on the show seems to be wallowing in romantic troubles, at least Nancy and Chris have a sure thing. I guess that's why they call us 'tent-pole' characters. We hold up the moral outlook of the show."

Other couples whose marital stability writers don't dare tamper with for fear of audience retribution are Mary and Jim Matthews on *Another World,* Tom and Alice Horton of *Days of Our Lives*—and for nearly twenty years, until the death of Melba Rae, Stu and Marge Bergman of *Search for Tomorrow*. A few years back, Irna Phillips had an argument with Harding Lemay, the new writer of *Another World,* over his intention to endanger Pat and John Randolph's marriage by having John cheat on Pat, who would become an alcoholic. Miss Phillips argued heatedly that long-time followers of the serial would never stand for the destruction of such a stable marriage. Mr. Lemay argued back that indeed they would. The show didn't lose viewers over the writer's breaking of the cardinal law of stable soap marriages, but then Pat and John *did* come back together and Bernice, the woman who came between them, *was* sent to an early grave.

Why do viewers love their soaps so and believe in them so fiercely? Chances are, if you've read about the serials in magazines, you've already come upon the typical sort of explanation that *General Hospital*'s Emily McLaughlin gives: "We are in their living room five days a week, leading a continuous life, so we achieve a kind of reality. That's why viewers think we're real people."

Other people prefer to emphasize the fact that as fiction the soaps are closer to reality than either movies or night-time television because on soaps even heroes can have weaknesses, suffer breakdowns, and even die. Soaps don't offer escape; they offer identification. People can pick out certain characters in the story who remind them of their own mothers, fathers, sons, daughters, grandparents, friends. A viewer once angrily said to Val Dufour: "I want to slap Rachel's face for being so mean to Russ because he reminds me of my own brother."

Both of these explanations for the surging popularity of daytime serials are true. Soaps certainly offer a look at reality, and they give millions of people an opportunity to become acquainted with a small group of interesting individuals who almost "live" in their homes for a half hour every day. It is the frequency of the contact and the unusual intimacy between the actor and the viewer that make many viewers feel there is no difference between the actor and his character. Hence, when an actor is written to, the letters are addressed to "Mrs. Joanne Vincente," or "Mr. Steven Frame," or "Jessie Brewer, R.N." rather than to the actors themselves. For many soap watchers, the stories and their characters are so real that it just doesn't occur to them that the actors' names are different from the ones they are given on the tube five days a week.

"It used to bother the heck out of me," says *The Guiding Light*'s Don Stewart, "that people would only know me as Michael Bauer. I was certainly glad that millions of people were finally seeing me in a television show—but I wanted them to know that I was an actor, Don Stewart, and that I was different from Michael Bauer. Lately, because of my singing career and all the magazine publicity, that's been happening, but it took a long time."

However, most serial actors are grateful to have their jobs and they good-naturedly accept the little quirk of being called by the name made up by some head writer. Mart Hulswit, *The Guiding Light*'s Dr. Ed Bauer, looks at it as funny and weird: "It's almost like having a twin brother that everyone mistakes you for." Eileen Fulton, *As the World Turns*' Lisa Shea, even admits that "sometimes we do the same things ourselves around the set, and call each other by our character names: 'Lisa,' and 'Wally,' and 'Bob,' and 'Nancy.' It just makes things easy because there are so many names to remember."

Steady viewers of the serials feel they are on a sort of first-name basis with the actors—who, after all, come into their homes, just like friendly neighbors, with all their personal troubles and concerns—and don't approach them at all with the same awe with which they approach other actors. In New York, where most of the serials are done, many of the actors ride the subways and buses and are always being stopped by men and women who just want to chat, shake hands, and say how much they enjoy watching them. Most of these encounters are pleasant, smooth, courteous, and thoroughly enjoyable to recognition-hungry serial actors.

But occasionally all the chummy familiarity leads to some embarrassment. One day a husband and wife found out that Don and Mary MacLaughlin lived near them and proceeded to pay an unannounced call to their Connecticut farmhouse. They felt so relaxed with their familiar Chris Hughes that instead of leaving politely after finishing the drinks offered them, they simply inquired, "Well, when are we going to have supper?" The MacLaughlins didn't exactly say what was on their minds after that request, but politely told the couple that they weren't prepared to offer dinner invitations that evening.

After Jacquie Courtney left *Another World* a few years ago to marry Dr. Carl Desiderio and live with him in Jackson, Mississippi, she thought she'd be able to take up the life of just another housewife. "But everywhere I went people would recognize me. In the beginning I tried to be as polite as I could when people came up to me and tried to start a conversation. Then when complete strangers started grabbing me from out of nowhere I was first annoyed, and then terrified. I even found myself being rude. One woman took hold of me, I said something sharp, and then she said under her breath, 'Huh! She's just like Rachel!' " Jacquie has since returned to the role of Alice.

Such encounters with the audience in the outside world are always a little surprising for daytime actors, for they see themselves as rather unimportant actors who are just doing their jobs. Larry Haines tells the story of the time he had gotten off from *Search for Tomorrow* to appear in a play. As soon as he made his entrance on stage, a woman in the audience stood up and shouted for all to hear, "Why, I know you. Stu Bergman! . . . What on earth are you doing up there?" Larry swears that another time, on his way to work one morning, he was followed and stopped on the Brooklyn Bridge by a policeman who wanted to know what was going to happen next to Joanne.

"Oh, the same thing happened to me!" insists Stefan Gierasch, who played the "wire man," Mr. Sykes, on *Another World.* "I was in a car with Mark Rydell, and a cop made both of us pull over to the side of the road. Mark asked me if we were going too fast. Before I could answer the cop yelled at Mark, 'Oh, my God, he's risen from the dead! It's Jeff Baker!' So help me, it really happened." Mark had been playing Penny's first husband, Jeff Baker, on *As the World Turns,* until he got tired of the part and, like Teal Ames on *The Edge of Night,* had to be killed off in a frightful auto accident.

After realizing that they have this kind of audience power, many soap stars attempt to further their careers by taking advantage of audience recognition. They're constantly rushing off to cities around the country doing stock plays and getting paid handsomely. In recent years stock company managers have discovered that soap actors would attract big theater crowds even if they were to do readings from telephone books. Many viewers in small towns travel hundreds of miles just to see their favorite daytime star in a play. Gene Bua (the late Bill Prentiss on *Love of Life*), Eileen Fulton, and Don Stewart were all able to further their nightclub singing careers with the help of their soap-star status. Don Stewart notes: "In the beginning I knew I was being booked just because I was a star on *The Guiding Light*. So I sang a lot of songs that I knew viewers would like, and kept away from rock. I even did a song written by Earl Wilson's son, called 'My Name Is Michael Bauer,' and a monologue about the character." All three singers, by the way, were soon swamped with booking engagements—primarily because of the original support of their dedicated daytime fans.

Being on a serial, though, and being popular with millions of fans, isn't always the key to surefire success in other fields. In fact, sometimes it works the other way. Stefan Schnabel recently auditioned for the part of a caretaker in the new movie, *The Exorcist*. The director, William Friedkin, loved the audition, and was just about to hire Mr. Schnabel. Then Friedkin asked, "What have you been doing? I haven't seen you in anything for years." "I've been playing Dr. Stephen Jackson on *The Guiding Light* for the last eight years." Friedkin thought a moment, then looked up, astonished, "Oh, no, I can't hire you for this film! Karl, the caretaker, is supposed to be a mysterious figure. Instead, everyone will be saying, 'There's Dr. Jackson!' " Friedkin, no dummy, knew that *The Guiding Light* had more loyal-to-the-death viewers watching it in one *day* than *The Exorcist* would have in a year.

Loyal, concerned, emotionally caught up, involved—all these words apply to the daytime fan. He is easy to knock because he is so vulnerable, because he wants as much life as he can get, and the daytime serials help him get it.

One female psychiatrist, a specialist in housewives' problems, once tried to convince a magazine writer that soap operas were watched because of a "low-grade constant depression" that most housewives suffer. Now this well-known and highly respected woman doctor was perhaps right that many housewives probably unconsciously would prefer to be doing something else—probably would prefer to be more actively involved in the world. It is true that many housewives do not have a healthy enough self-image. But soap watching, if anything, certainly is not a *symptom* of low-grade depression, but a way of combating it by helping to bring women into contact with a world of "real" emotional involvements. Also, the soaps don't put women down—women on serials are shown not only as housewives, but as doctors, lawyers and judges. That certainly helps to improve the woman's self-image. It also teaches her something important about the harder aspects of living. "Too many people sneer at soap operas," said Dr. Paul Rosenfels, a well-known New York analyst who is deeply concerned with the way mass media influences peoples' lives. "It's just about the only form of television that shows people how to face up to the problems of divorce, losing a child, death, illegitimacy, or infidelity. People who watch the serials see these problems portrayed realistically, and it helps them cope."

Dr. Rosenfels wasn't just referring to the effect of daytime serials on women but on men as well. It is a fact that nearly a full fourth of the viewing audience is male. Many people are surprised to learn this. But in a world where almost every family is affected by personal conflicts of some sort—the divorce rate has leveled off, according to recent statistics, at a constant rate of 50 percent—why shouldn't men become just as involved in the day-to-day problems faced by soap characters? "Men are always writing to me," says Mary Stuart. "Why, I have a fan club made up solely of vice-presidents who watch *Search* during their lunch hour." Both Lee Patterson (Joe Riley on *One Life to Live*), and Don May (Adam Drake on *The Edge of Night*) are constantly amazed by the number of truck drivers and gas station attendants who greet them with a "Hi, Joe!" or "Hi, Adam!"

After the die-hard cynic has stopped his derisive laughter at the daytime stories, which are closer to reality and more up-to-date than the formula-made nighttime TV shows he watches, and after he has stopped guffawing at the people who sit before TV sets, misty-eyed at the reconciliation between two lovers after much misunderstanding—let him ponder the case of a nurse at a cancer ward who wrote into *Another World* to find out what lay ahead for the characters since many of her patients feared they would never find out. The producer wrote back and wanted the nurse to assure the patients that everything would turn out fine. Such strong connections between fiction and the well-being of the audience seldom exists anywhere else but in the world of daytime serials.

That is precisely why so many celebrities and intellectuals cling steadfastly to their favorite soaps, which can be quite uplifting and reassuring about the possibilities of human fulfillment and interrelationships, and everyone needs reassuring. How many viewers, for example, will forget the day *As the World Turns'* Kim Reynolds lost her baby and was comforted by her sister, Jennifer? The writing and acting in this scene was superb. And how many will ever forget the day that *Another World*'s Alice and Steve finally met after nearly a year of separation and misunderstanding? The scene was so beautifully moving that it was replayed weeks afterward on *The Mike Douglas Show* and received quite an ovation. The cynics and snobs should realize that the soaps aren't addicting because the people who watch aren't smart enough to resist the habit; on the contrary, it's the clever people who realize that the daytime serial world is where it's at.

ᦕ VIII ᦖ

Famous Bloopers, Gags, and Mishaps

DAYTIME ACTORS LOVE to tell funny stories about their bloopers—which happen to the best of them because of their hectic working schedules. *As the World Turns'* Helen Wagner always laughs when she thinks about the time she and Rosemary Prinz were playing a scene and Helen passed a tray to her and said, "Have some more pennies, Cookie?" And if John Larkin were alive today he'd still be embarrassed about the scene in which he, as Mike Karr on *The Edge of Night,* came through a door and yelled at the cameras: "Hello, all you folks out there in TV land," and then started cutting up and dancing around. He wondered why none of the other actors were laughing along with him. When the commercial break came, he found out that he had mistaken the live broadcast for the dress rehearsal and that ten million people or so had watched the whole charade. John was destroyed.

These mishaps always seem funny in retrospect—and long-time soap lovers can probably add a whole list of the ones they remember best—but when they happen to an actor, the embarrassment of making a fool of himself in front of millions of viewers may make him seriously consider going for a rest cure in some Swiss sanitarium.

Mistakes on soap operas were much more dreadful for the actors way back when all the serials were live. Then a goof couldn't be bleeped out or retaped. Every word an actor said—and sometimes every word he *couldn't* say—was broadcast. According to Val Dufour, a star who had been imported from Hollywood in the fifties to appear on her very first television serial—*Concerning Miss Marlowe*—had been in the middle of a scene with her French maid when the telephone rang. It wasn't supposed to ring in the script. The befuddled star simply picked up the phone, handed it to her French maid, said "It's for you!," and walked off the set. The horrified French maid had to improvise a telephone conversation for the rest of the scene. (Carol Burnett recently did a take off on that sort of soap blooper when she and the late Betty Grable were doing an "As the Stomach Turns" comedy skit. Carol says to Betty, "Isn't that the phone?", and two seconds later the phone rings.)

Val Dufour also recalls a calamity years ago on *First Love* that almost got its three stars—himself, Patricia Barry, and Rosemary Prinz—their pink slips. The show was live, and on this occasion the head writer, Monia Starr, had written a "Friday cliffhanger" in which Val, as jet engineer Zack James, witnessed an awful plane crash in one scene, and then rushed off to tell his wife (Pat Barry) in the next scene: "Chris cracked up the plane." was the line. While Pat was to register anguish, the pilot's wife (Rosemary Prinz) was to break down in tears. That would end the Friday show, leaving the audience to wait on pins and needles till Monday to find out if the worst had happened to Chris. "Everything went fine," said Val, "until that last scene. I came rushing through the door and said to Patricia, 'Chris crapped . . .' I was so horrified at what I had said on live TV that I just stopped, and then continued in a very small, timid voice, '. . . up the plane.' The camera panned over to Pat Barry, who by now was gagging with her effort to stop laughing, and then to Rosemary Prinz, who was roaring. The show ended and the director was furious. Among other things, he yelled at me, 'You shouldn't have stopped after "crapped!" That just made it worse.' But viewers wrote in and said they loved our goof."

Some actors call these tongue-twister stories. Ruth Warrick (now Phoebe Tyler on *All My Children*) says her favorite one happened during her brief part on *The Edge of Night*. Again, it was a Friday-cliffhanger show, and it was supposed to end with a close-up of a man talking about his wife and child. "He was supposed to say, 'But you know I love Betty Jean and Budd.' And the camera comes in on a big close-up and he says, 'But you know I love Betty Jean in bed.'" Again, live, Eileen Fulton was supposed to be introducing a young girl to a man on *As the World Turns*: "I should have said, 'I want you to meet so-and-so.' But instead I said, 'I want you to make so-and-so.'" In both cases the audience must have thought that the TV code of ethics had changed drastically.

Many daytime actors have to play professional-looking and -sounding doctors and lawyers, and they do such a good job at it that some viewers actually write in asking for medical and legal advice. In real life, however, most doctor-actors "wouldn't know a scalpel from a swizzle stick," as the late Ed Zimmermann, who played Dr. Joe Werner on *The Guiding Light,* was fond of saying. Those worried and serious looks on the faces of soap professionals always impress viewers, but often they come from a deep-down dread that all those technical medical or legal terms the actor learned the night before will get bollixed up when he finally has to say them. Playing Andre Lazar on *The Edge of Night,* Val Dufour once had to describe to Antony Ponzini, playing fellow partner-in-crime Tony Wyatt, how a third accomplice had died. "It was one of those two-part Latin disease terms," says Val. "The night before I thought I had it memorized, but on air I just completely forgot it. So I just made up a name. I said, 'He died of *nebullosic fibrosis.*' Tony was supposed to repeat the disease-name that I had forgotten, and when I said the crazy thing, he stammered 'What?' Now I couldn't even remember what I made up, and improvised, 'Well, go look it up in the medical dictionary, dummy!'"

That story is topped only by the one Ed Zimmermann

related when he appeared on *The David Frost Show*. "I'm terribly nearsighted. I mean, I can't even hear very well without glasses. One day I had to do my second big operation on *The Guiding Light*. I had to remember the names of so many instruments—sutures, clamps, and stuff—I didn't have the foggiest idea of what they were. They all became a jumble in my mind. I just had to get all those lines out, so I decided to wear my contact lenses on that particular day so that if I had to look at the teleprompter I would be saved. At the crucial moment in the operation I saw this nice little gray contact lens flip up in the air and go right into the wound. And then, you know what happens—you begin to think of all kinds of extraneous things instead of what you're supposed to think of. I thought of that contact lens in that poor man's stomach. I didn't know what I was supposed to do next. We have real nurses working with us during operations, and those ladies were looking at me as if they were saying, 'Come on, dummy, do something.' And then there was this awful pause. The teleprompter kept going, and I looked at it; the man running it had madly put it in reverse. When I looked it was running backwards! I decided at that point that I was either dreaming, or if this was happening I had better do something fast. And I started giving all kinds of weird commands. I didn't even sew up the wound, I sewed up my glove. Fortunately the nurses saved us." Ed said the incident was funny to think about later on, but was sheer hell when it was happening.

During those operations, by the way, the blood that you see is a red-colored liquid that is specially formulated to stick to rubber gloves, instruments, and clothing for added realism. The "blood" is brought from makeup to the "operating rooms" by the pailful. Once, during dress rehearsal for an operation, Ed Zimmermann suddenly had to stop in the middle of an incision and complain, "I can't go on! I have blood all over my script."

A well-known character actor came on *The Doctors* for a "one shot," and not only couldn't remember the medical terms, but couldn't remember anything else either. Says Jim Pritchett, describing the scene, "He walked in the front door and was supposed to be furious with some younger doctor on the staff. And he said, 'Matt, I'm not going to—I'm not ... not going to—I—I ...' And he couldn't think of the first line. So I said, 'What's the matter, Doctor? I suppose you're upset about young Dr. Sloan again.' 'Yeah, that Dr. Sloan, he's—he's—he's ...' 'What seems to be the trouble? Is it the Harrison case again?' 'The Harrison case!' So we went through an entire act of about six minutes, and he could not think of a single line. He was so shook he couldn't even see the teleprompter and he would repeat everything I said, and then he would stop. We took him all the way through and when the poor man finally finished the thing he walked out the door and out of the studio and out of the building, and he's never been back since."

That's an extreme example of an actor "going up," or forgetting his lines. Most of us who watch daytime serials see actors who hesitate on their speeches longer than necessary, stumble on their lines, miss their cues, or suddenly have to look up from the person they're talking to before saying another word. The pause permits him to look at the teleprompter, a small black box with all the actors' speeches written on an electrically moving scroll. Although actors abhor having these inevitable moments of weakness exposed to vast numbers of people, most viewers are sophisticated enough to realize that going up and stumbling do not indicate any lack of ability, but rather a lack of adequate rehearsal time.

Some actors don't actually go up on their lines, but often have trouble with the names of other characters. And on soaps, character names are repeated incessantly in the scripts, primarily to help viewers follow scenes even if they have to go away from the TV to do chores. Why the special trouble with character names rather than with lines? It is simply that actors on daytime serials grow to know each other so well over a period of time and are so used to calling one another by their real names off-screen that it's sometimes an effort to play a scene with a friend and have to call him by a made-up name. Val Dufour confesses that on *The Edge of Night* he had an on-the-air habit of calling Phil Capice "Ray," for of course the character was played by Ray MacDonnell.

On the same show Jered Holmes, playing Brian Blake, once tried to correct a mistake with names and only made it worse. He said, "Rachel is the father of Steven's child . . . er, I mean, Steve is the mother of Rachel's child." The other actors in the scene (including Val Dufour, who recalled this incident in an article for *Afternoon TV*) had quite a time keeping straight faces.

Then Don MacLaughlin, as Chris on *As the World Turns*, remembers years ago that he was having a scene with Les Damon, who played his best friend, "and I suddenly couldn't remember that his name was Jim. So I called him by my own brother's name, Peter."

Lest it be forgotten that serials are seen as well as heard, we must not neglect mentioning the by-now thousands of visual catastrophies that have been seen on the TV soaps. When these technical errors happen, daytime actors are as resourceful and courageous as can be imagined. What greater horror, for example, than to be playing in a daytime TV serial and suddenly have the wall cave in on you while you're trying to recite your lines? That's exactly what happened to Joy Nicholson and Leonard Valenta (now the highly successful director of *As the World Turns*), when, while they were appearing on an April 12, 1942 episode of *Last Year's Nest,* one of the set walls suddenly collapsed. "We were in the middle of a love scene," says Valenta, "and Joy, who was nearest the wall, simply leaned against it and played the rest of the scene holding it in place."

Leonard Valenta also remembers when, a few years later, he was appearing on a Western-type serial called *Action in the Afternoon* and could expect any one of a number of things to go wrong almost every episode. "It was live, of course, and we did it outdoors. Sometimes in the middle of scenes planes would roar overhead—which was pretty embarrassing, since this was supposed to take place in the Old West. On one show there was supposed to be a gunfight, but the ground was so muddy that the actors kept slipping and dropping their guns. Eventually,

out of five gunfighters, only one actor was left holding a
gun. He didn't know what to do with it, so he just threw
it at the others."

Similarly, Jim Pritchett tells of the time another one-
shot actor was called in to perform a brain operation with
him on *The Doctors*. (Matt Powers is a thoracic surgeon,
so he had to be assisted by a brain surgeon.) "This gentleman was going through the whole procedure, and he
called for a chisel. He got his chisel. Then we had a few
more lines of dialogue, and he was supposed to get a mal-
let to start working on the skull. He said 'chisel' by mistake. So they gave him another chisel, and he found
himself with two chisels. Then he just shrugged and
hammered one chisel with the other chisel."

Actors are in the habit of rehearsing without actual
props until dress rehearsal and broadcast. Once, on *The
Edge of Night*, an actor was supposed to end the show
with a teaser telephone conversation. He spent the whole
day rehearsing the difficult speech by holding his hand up
to his ear, as if it were a phone. When the phone rang
during the live broadcast, he held his hand up to his ear,
instead of picking up the phone, and started talking.
Meanwhile, he just happened to glance at the monitor and
saw himself standing there like an absolute idiot talking
into his hand. After the broadcast, the shattered actor
confessed that he had considered making some sort of
mad speech about why he was talking into his hand instead of the phone, but he decided not to bother.

"I remember one time," says Don MacLaughlin, "that
Helen Wagner was supposed to be serving me cherries
jubilee on the air. You know what cherries jubilee is—you
pour liquor on top and set it on fire, and then you serve it
as soon as the fire goes out. Well, we had such trouble getting the cherries jubilee to light during rehearsal that we
poured literally half a bottle of cognac on top so it would
light properly on air. Came air time, a match was set to
the dessert and it exploded in flames and wouldn't go out!
I had to eat the cherries, flames and all, because I had
lines later that referred to how wonderful my dessert had
been. So there I was, on camera, trying to eat those flam-

ng cherries. I felt like a fire-eater in a circus—and it must have looked absolutely ridiculous to viewers."

Don, like most soap actors, doesn't realize how much most viewers relish those funny technical disasters. Mistakes on the soaps remind the audience that no one is infallible, least of all those gorgeous TV people. Then, too, these mishaps give many viewers yet another reason to love the actors, since imperfect people are easier to love than perfect ones.

However, not many viewers caught on when Don MacLaughlin and Rosemary Prinz once handled an on-the-air catastrophe so beautifully. The two were reciting their lines for several minutes in the Hughes's kitchen while working around a real oven. Suddenly the timer began ringing. Says Don, "Rosemary and I had a long ten-minute scene to get through, and after a few minutes we just started improvising lines. 'Gosh, Penny,' I said, 'what's wrong with that darn oven?' 'I don't know, Dad,' said Rosemary, 'we were trying to get it fixed this morning.' All through it Rosemary and I managed to stay in character, and we referred to each other only by our story names. Finally a stagehand crept up out of sight of the TV camera and managed to shut the timer off. Meanwhile, Rosemary and I had used up all this time talking about the timer, and we still had all this dialogue to get through. Well, somehow we were able to condense our lines and still get across the sense of the scene. It all looked very real. Viewers probably thought the oven business was planned that way."

Dean Santoro, who played the late Paul Stewart on the same show, will never forgive a fan magazine for running a cartoon of his losing his hairpiece on air. "It was so embarassing," says Dean. "Right in the middle of a scene my wig falls off and all I could do was pick it up and put it back on. And then I got so many letters from viewers who saw it and said they didn't realize that I *had* a hairpiece. The magazine cartoon wouldn't have been so bad, would have even made me laugh, if only they had waited a few months for the whole dreadful incident to die down."

Such accidents happen in the excitement of trying to

give a first-class performance after just a few hours of re
hearsal. Jordan Charney, playing Sam Lucas, had a nea
disaster on *Another World* because he was too relaxed
During a scene, Sam was supposed to be lying in a hospi
tal bed, dreadfully ill, being comforted by Lahoma
played by Ann Wedgeworth. Well, Jordan, who is alway
cool and collected anyway, had gotten so relaxed lying i
bed during the dress rehearsal that during taping he ha
fallen asleep. Ann delivered her first line to him. No re
sponse. She repeated the line—Jordan was supposed to b
making low moans, but he wasn't saying anything. A
Virginia Dwyer remembers the rest: "Ann managed t
wake Jordan up and Jordan, startled from sleep, manage
to realize what was happening—that the cameras wer
rolling. And then he delivered all of his lines perfectly
Oh, it was funny, and we've never let him forget it either
Jordan Charney is probably the most relaxed man wh
ever lived."

If you think that some of these unintentional on-the-ai
soap catastrophes are funny, you should witness some o
the quite intentional madnesses actors perpetrate aroun
the studios. In fact, some of the funniest comedy bits ar
performed off-screen—principally as a means of getting a
least some comic relief into the often unrelieved serious
ness of the afternoon dramas. On-screen, for instance, Bol
Hughes of *As the World Turns* suffers one tragedy and ro
mantic heartbreak after another; but around the set, acto
Don Hastings is Mr. Court Jester himself. During re
hearsals he manages to crack everyone up with his smar
remarks, and he usually gets back as much as he dishes
out. In the middle of a tearful scene in which Dr. Hughes
is pondering the fate of an injured young girl, Don quips
"I don't zink zis patient will live through ze night!" An
someone immediately counters, "Doctor, you're turning
blue! I don't think you'll make it either!" Then Dor
again, "It must be the new brand of pipe tobacco our di
rector is using!" And so it goes. The writers of *As the
World Turns* should really use Don's comic gift for the

character of Bob Hughes. The audience would adore seeing this side of Don Hastings.

Occasionally writers do become aware of an actor's comedic talent and attempt to inject humor into some of his scenes, if the story permits. It is usually hard to put comedy into a daytime serial because the going theory is that the audience wants to become emotionally involved with serious problems. Millee Taggart, playing Janet Collins on *Search for Tomorrow*, broke the Law of Sacred Soap Seriousness on the show when she and Larry Haines, who plays her father, Stu Bergman, started playing some of their scenes for laughs. "I thought the show needed it," says Millee. "Afternoon audiences like to laugh occasionally. The writers saw that our brand of humor was working and began to write comic scenes for Larry, John Cunningham—who plays my husband, Wade—and myself. I think it would help all serials if they started doing a little of the same thing." To keep their funny bones limber, Millee and Larry are always pulling elaborate gags on each other on the set of *Search*. For example, after Janet's former husband, Dan Walton, had died of a rare blood disorder, Janet was supposed to receive his ashes in an urn. During the run-through just before Dan's "funeral," Millee spilled the ashes all over the floor; Larry came up with the line, "That's Dan all over." Everyone laughed. Then Millee looked up and collapsed with mirth, for there was Ron Hussman—the deceased Dan Walton—who was paying a social visit to the set wearing a home-made wire halo. Another time, it was Millee's turn. She put on a pair of platform shoes but didn't tell Larry; she then proceeded to play a dress-rehearsal scene sitting on the couch with Larry Haines, who's sensitive about his height. When she stood up, "he did the biggest double-take I've ever seen in my life," one observer remembered. The whole cast enjoyed that one.

Young actors who are good sports are always the objects of gags played on them by the technical crew—sort of the crew's way of saying "we like you." Cathy Bacon, who played Sally Bridgeman Rollins on *Love of Life,* was always getting kidded. Once, in the story, Sally was supposed to be having a simple ham sandwich at her book-shop. During dress rehearsal the prop men set up fried chicken and champagne as a practical joke on both Cathy and the director in the control room.

Jada Rowland, *The Secret Storm*'s Amy, was called "the rock" by the crew because she would take the most insane sort of gags with a good-natured smile. In one scene she was supposed to pour ashes in a trash can. Before she did it, the crew took her shoes and hid them in the bottom of the can. Jada had to walk home that night with the world's filthiest shoes!

Just to get a laugh out of the director of *All My Children,* the crew bound up Charles Frank (playing Jeff Martin) with ropes and then gagged him. Then there was the time Charles hid under the nurses station and played with Mary Fickett's (playing Ruth Brent) legs during taping. Ruth had a hard time trying not to giggle.

Finally, the *piece de resistance* of soap opera gags. It was Bob Short's twenty-fifth anniversary as head of daytime serials for Procter and Gamble Productions in Cincinnati. The whole cast of *As the World Turns* and various actors from other P & G soaps got together with Ed Track, Bob Short's assistant, to roast Bob in a mock half-hour soap episode. It was a terribly funny and campy script, written by Ed Track and directed by Dan Levin, the former director of *Search for Tomorrow*—and taped at the *Search* studio. Essentially, the episode involved a courtroom scene, and Bob Short was on trial for "ruining the minds of American womanhood." The soap was re-hearsed, and then taped, with Val Dufour playing the district attorney, Larry Haines playing the judge, Ann Wedgeworth and Mary Stuart as witnesses for the prosecution, Charita Bauer and all the actors of *As the World Turns* as jurors, and Don MacLaughlin as the final Voice of Reason.

Mary Stuart came to the witness stand and told Val that "my whole life is shot to hell" because of Bob Short and having to play on a soap opera year after year. Ann Wedgeworth then came to the stand and said that she was just an ordinary housewife until she had been "enslaved by the soaps." How could Bob Short do that to her? "My husband left me because I had neglected him for my serials, and then my baby died while I was watching *As the World Turns*. Well, Franny was being killed by Ellen because Franny was about to reveal the truth about Dan's illegitimacy. Well, I just *couldn't* miss that!"

Ed Track gave his testimony, playing a kind of Captain Queeg nervously fidgeting with steel balls in his hand. There was more testimony. One witness said that Bob Short had changed over the years. "He used to be so moral. Even the word *intersection* would make him blush." Finally Don MacLaughlin, as the Voice of Reason, ended the whole pretend-soap by summing up the feelings of all the actors: "Bob, everybody loves you."

When Bob Short finally received the tape in Cincinnati, he was entranced.

So, you see, it's not all tears and seriousness behind the soap bubbles.

◄§ IX §►

*"I Suddenly Realized
I Had Become My Character!"*

Another World's Virginia Dwyer tells an incredible but true story: "I had been playing Mary Matthews for a couple of years. One afternoon I returned home from the studio and I began poking around in my clothes closet. Suddenly I reeled from the shock. Every article of clothing in that closet was Mary's, not mine. Every dress and every coat was exactly her—ultraconservative. I panicked. I scooped all the clothes up in my arms and threw them out! I had forgotten who I was. I had become Mary Matthews."

It is an accepted fact that some viewers believe that the characters on serials are real people. These delusions often cause extreme and questionable behavior. Why is it so easy for even the most intelligent serial viewers to be momentarily confused, partly deluded? Is the line between this peculiar kind of fiction and what is *really* happening to real people so thin? And, while one wonders about these viewers, what about the many daytime actors who also become confused over who they are, on camera and sometimes off?

This is indeed an eerie psychological situation. When you think of it, though, it's not so surprising. If watching the same people discuss and play out their personal problems day after day on the television screen begins to convince some viewers that these characters exist, then shouldn't it be just as easy for the actors to find, despite themselves, that they are gradually *changing* into those characters? Of course, it's much more of a shock for the actors to discover themselves in the act of identifying than for the viewers, who want and sometimes need to believe. It was certainly a shock for Virginia Dwyer, who basically sees herself as Mary Matthews' complete opposite. Where Mary Matthews is conservative and sort of dowdy, Virginia sees herself as vivacious, dressy, creative; but day after day of playing a rock instead of a zephyr took its toll on her psyche. Another long-time soap actress became severely depressed and finally went to see a psychiatrist. It was revealed in analysis that her "sister" had died in the story, and she was unconsciously grieving over the loss of her make-believe relative. And Val Dufour says that as John Wyatt on *Search for Tomorrow* he's always wearing $300 Bloomingdale suits, $38 custom-made shirts from Paul Stuart's, jewelry, big diamond rings, wrist and neck chains. "I've never dressed that way in my life. But now that I'm doing it on the show, I suddenly find myself buying fancy suits, the same sorts of jewelry, tight shirt collars. I stroll through Bloomingdale's looking at John Wyatt type clothing, and I ask myself, 'Why am I doing this?' " One talented woman who plays a serial bitch—but is ordinarily a sweet person in real life—confesses that she becomes so engrossed in her character that she often finds herself snapping at her husband and children for no reason at all.

Here, then, is a case of *some* viewers who begin to feel fervently that the soap actors are their characters, and *some* soap actors who begin to feel that they too are their characters, and usually resent the feeling—all trapped, viewer and actor alike, in the complex, involving world of the daytime television serial.

The soap opera world wouldn't be nearly so complicated-bizarre if it weren't for the intervention of minds and wills, other than those of the actors and audience, in height-

ening the metaphysical confusion. "Fate," too, plays
its part and adds to the eeriness. For soap opera not
only imitates life in its realism, but life in turn imitates the
soap operas. For example, about six years ago, Gene Bua
and Toni Bull were introduced on *Love of Life* as Bill
Prentiss and Tess Krakaur. The characters were young
and in love and, naturally, were confronted with many
problems. Bill, naive and impulsive, was a talented singer;
Tess was somewhat spoiled, unsure of what she wanted
out of life, but basically a good person. On the show, Bill
began to teach Tess the real meaning of the word *love*. He
became her love guru. Tess married Bill, divorced him,
and then married him again. In real life, Gene Bua and
Toni Bull—who, like all soap actors playing a romantic
couple, had to work together every day—became attracted
to each other and fell in love. There's nothing unusual
about that; many actors who work together fall in love.
But here is the coincidence: Gene had become Toni's
teacher, her guru, and he even referred to her later as a
love child! There is no doubt that their love affair was
progressing in real life just as it was in the story, even to
the imitation of little details. For instance, Bill would sing
on the show and Tess would always remark how terrific a
singer he is, and Toni would later say the same thing
about Gene's singing when talking to interviewers. After
Gene got his divorce from his first wife and married Toni,
the viewers of *Love of Life* found out about their marriage from the fan magazines. One can't blame soap opera
viewers for listening, at this point, to every word Tess and
Bill said to each other and believing that these were ex-
changes between a real husband and wife. Viewers were
observing the problems of a real couple—and Toni and
Gene were more or less playing themselves.

Since soap opera fiction now paralleled real life, the
producers of *Love of Life* began to add to the strange
transference process by manipulating the story in a peculiar way. If viewers saw Bill and Tess as an off-screen real
couple, what better way to skyrocket ratings than to kill
off Bill and have Tess grieve over him? The grief would
surely be heightened since Toni would be acting out grief

for her real husband. Viewers would naturally see that Toni was grieving for Gene. And that is exactly what happened. Toni Bull Bua gave the most beautifully convincing performances during those many grief-stricken months, and people believed what they saw, believed they weren't watching fiction at all.

Says Toni Bull Bua, "In the beginning I was all choked up at the idea of the producers killing off Gene—I couldn't understand why they'd want to do it, especially since Gene and I fell in love on the show and were married in real life well after our characters were married. It was unavoidable—the story of our own love affair became intertwined with the story of Tess and Bill. When they finally killed off Gene and I had all of those scenes to do bemoaning Bill's death, I was determined to prove to all the viewers how much I loved Gene by doing the best job I could in playing the bereaved Tess. After all, to many people it was almost as if Gene had *really* died. I wanted them to see how much Gene meant to me."

The producers exploited the situation to the *nth* degree. They even convinced a reluctant Toni to do promos of black-togged Tess weeping over Bill's coffin, and they showed them for many afternoons with an announcer overlay: "Tess grieves for her beloved Bill ... Watch *Love of Life!*" Both Toni and Gene deeply resented the way the show's producers had manipulated them and their followers for the sake of the show's sagging ratings—which, by the way, did go up and stay up for a long time after Bill's death.

Gene and Toni Bua didn't necessarily suffer any delusion about who they were in real life, nor any confusion about their identities as people. But, on the other hand, it is evident that there was a kind of cryptic interplay between the audience, the characters, and the actors themselves—something you wouldn't expect in any other art form. Situations such as this are possible because the soap actor plays his character for a long period of time, on an almost daily basis, and because he is often type cast in his part. The head writer begins to shape and develop a character based on the personality characteristics of the particular actor. Many daytime performers put it bluntly: "I'm playing myself."

Naturally, if you get enough people together on a soap who are, in a sense, playing themselves—with the writers figuring out plots that grow out of these characters—it's hardly surprising that actors behave toward one another on the sets the way their characters do in the stories! Helen Wagner and Don MacLaughlin, although happily married to other mates, make no bones about the fact that they feel almost married to one another after eighteen years of TV marital bliss as Nancy and Chris. They usually spend the whole day together at the studio on Fifty-seventh Street going over their scenes. "Helen's a hard taskmaster," Don says appreciatively, as if he were talking about the expectations of his wife. On the set, they have formed a sort of marital relationship somewhat similar to their characters', with Helen the perfectionist and Don going along with her ideas. "She's usually right, anyway," he says. Many of the kitchen scenes on the show, showing Nancy kneading some life into a piece of dough or cutting carrots for a stew, came about because Helen is such a good cook herself. She even distributes recipes to other members of the cast with titles like "Nancy Hughes's Lemon Chicken" just as her character does on the show.

After twenty years of kissing and exchanging endearments on *Search for Tomorrow,* the late Melba Rae wasn't just joking when she referred to Larry Haines as her "second husband." At the time of her tragic, untimely death, more than one actor on *Search for Tomorrow* reported, "It was as if Larry had lost his own wife!"

Teri Keane remembers arriving at *The Edge of Night*'s studio one morning to start rehearsals with Mandel Kramer—they had been playing Mr. and Mrs. Bill Marceau for some years. He suddenly reached into his pocket and then asked her, "Where are the tickets? Did I give them to you?" Says Miss Keane, "I said, 'I'm not your wife, Mandy,' and he looked embarrassed." The odd thing is that Ruth Kramer, Mandel Kramer's real-life wife and the mother of his children, looks exactly like Miss Keane from certain angles.

On *The Doctors,* Carolee Campbell and David O'Brien (as Carolee and Steve Aldrich) have been playing husband and wife for nearly eight years; they now feel so drawn to each other that they both swear they'll quit the program if the other leaves. Miss Campbell adds, "I think the producers made us get married on the show in the first place because they could see how much we liked one another." She's happily married to actor Hector Elizondo and David's a debonaire, semiconfirmed New York bachelor—yet, did the soap situation fulfill a sort of platonic-love wish on the part of both people? Were the writers satisfying not only the audience's fantasies about these two attractive people, but also those of the actors themselves?

The examples of TV soap marriages that carry over into real life seem endless. These off-screen relationships are just like the on-screen marriages or love affairs except that they are devoid of the mystery—and headache—of sex. Ron Tomme is probably around his soap opera wife, Audrey Peters (they play Van and Bruce Sterling on *Love of Life*) more than his own girl friends. In magazine interviews they talk incessantly about each other, about each other's good qualities. Audrey Peters's son, Jay, called Ron Tomme Uncle Ron for many years. Both Audrey and Ron are divorced from their past mates and swear that their unpleasant connubial experiences leave them without any desire for remarriage. Again, one can speculate: Has the on-screen and off-screen "marriage" so satisfied these two, giving them the stability of a relationship they unconsciously need, that they may now scoff at real marriage?

The bonds are very strong behind the scenes of the soaps, not only among the on-screen romantics. Playing mother or daughter, for example, is a surefire way to gain a "second relative." When Eileen Fulton of *As the World Turns* decided to elope with Danny Fortunato, "the one person I so wanted to tell, but couldn't, was Ethyl Remey, who plays my mother on the show. Why, in so many ways she's just like a real mother to me." On the set of *Another World,* Jacquie Courtney and Virginia Dwyer conduct mother-daughter chats. "Oh," says Virginia, "it has been very much like watching your own daughter grow up. When she came on the show she was just going on seventeen, and we used to talk about her boyfriends. Now that she's more grown up, we're just as close, only we talk about her baby instead of her dates."

It's as if a nonverbal dialogue were going on among soap-opera actors, in which each one says, implicitly, to the other: "I play myself but pretend I'm playing someone else. *You* pretend to play someone reacting to someone else, but you're reacting to *me,* your friend, in reality. The audience is asked to believe that they are just watching me play someone else, but deep down they know, and I know, they're watching *me* play *me.* We all pretend that we're not who we are!" Jim Pritchett, *The Doctors'* Matt Powers, recently admitted that he was aware of a change in his own on-camera personality with each new "Maggie" that he'd play opposite: Ann Williams, Bethel Leslie, and finally Lydia Bruce. In daytime television serials it's as much *re*acting to a real-life situation as it is *play*-acting a fictional one.

In so many other ways, real life often determines the course of a story-line, and even begins to extend its boundaries into new dimensions of intrigue. When Robin Strasser went to the producers of *Another World* and announced that she was going to have a baby, they were faced with a typical problem: what to do with Rachel? Writing her out of the story was impossible and trying to hide her stomach behind rose plants or photographing just head shots for six months would have been inconvenient. And so the real-life pregnancy was written in, inspiring a thoroughly exciting story-line in which the character Rachel was married to one man but was having the child of another man who was in love with another woman. That story, created by a real situation, has been going on ever since. The agony for Steve, Alice, Rachel, and Jamie started the day Robin Strasser and husband, Larry Luckinbill, conceived their first child.

The same thing happened a year or so ago on *General Hospital,* with Sharon DeBord; but this time the actual pregnancy wasn't just any old conventional one, like Miss

Strasser's. In this case the actress was not married. Naturally the fan magazines generated a great deal of publicity
about Miss DeBord's decision to have a baby though still
single—with many comments about her courage and mo-
dernity. Meanwhile, viewers were watching her character,
Sharon Pinkham (same first name!), have a baby in the
story. The show's producers, after the initial panic subsided, first considered making up a story about some
phony husband, "because we thought it might be too
much of a shock for viewers," then, later, Miss DeBord
convinced the producers to tell the truth. It turned out
that Miss DeBord's followers at home came through with
many wonderful letters of encouragement and approval.
"Now that the audience knows the truth," said a member
of the production staff, "we haven't gotten one single letter
here criticizing her, or complaining, only letters compli-
menting her on her attitude." Two stories, then, the real
one and the fictional one, were running parallel for viewers, who could decide which one they liked better. *General Hospital* became a "three-dimensional soap," taking
place on-screen, off-screen, and even on another serial—
an ABC one, naturally! That is, *One Life to Live*'s Antony Ponzini (he plays Vince Wolek) made a trip to Hollywood, became completely taken with Sharon, married
her, took her off *General Hospital* and brought her back
to New York, where *One Life to Live*'s producers began
talking about hiring her for that show. It all seemed endless and fantastic. Viewers were beginning to wonder as
much about the actors as about the characters. Will
Sharon DeBord and Antony Ponzini find happiness
despite their complicated situation? Will Vince Wolek
marry Wanda Webb on *One Life,* or will he find a new
love with a new character played by Sharon DeBord Ponzini? What will happen to Sharon Pinkham on *General
Hospital*? Will the stories in fan magazines now become
more interesting than the soap stories themselves?

Producers, however, most often decide not to inflict an
actress's pregnancy on her character (it can't always be
worked into the show), but go through all the rigamarole
of hiding her behind plants and vases, photographing her

sitting down or always above the waist. Naturally, when an actress is in this condition she can't do much more than recap work—just talking about other people, commiserating. Steady soap viewers are rather sharp and almost always know when the producer and director are trying to pull the wool over their eyes about what's happening to their favorite actress; they know what all that hiding-behind-the-plants-and-always-sitting stuff is about, and invariably they get a glimpse of the *enceinte* stomach anyway. But there are other giveaways. Once the director of *The Edge of Night* had been terribly clever in hiding Ann Flood's pregnancy from the audience without too many obvious devices. But one woman wrote to Miss Flood and said that she knew that she was pregnant because her eyes gave her away. "A woman's eyes are always the best way of telling," wrote the viewer. Miss Flood said that she was touched and will never forget the incident.

Not only pregnancies, but illnesses and the actual deaths of actors must be written into the scripts. When an actor gets sick, it's usually a matter of finding a substitute. Producers, however, know from past experience that seeing a new actor or actress in a role can cause heart palpitations of anxiety in many viewers from the fear that a well-loved actor has been replaced. So at the first appearance of another actor replacing the bedridden one, an announcer always says, "The part of so-and-so will be played today by so-and-so, during the absence of so-and-so." Sometimes the producer will even tell viewers that the actor is sick, if he is to be gone for some time. "The part of Tony Vincente will be played by Robert Loggia during the illness of Tony George," came the announcer's voice every day on *Search for Tomorrow*. Viewers were being told, in effect, that their *Search* favorite was gravely ill (otherwise why would he have been away so long), perhaps even dying. An avalanche of get-well cards came, for Mr. George's followers were indeed deeply worried. It turned out they had good reason to be. He was being operated on for possible cancer of the right lung. The tumor was discovered to be benign. "I can honestly say," said Mr. George, "that all of those letters and presents I got from the viewers helped me over a rough time. I was back on the show sooner than I expected to be." The viewers at home and the actors on the serial were busily creating their own soap story while the writers of *Search* were formally creating quite another, and both stories ran parallel, ultimately enriching the show.

The most dramatic incursions from real life into the serial world happen when an actor suddenly dies. Not only is the death thoroughly devastating for the audience, which by now has accepted the performer as a regular member of the family, but it also causes confusion since the tragedy is often played out all over again in the serial story-line. The deaths of Ed Zimmermann and Theo Goetz of *The Guiding Light* were already discussed. Then there was Melba Rae.

On one terrible Monday morning—December 27, 1971—photographer Gilbert Shawn called John Edwards, the producer of *Search for Tomorrow,* to let him know that his wife, Melba Rae, had collapsed while getting ready to leave for the CBS studio, as she had left on so many mornings during her twenty years as Marge Bergman on the show. In a coma, she was rushed to New York Hospital, where her ailment was diagnosed as a cerebral hemmorhage.

That Monday afternoon, after the show's taping, most of the cast came to see the unconscious Melba. She never woke up. Two days later, on December 29—shortly after the cast Christmas party attended by Mary Stuart, Larry Haines (Melba's TV husband for twenty years, Stu Bergman), Leigh Lassen (Patti Tate), and Carl Low (Dr. Rogers)—Melba Rae, at age forty-nine, was dead. New Years, unlike Christmas, wasn't to be as happy for the actors of *Search*.

Viewers found out immediately. That Wednesday, when Melba died, an epitaph was shown at the start of the show: "IN MEMORIAM—MELBA RAE (MARGE BERGMAN)." Later, at the end of the same program, an equally simple announcement was made: "The cast and

crew wish to express their sorrow at the passing of Melba
Rae." Behind the scenes a quick decision was made.
Marge would have to die on the show, since no actress
could possibly replace Melba Rae after twenty years.
Rather than overburdening viewers with the sorrow of
first experiencing Melba's death in real life and then having to witness the same event on TV, the producer of
Search for Tomorrow planned to keep any mention of
Marge Bergman out of the story for two weeks. Then the
actors would speak of her as if she had died six months
before and all the tears surrounding her sudden death had
already been shed. Such a plan was easier on the actors as
well as on the viewers, for it saved them from having to
relive the original shock of seeing Melba taken from them
without warning. She had been a lovable woman, and indeed her most characteristic line on the show—"Oh, Jo"
(or, "Oh, Stu"), "it's not as bad as you think!"—was typical of Melba herself.

Although the audience and actors of *Search* were ini-
tially spared the ordeal of having to play-act the heartbreak
that had befallen them, for several years now much of
their conversation and many of their actions on the show
have centered around Miss Rae's death. Stu Bergman's
whole story, now, is that of a man who cannot let go of
the memory of his wife. One can only imagine that the
scenes in which Larry Haines reminisces about his dead
wife are indeed difficult for him. Melba and he had grown
so close on the show that she would often call him Gilbert (her real husband's name) by mistake, and right after her death Larry's fellow actors offered their sympathies as if they were consoling her real husband. One
recent scene had Larry leaving the house in which he
and Marge had lived in Henderson for so many years,
to move in with his daughter, Janet Collins (Millee Taggart). As he left, he broke down in tears: "Oh, Marge,"
came his sigh. It's impossible to conceive that Mr. Haines
was not thinking of his dear friend Melba Rae at that
moment.

Some people may complain that the soap producers
are tastelessly capitalizing on the death of an actor when

hey simultaneously have his character die on the show ince soap deaths tend to raise the ratings. On December , several weeks before the real-life tragedy of Melba Rae's leath hit *Search for Tomorrow, Love of Life*'s Fred Stewrt, who played Alex Caldwell (the husband of Van's nother, Sarah), keeled over while doing a scene at the Acors Studio. Moments later he was dead of a heart attack. Now, after the shock of the death had passed, the producer of *Love of Life,* Freyda Rothstein, had to deal with ome immediate problems—namely, what to do with the lead man's lines. After some quick rewriting, all Mr. Itewart's lines were absorbed by other actors. But bigger problems still confronted Miss Rothstein. Should Alex Caldwell die on the show, too? Should another actor be prought in to play him? The producer thought that capiializing on Fred Stewart's death with a simultaneous story leath would have been too gruesome, tasteless. Instead, he took a chance that the audience could accept another actor in the role, and eventually hired Charles White, who ooked a lot like Fred Stewart. The transition was successul. Only a few viewers wrote in to express their regret over Mr. Stewart's death; one woman even sent a sympathy card to Joanna Roos, who played Sarah Caldwell.

Both *Search for Tomorrow* and *Love of Life* opted for different courses of action in dealing with the clash between real life and ongoing serial life. Both seemed valid choices. Yet it was *Search for Tomorrow* which extended its boundaries by allowing its viewers the release of grieving over the death of one of its actresses. *Love of Life*'s viewers did not experience the same release when Fred Stewart died. The show just pretended that Alex Caldwell lived on in spite of Mr. Stewart. There was no announcement of the actor's death. Possibly many viewers felt the way children feel when their elders foolishly—and cruelly—try to hide from them the grim reality of death.

Another instance when viewers did not immediately know of a death in a serial family was some years ago on *The Edge of Night,* when Peggy Allenby (she played Adlie Grimsley) suddenly died. Mary K. Wells (she played, Louise Capice), a close friend of the dead actress, was

chosen to say Miss Allenby's lines on air only two hou
after learning of her friend's death. Viewers weren't awa
of why Miss Wells was having a particularly difficult tir
with her speeches that day, nor were they aware that th
were witnessing a mini-soap opera within the regular so
opera.

Six or seven years ago, such behind-the-scenes melodr
mas could easily occur without many viewers being awa
of them. But these days, with the advent of the daytin
TV fan magazines, viewers know about almost everythi
that happens. Deaths, births, marriages, divorces, ar
other personal events in the lives of soap opera actors a
reported instantly in the two million or so monthly issu
of *Daytime TV* (Sterling Publications), *Afternoon T*
(Tower), *TV Dawn to Dusk* (Ideal), *TV By Day* (Mag
zine Management), and *Daytime TV Stars* (Dell). Unli
scandal-prone movie and nighttime TV fan magazine
these publications attempt to be more factual. Because t
magazines enjoy the high opinion of soap producers ar
actors, they almost always offer stories based on actual i
terviews.

Such magazines contribute a great deal both to t
shows and to their readers by extending to real life t
boundaries of continuing daytime fiction. Readers know
ing that *The Doctors'* David O'Brien is essentially a lone
bachelor although he plays the happy husband and fathe
Steven Aldrich, can perhaps better understand his style
acting. When viewers discover what an actor like Dea
Santoro (in the role of Paul Stewart) has to say abo
his being suddenly killed off on *As The World Turns*, the
feel, if not better, at least more relieved about his su
den departure. One magazine even offers in-depth r
views of all the serials, something the viewers never ha
before. Two million copies a month of various soap mag
zines displayed on all the country's newsstands migi
cause a number of people to stop and reconsider t
merits of daytime serials. Mike Douglas recently intro
duced *The Guiding Light's* Don Stewart as his Christm
Eve cohost. Without naming the source, he referred t
Don as "having recently been voted Best Actor on Da

me Television." The source of his information hap-
ened to be the January 1974 issue of *Daytime TV
tars*.

Daytime serials, as their radio ancestors did, incorpo-
ate tales of self-sacrifice and heroine-ism, faithfulness and
ntegrity—stories of people who might be described as ab-
olute paragons. Nancy and Chris Hughes seldom argue
nd are always worrying about their friends and relatives
n Oakdale. Bay City's Mary and Jim Matthews spend
leepless nights worrying about other people's troubles.
Nurse Martha Allen of *The Doctors* racks her brains
earching for the best advice to give problem-ridden as-
ociates. Certainly such individuals do exist in real life,
ut the viewer probably considers it unlikely that the acors are as pure as the characters they portray. And of
ourse they're not. But in one important way they are as
elf-sacrificing, long-suffering and ever-faithful as their
erial counterparts: they work day after day on daytime
elevision. Any actor who does this is by the nature of
is existence a full-blown, self-sacrificing soap opera hero
r heroine. That exhausted look you see on an actor's
ace during a grueling crisis in the plot is often real.
These poor actors have to get up at an unreasonable
our of the morning—usually 6:00 A.M., and if they live
ut of town, 4:00 A.M.—stumble to studios, perform a
half-hour TV drama after only a few rehearsals, do pre-
hearsals for the next day's show, get home just in time to
watch their children go to bed, and then spend another
three hours studying lines for the next day's show. Some
actors, who are important characters, must repeat this ex-
rcise four or five days a week, year after year. If they
have other acting jobs as well—say, in a Broadway
play—their health, or looks, or both, may well begin to
deteriorate.
Don May is perhaps the self-sacrificing daytime hero of
all time, a sort of male Stella Dallas. Six years ago, when
he came on *The Edge of Night,* he moved his wife and
two boys from Hollywood, where he had been working in
films, to New York. He wouldn't permit his family to live

in the city itself—an unattractive environment,
thought, for two young boys to grow up in. So he boug
a sprawling and handsome home for them in Cold Spri
Harbor, Long Island, two hours away from the city. B
cause of his concern for his family, Don May has spe
the last six years getting up at dawn, driving for two ho
into New York City, putting in a full day's work portra
ing private detective Adam Drake (for a live show, t
most nerve-wracking kind of program), and after t
2:30–3:00 P.M. (EST) broadcast, conferring on the ne
day's show. He finally leaves the studio at 5:00 P.M., ge
ting stuck in traffic jams on the Long Island Expresswa
and arrives back home at about seven or eight in th
evening. He may go through this routine five days a wee
since Adam Drake is the principle character on the sho
Why on earth does he do it? "I guess," he admitted, "I c
sometimes feel like a rat on a treadmill. But essentially
do it for my family. My part pays me well, and th
means that I can give them a secure, good life. And m
wife makes it easier for me. She takes care of all my co
respondence, appointments, and the paper work that mu
be done. That leaves me just about enough time at nigl
to study my script and go to bed."

Another World's Victoria Wyndham, who pla
Rachel, lives out in Connecticut and drives into work
5:00 A.M. with her investment-counselor husband, We
dell Minnick. "We don't get back until after the childre
are asleep," she says. "We see them on weekends and tr
to make up for lost time then. During the week they hav
a governess who looks after them." Victoria says that n
being able to see Darian, age four, and Christian, three,
pretty hard for her, but she considers it even more impo
tant for her and Wendell to give them a pleasant and sa
home. That's why she—and her long-suffering hu
band—endures her schedule.

But let's not carry these anecdotes and parallels too fa
Virginia Dwyer is Virginia Dwyer, and Mary Matthew
is Mary Matthews. Most soap actors live different liv
from those of their characters, and the continuing seri
stories, although often inspired by real situations, are mos

definitely created in someone's head and are not, as some viewers may think, made up by the actors as they go along. Nonetheless, it was amusing, if not altogether surprising, to hear Don Stewart admit on *The Mike Douglas Show*—after voicing some rather weak objections to being called Michael Bauer by people who meet him on the street—that it really didn't matter because "Don Stewart *is* Michael Bauer, after all."

❧ X ❧

Mary Stuart

FEW DAYTIME SERIALS can boast of having only one star, but *Search for Tomorrow* can—Mary Stuart. She's on the program an average of four times a week. Viewers have watched her live through the deaths of husbands, the loss of lovers, the threats to daughter Patti's happiness, and the troubles of her friends. Twenty-three years is a long time, and Mary Stuart and her audience are all practically family by now.

Sitting in her living room, where her mother is serving tea—pictures of her two nearly adult children, Jeff and Cynthia Krolick, close by—Mary jokes about her special daytime TV status: "I've told others this before, but I'm probably the world's oldest living ingenue." "Oldest?" Perhaps—but somehow still youthful as the ever-attractive Joanne. Mary has a graceful figure, wears clothes (on and off the show) like a fashion plate, has smooth, line-free skin, and pure, deep blue eyes. Those eyes, the haunting shape of the mouth and the slightly protruding chin, and the bell-like clarity of her speaking voice are the most instantly attractive things about Mary. Back in 1951, when this lovely lady was hardly into her twenties, she and *Search for Tomorrow* met daytime television audiences for the first time and—seasoned and made somewhat more interesting by age and the complexities of a well-developed personality—they are still on the air today.

"Many viewers think that Joanne and I are one and the same person and believe that I just make up her words on the show myself. I think that's the greatest compliment an actress can receive, to be told that she is so convincing that she *must* be living out her own life on television. Actually Joanne, as a character, is very dear to me because I've lived with her so long and because we are so much alike. We both want to do what is right, and we've both been growing more mature as the years have flown by—perhaps we're only different in that Joanne is so much more concerned about the people around her than I can allow myself to be. I'm more of a loner, at least that's the way it's been since my divorce six years ago. I prefer to spend my time sitting quietly at home writing lyrics for songs. I have little social life outside of my friendships with the actors on *Search*. I suppose I would like to have other friends, but I have a greater need to spend my time alone being creative."

As she spoke, Mary's mother, Mrs. Houchins, came into the room to tell Mary that her ex-husband was on the phone. After she spoke to him and returned to the living room, Mary announced, "Well, you know I'm still good friends with Richard. I'm still good friends with *all* of my husbands!" Let's see—she was referring to one other real-life spouse from many years back; and to Johnny Sylvester, who played Keith Barron, Joanne's first mate; and to Terry O'Sullivan, Jo's second husband, Arthur Tate; and to Bob Mandan, who was her almost-husband, Sam Reynolds, for four years; and finally to Anthony George, her third and current husband, Tony Vincente. "I adore Tony," says Mary. "I hope we stay together a long time. And I loved Bob Mandan; I was sorry when he decided to leave the show. But I'm friends with them all."

Mary and Joanne's lives have intermeshed, obviously—but then, real life and soap opera fiction tend to do that.

How does a person become a Mary Stuart? How did

Mary herself find her tomorrow on the show that has always been searching for that very thing?

When Mary Stuart Houchins was growing up in Tulsa, Oklahoma—where her parents had moved after her birth in Miami, Florida—she once picked up a movie magazine that said radio serial actresses received five hundred dollars a week and only had to work three or four hours a day. Mary knew of the serials way back then and occasionally listened to them. "I said to myself, 'Now that's what I'd like to be, a serial actress who earns five hundred dollars a week and still has time to raise a family.'" Years later, when Mary was hired for one of television's first daytime serials, *Search for Tomorrow*, she was offered a starting salary of five hundred dollars a week. It was like a prophecy come true.

But then, such occurrences were not and are still not unusual in the life of Mary Stuart. For once Mary sets her sights on a goal, she never stops to consider that she might not achieve it, works doggedly to get it, and then holds on to it. So it was no accident that Mary wound up at the top of her chosen profession. Mary sums herself up: "I'm a settler. I liked my job on *Search* and I stayed, even though sometimes there were obstacles." Her son, Jeff, now eighteen, adds: "Mother is a hard worker. She's always achieving something. She pushes herself too hard sometimes, I think, because she remembers what it was like to be poor when she was a child."

As a little girl during the Depression, Mary Stuart Houchins moved a lot with her parents—her father was a car salesman. She hated sitting still in school, although she was considered terribly bright, but loved to play-act in front of other people. One day she decided she would be a famous actress, and that was that. But by her late teens no producer had discovered her yet—even though she *had* appeared in numerous school plays and other local productions!—so she decided to take the matter into her own hands and come to New York for auditions. At the first sight of young Mary Stuart, casting directors did not bubble with enthusiasm. In fact, Mary soon had to face the fact that she needed a job to support herself. So, in true Mary Stuart style, she simply walked up to the nearest hat-check girl and said, "How do I get a job like yours?" When the procedure was described, Mary wound up checking hats and coats at the Roosevelt Grill. "I'd get bored just standing around, so I asked to sing some songs with the band, songs I had written myself." Joe Pasternak, the Hollywood producer who created so many stars at MGM, happened to be there one night when Mary was singing. "After I had finished he came over to me and asked if I wanted to be in the movies. I laughed at what I thought was a joke and walked away. Then one of the girls at the lounge told me that he certainly wasn't kidding. When I returned he told me to come to the Waldorf the next day for a screen test. I was awful. After it was over, Joe Pasternak walked over to me and said, 'You can't sing and you can't dance. You're funny-looking and I have no idea if you can act. But you've got something.' So I got a contract and went to Hollywood at the age of eighteen."

Mary's childhood ambition to become an actress whom millions would see up on the screen was beginning to come true—Mary never doubted that it would. Later the screen would become the TV tube, but it was much the same thing. Also at the age of eighteen, Mary married for the first time. It's funny how these two milestones in her life happened simultaneously—almost funny. No soap, nighttime sit-com, or screen writer could come up with *this* irreverent hodge-podge of events. It seems that before the Pasternak audition Mary had been living in a rooming house on Lexington Avenue which, unbeknown to her, was filled with streetwalkers. At night, during working hours, the girls would lock her out of the house and Mary would have to sit on the steps and wait. One young man, a painter, had an apartment nearby and would invite the young actress to wait in his apartment until the customers had left. They soon grew close. When Mary told him about the MGM Hollywood contract, he warned that she would probably do something as silly as taking an apartment in such a building out in Dream Factory, U.S.A., and insisted that they go out there together as Mr.

and Mrs. By the time Mary Stuart got to Hollywood to begin making grade-B movies, she was a young wife.

Mary, who had to keep secret her marriage to the young painter—young starlets then were supposed to be single, for the publicists—made some twenty movies in the four years (1946–50) that she was in Hollywood. From the start, the studios tried to make her look like a sex symbol, a glamour queen. Warner Brothers cast her as one of Errol Flynn's sultry lovers in *The Adventures of Don Juan;* Columbia put her opposite Preston Foster in *Thunderhoof,* making use of the young actress's exquisite bare shoulders. She looked glamorous enough in these films, but essentially Hollywood's campaign to make her into a sexy doll for publicity purposes failed dismally. Mary confesses that she didn't know the first thing about buying dresses, applying makeup, doing up her hair. She was still Miss Practical, even prefering to make her own clothes.

She and her husband built their own house with nothing but their own four hands. It was not so much an economy measure as a reaction against the whole ready-made life, all preplanned and conceptualized, that Metro and the other studios had cut out for her. Mary and her first husband spent a whole year building their home on Laurel Hills Road in Laurel Canyon, quite near where Elizabeth Taylor and Michael Wilding lived a few years later. The house is still standing today.

The actress's marriage to her painter husband dissolved after two and a half years. "It was just a problem with our careers. He had to move back to New York to work and I was stuck in Hollywood. Our marriage just couldn't work out."

Not only did the marriage not work out, but Mary was becoming distraught with the loneliness and inherent isolation of the Hollywood life. This was not really the life for a self-made young woman who liked to make her own dresses and build her own home. People were always trying to make her into something she was not. Besides, young Mary Stuart had quite a reputation for being a hard and productive worker, and she felt that her talents

were being abused for the sake of productivity. The end
of her cinema career came in 1950. "I remember I suddenly decided that I had to get out of Hollywood. I was
supposed to go into a picture that Ida Lupino was directing. But one morning just before that I was told I was to
cover for another actress whom I didn't even know. That
was it for me. By eight o'clock that evening I was on a
plane to New York—I had sold my horses, my car . . .
just left my house and gave orders to my housekeeper to
have everything else forwarded to New York. She did
send everything, except my jewelry and my furs. But pos-
sessions didn't mean a thing to me—and they still don't."

After having every little detail of her working life
planned for her out in Hollywood, Mary was now engaging in her own little orgy of career planning. "I gave
myself exactly two weeks to find an acting job in New
York. If I didn't, I was going to go out to Texas to sell
heavy farm equipment with some stuntmen I'd met on a
western picture. Two of us were going to put up the
money and the other two were going to sell. Well, I
thought it was better than starving for art someplace."

After she had been in New York for about ten days,
she and *Search for Tomorrow* unofficially came together,
although Mary didn't realize it at the time. She and
Time-Life executive Richard Krolick, whom she had met
in California before her divorce, had resumed their friendship in New York. Richard invited Mary to have lunch
with him and Roy Winsor, a friend in the advertising
world. Richard was late for the meeting, so Mary and
Roy, total strangers, were stuck with each other's company. "I really didn't know what to say to him," says
Mary, "so I just started making haphazard conversation.
He was involved with TV producing, and I had done a
number of TV game and talk shows—they had them in
those days, too—and I just happened to say that I felt
that television wasn't satisfying the needs of women. Radio wasn't either. 'Women are too perfect on radio and
television shows,' I said. 'Women can't see themselves.
Their needs aren't satisfied. Why can't television do something real for them?' I don't even think I was all that sure

of what I was talking about, but I had to say something. Roy then said to me, 'You should play the lead in that kind of TV program.' "

Mary didn't realize it then, but Roy Winsor, a radio and television production executive for the old Biow ad agency, was already in the process of talking with Procter and Gamble about a new afternoon television serial that P & G would sponsor. Roy Winsor says today that he was deeply impressed with Mary Stuart during that first meeting and had her in mind for the lead of the new serial from the start. "And why not?" says Roy. "Mary Stuart had all the qualifications: she was attractive, and I knew that she had the experience and was a hard worker. Obviously that first meeting brought us all tremendously good luck. I don't think we could have come up with a more perfect Joanne if we had searched the world."

Mary, however, didn't know anything about the projected new serial, nor about the impression she had made on its producer. Meanwhile, she and Richard Krolick, both newly divorced, began dating seriously. Mary, for the moment, gave up the idea of selling heavy farm equipment and enrolled in an acting class. Four months after her first meeting with Winsor, a man who had been watching her perform a scene in class came up to her and said, "Hello, Miss Stuart. I'm Charles Irving. Roy Winsor wants you to star in his new daytime television serial. Your salary will be five hundred dollars a week." Mary replied: "Super." That's how *Search for Tomorrow*, currently television's longest-running daytime drama, hired television's longest-lived daytime heroine. Without realizing it, Mary had auditioned for the show during that acting class. Charles Irving, you see, was the show's first director and coproducer.

Shortly before the first live air date, Roy Winsor and Procter and Gamble finally hit upon the title they wanted for the series. *Search for Happiness* had been rejected as being too saccharine. The first P & G products to be advertised on the program were items such as Spic & Span, and Joy dishwasing liquid, which Winsor says caused him to wonder if there wouldn't be some obvious conflict be-

Adam and Nicole finally marry. Today's daytime television serials are expensive and elaborate—many times the cost of the early fifteen-minute radio and television soaps. This ornate wedding scene on *The Edge of Night* in 1973, for example, cost a small fortune to produce. From left: Alan Feinstein (Dr. Jim Fields), Johanna Leister (Phoebe Smith), Forrest Compton (Mike Karr), Don May (Adam Drake), Ann Flood (Nancy Karr), Maeve McGuire (Nicole Travis), Ted Tinling (Vic Lamont), Teri Keane (Martha Marceau), and Mandel Kramer (Bill Marceau).

1

A radio family makes it to TV. Few daytime serials were able to make the transition from radio to television. A shining example of one that did is *The Guiding Light.* Another was *One Man's Family,* created by Carlton E. Morse. *At top,* the Barbour radio clan, toasting their twenty-fifth anniversary, included, from left: Mary Adams (Mother Barbour), Page Gilman (Jack), Barbara Fuller (Claudia), Russell Thorson (Paul), Bernice Berwin (Hazel), and Anthony J. Smythe (Father Barbour). *Right,* the Barbours, debuting on NBC daytime TV in 1954, included: above—Martin Dean, Linda Leighton, Ann Whitfield, Russell Thorson (again as Paul); below—Theodore Von Eltz (Father Barbour), and Mary Adams (again as Mother Barbour). 2

She only looks old. Famous daytime radio actors always had to be made up to look like their soap characters when they appeared in public. For example, Virginia Payne, who played Ma Perkins for twenty-seven years, was still a handsome young woman when this publicity photo (with Ned Dearborn, president of the National Safety Council) was taken in 1947! Many eyes became misty when wonderful *Ma Perkins,* which premiered in 1933, left radio forever on November 25, 1960.

A star of radio serials, now a star of a daytime TV serial. Virginia Dwyer played Chrystal Shields on the CBS radio soap, *Joyce Jordan—Girl Interne,* in the forties *(below, left)*—as well as other sudsy radio heroines. Unlike some actors and actresses, Virginia had no trouble whatsoever making the transition to television soaps. Today *(right)* she's as attractive as ever in her role as Mary Matthews on NBC's *Another World.*

Gone but not forgotten. In twenty-five years of daytime serial broadcasting, fifty-four serials have come and gone. Most of them are still remembered by viewers. Here are six from the defunct fifty-four. *Opposite page, top:* Patricia Allison, Iris Joyce, Nuella Dierking, Wynne Miller, Jacquie Courtney, Esther Ralston, and Michael Keen in *Our Five Daughters,* 1962, NBC; *bottom left:* Ann Flood and Bob Mandan in *From These Roots,* 1958, NBC; *bottom right: the* Dyan Cannon and Ronald Foster in *For Better or Worse,* 1959, CBS. *This page, top left:* Val Dufour and Patricia Barry in *First Love,* 1954, NBC; *top right:* Mary Linn Beller and Lois Nettleton in *The Brighter Day,* 1954, CBS; *bottom:* Gale Sondergaard, Patty McCormack, Geraldine Fitzgerald in *The Best of Everything,* 1970, ABC.

"Bauer Power." For more than twenty-seven years, daytime radio and televisio audiences have lived through all the sad and happy times of the close-kr Bauer family of *The Guidin Light.* But before the Bauer family came into promi- nence, the show was peo- pled with church pastors and their families. *Left, top* Hugh Studebaker (left) pla the role of the kindly minis ter, Dr. Charles Matthews, while Willard Waterman an Betty Lou Garrison play an ex-convict and his girl- friend, on the CBS radio show in 1947. That same year, Theo Goetz came on radio as Papa Bauer, and two years later Charita Bauer joined as his daughter-in-law, Bert Bauer; *bottom:* the two are seen years later on the TV show with Bob Gentry, who used to play Bert's son, Dr. Ed Bauer, as an adult.

Michael Bauer was born on radio, and shortly afterwards (when the show was on both TV *and* radio in 1952) he could be seen growing up on television. *Above:* little Michael was played by Glenn Walken, shown sitting on Papa Bauer's lap in a 1955 scene from the TV show. *Above, left:* Today, Michael, as a forty-ish adult, is played by dynamic Don Stewart, shown in a scene with his "mom," Charita Bauer. *Below:* a gala celebration for *The Guiding Light*'s thirty-fifth anniversary in broadcasting.

A dangerous profession.
Eileen Fulton was an ins[...]
success when she came [...]
As the World Turns in 19[...]
as the conniving young
troublemaker, Lisa Mille[...]
fact, so good was Miss
Fulton at playing the lyin[...]
scheming "bitch" of the
story that she began rec[...]
ing threatening letters a[...]
even more frightening
"hate" phone calls from
furious viewers. Utter
strangers even slapped [...]
face. Eventually a securi[...]
guard had to escort her [...]
her way to work in the
morning.

**Happy wedding annivers[...]
Nancy and Chris!** Helen
Wagner and Don Mac-
Laughlin of *As the World*
Turns show how many
cards, telegrams, and let[...]
they received when Proc[...]
and Gamble decided to a[...]
viewers to send congratu[...]
latory messages for their
characters' fortieth wedd[...]
anniversary.

Classic love triangle. Alice loves Steve *(above)*, Rachel loves Steve, and Steve loves Alice and half-loves Rachel. How will it all end? The ups and downs of this delicious romantic confusion have been keeping viewers of *Another World* enthralled for the last five years, and the show at the top of the ratings list. The parts are played by three sensitive, skilled actors: Jacquie Courtney as Alice Matthews, George Reinholt as Steven Frame, and Victoria Wyndham as Rachel Davis. James Douglas, in turtleneck, plays Elliot Carrington, the writer who comforted Alice when it seemed she had lost Steve to Rachel for good. She hadn't.

e romance of Joanne Tate. *Search for Tomorrow*'s Joanne Tate,
ayed by Mary Stuart since September 3, 1951, was and has always
een daytime TV's answer to radio's *Romance of Helen Trent, Stella
allas,* and other heroine-oriented radio soaps. TV watchers have
een engrossed for more than a score of years by Joanne's unshak-
ole faith that she'll find her tomorrow, despite her many troubles and
ose of the people around her. *Opposite page, top:* Joanne Tate hav-
g a Thanksgiving with her daughter Patti (Lynn Loring) and husband
rthur Tate (Karl Weber, who briefly replaced Terry O'Sullivan);
ottom left: Joanne laughing with Allison Metcalf (Ann Pearson);
iddle right: Mary Stuart as a dignified, beautiful young woman when
e first came on the show; *bottom right:* Joanne some fifteen years
ter with her new husband, Dr. Tony Vincente (Tony George).

tending the twenty-second anniversary of *Search for Tomorrow*
ere the show's stars. From left: David Ford (Karl Devlin), Val Dufour
ohn Wyatt), Peter Simon (Scott Phillips), Billie Lou Watt (Ellie
arper), Ray Belleran (Tommy Berman), John Cunningham (Wade
ollins), Millee Taggart (Janet Collins), Courtney Sherman (Kathy
hillips), Tommy Norden (Gary Walton), Anthony George (Tony
incente), Mary Stuart (Joanne Tate Vincente), Joan Copeland
ndrea Whiting), Carl Low (Dr. Bob Rogers).

The two Vans. When *Love of Life* premiered on September 24, 1951, Vanessa Dale was played by Peggy McCay. *Left:* Van (Peggy) as an unmarried woman, her main concern the happiness of her nephew, Beanie Harper. After Miss McCay, the role went to Bonnie Bartlett for a few years, and finally to Audrey Peters, who has played the part longest. *Right:* Van (Audrey) during her recent on-screen marriage to Bruce Sterling (played by Ron Tomme). Van had originally married him after her first husband, Paul Raven, was thought to have died in a crash.

Who's who? At publication time the cast of *General Hospital*—ABC's phenomenally successful afternoon serial—included (from left): Rachel Ames (Audrey Baldwin), John Beradino (Dr. Steve Hardy), Paul Savior (Dr. Tom Baldwin, temporarily written out of the plot), Craig Huebing (Dr. Peter Taylor), Shelby Hiatt (Jane Dawson, R.N.), Emily McLaughlin (Jesse Brewer, R.N.), Ray Girardin (Howie Dawson), Martin West (Dr. Phil Brewer), Peter Hansen (Lee Baldwin), Sharon DeBord (Sharon Pinkham, R.N., temporarily written out), and Elizabeth MacRae (Meg Baldwin, soon to die). There are other actors in the cast, but these are the show's "old-timers."

Daytime stars have come into their own. Most talk shows these days are inviting soap actors and actresses to appear as guests. At one time such a thing would have been unheard of. *Top:* Mike Douglas chats with Mary Stuart, David O'Brien (Steven Aldrich on *The Doctors*), and—sitting between Florence Henderson and Tiny Tim—famous serial writer Agnes Nixon. *Middle:* another time, Mike talks with Don Stewart (Michael Bauer on *The Guiding Light*) and Hugh O'Brien. Don, an accomplished nightclub performer as well as an actor, sang a few songs on the show. *Bottom:* teenagers join the rank and file of daytime serial addicts as they greet Jonathan Frid (who played Barnabas on the old *Dark Shadows*) by the thousands wherever he goes.

"Will Amy work for peace? Wi[ll] Phillip enlist? Will ..." When A[ll] My Children began in 1970, its main character, Amy Tyler (pla[yed] by Rosemary Prinz), spent as m[uch] time joining anti-Vietnam War rallies as she did fighting to ke[ep] her illegitimate son, Phillip (Richard Hatch) from finding o[ut] that his real father was Nick Da[vis] (Larry Keith).

Black story lines. For several y[ears] now, a number of daytime sho[ws] have been presenting blacks i[n] romantic story lines. On The Doctors, Dr. Hank Iverson (pla[yed] by Palmer Dean) is in love with nurse Lauri James (Marie Thor[n).

Teenaged dope addicts. One L[ife] to Live had a story line in 1970 involved the drug addiction of Cathy Craig (then played by A[my] Levitt). She was rehabilitated o[n] the show by joining real self-h[elp] therapy groups at New York's Odyssey House, which helps young addicts.

sanity, incest, and you ...me it. Devotees of *Days ...Our Lives* have thrilled for ...ght years to its many elec- ...c plots involving rape, ...cest, mental illness, male ...potency, abortion, and ...sband-murder. Central to ...e story are Dr. Tom Horton ...ayed by Macdonald ...rey) and his daughter-in- ...v, psychiatrist Laura ...rton (Susan Flannery).

...ychosexual marital in-...mpatibility. When *How to ...rvive a Marriage*'s Chris ...d Larry Kirby (played by ...nnifer Harmon and ...chael Landrum) realized ...er twelve years that their ...arriage lacked both ...aturity and the excitement ...sexual compatibility, they ...ch reluctantly agreed to ...through the pain of a ...vorce—despite the hurt ...ey were inflicting on their ...le girl, Lori. Deep delving ...o such contemporary ...oblems are typical on this ...rial.

...e restless young, the ...xious old. Basically, *The ...ung and the Restless* is ...out the sexual restless-...ss of young people and ...e anxious interfering of ...eir parents, such as the ...ooks (played here by ...orothy Green and Robert ...olbert). There's more frank ...k about sexual relations ...this show then has ever ...en heard before on a TV ...ries.

At last... the Emmy! *Top:* Jim
Pritchett, Gerald Gordon, Lydia
Bruce, David O'Brien, and Elizabe[th]
Hubbard helped *The Doctors,* in 1[9--]
win the very first Emmy Award giv[en]
to a daytime serial. *Bottom:* Mary
Fickett, who plays Ruth Brent on *A[ll]
My Children,* received an Emmy
Award in 1973 for "Most Importan[t]
Contribution to a Daytime Drama."
She gave a stunning speech again[st]
war on the show when news came [of]
her "son" Phillip's death in Vietna[m]

tween the serious nature of the drama they were presenting and the happy-go-lucky, our-suds-will-solve-all-your-
problems sound of the commercials. Of course, today's
viewers are used to the inane contrasts between the commercials and the drama. Agnes Nixon was hired by Winsor as the first head writer but was replaced after thirteen
weeks by Irving Vendig, a master of melodrama who
wrote the show for the next seven years. About this time,
Mary Stuart became Mrs. Richard Krolick.

On September 3, 1951, viewers first saw *Search for Tomorrow* on CBS-TV in a fifteen-minute live broadcast. It's
doubtful whether any of the viewers who saw it recognized that sweet young housewife—her hair done up in a
plain bun at the back, a loose-fitting housedress buttoned
up to the neckline, walking around in the plainest sort of
kitchen set—as the same sexy, bare-shouldered movie
queen who appeared in twenty adventure films and countless lusty Hollywood publicity stills.

The story at first was simple. Joanne and Keith Barron
were happily married; they had a little daughter, Patti,
and were somewhat hovered over by Keith's possessive
parents. After six weeks Keith was killed in an automobile
accident, and so began Joanne's troubles as a young, widowed mother. (For a complete rundown of the ins and
outs of the story from the very start, see page 305). About
two months after the show started, Marge and Stu
Bergman came into the story as Joanne's next-door neighbors. They had a young daughter, Janet.

The original cast, in the show's first few months, included:

MARY STUART (Joanne Barron)
LYNN LORING (Patti Barron)
JOHNNY SYLVESTER (Keith Barron)
CLIFF HALL (Victor Barron, Keith's father)
BESS JOHNSON (Irene Barron, Keith's mother)
LARRY HAINES (Stu Bergman)
MELBA RAE (Marge Bergman)
ELLEN SPENCER (Janet Bergman)

The show's appeal for viewers was almost instantaneous. It had a taste of real life about it: quiet scenes between a mother and child, typical in-law problems, the helplessness that families feel when confronted with sudden death. Some light comedy was supplied by Larry Haines and Melba Rae as the Bergmans, who were always around with a smile, a joke, and an outstretched hand when things got a bit rough for Jo. This touch distinguished Winsor's new TV serial from so many of the unrelieved ones that had preceded it on radio.

"But essentially, we did get the idea for *Search* from radio," Winsor says today. "I wrote the original presentation for the serial and saw Joanne as a kind of young Ma Perkins, the sort of woman who cared about her neighbors' problems, who would offer help to others, and who could face her own personal troubles with dignity." Mary says she recalls in the beginning there was talk about using a nineteenth-century novel called *What Every Woman Knows* for thematic purposes on the show, but she can't say how much the book was used.

Themes, of course, are important, and obviously the right one was chosen for *Search,* but it is the day-by-day story and the talent and appeal of the actors that bring life to a serial and capture the imaginations of the audience. Mary Stuart's portrayal of Joanne was so skilled, compelling, and realistic that after a while she became the show, at least for viewers. She had somehow learned, overnight—and obviously without too much help from the kinds of films she'd done in Hollywood—how to quietly project emotions that viewers realized were probably unbearable for the character. When Jo's first husband was killed, for example, the realism of Mary's somewhat underplayed grief was stunning. After a while, millions at home began to hope and pray that she truly would find the "tomorrow" she sought. Not surprisingly, Mary's character has been going strong for nearly a quarter of a century, for the Joanne that Mary Stuart created way back in 1951 was a perfect welding of art and real life.

"I'm positive that's why *Search for Tomorrow* became so popular and stayed that way ... it was Mary," says

Lynn Loring—now Lynn Thinnes, wife of Roy Thinnes and the mother of five-year-old Christopher. "After a while it wasn't just acting for Mary. Six months after the show started, she *became* Joanne. That's how the character became so real. I remember when I first met Mary she was a gorgeous, young, and vibrant woman—she couldn't have been, oh, much more than twenty-two. I remember when I was a girl I saw a painting of her with that lovely oak-blonde hair falling down over her shoulders. Then slowly, as she got into the part, Mary started looking older, wearing dresses like Joanne. But I think that was only because Mary took her work so seriously. You know, she was so concerned about the program and the character that she used to go out and do the marketing for Joanne's refrigerator herself! That's unheard of in television work! Because of Mary, a television show, for the first time, had a kitchen that really resembled a kitchen. She decided what it would look like, the kind of food that she would chop during a scene, how she would do it. It was her worrying over details like that that made *Search for Tomorrow* more real for the viewers."

Mary certainly doesn't resemble that old, ultraconservative, ideal-housewife type today. When I asked Lynn about that, she said, "I saw Mary one day six years ago, right after her divorce, and she was suddenly a different person. She was much more like the woman in the painting, the woman I had met when the show first started. I think she seems so much younger these days. Obviously Mary must have gone through psychological changes recently."

Lynn Loring grew up on *Search for Tomorrow* and even learned how to read by using her scripts. She was six when she came on the show and left when she was sixteen. There was a close mother-daughter relationship between Mary and Lynn in those days. "It wasn't just acting," says Lynn. "Mary was like a second mother to me. We spent a great deal of time together off the show. I think she thought of me, too, as her daughter. She cried at my graduation. As soon as she heard that organ music, the tears started coming. I'll never forget a few years later

I was with a date who said to the waiter, in front of Mary, 'Scotch and water, please,' and Mary shot up with, 'Oh, no! Not when you're with Lynnie,' just as if she were protecting her daughter. I felt so close to Mary, I even used to go over to her home to do my homework, and later, after I had left the show, I'd still keep on going over to the apartment."

How much like Joanne Tate *was* Mary Stuart? "Oh, almost exactly like her," says Lynn. "I haven't seen much of Mary in the past few years, and so I really don't know how she is with people these days, but I remember that she was always concerned about the welfare of others, just like Jo. She'd listen to people's troubles—she was always just wonderful that way. And she was a dedicated wife and mother. I know Mary probably hasn't told this to you, because it's something that she doesn't like to admit, but she used to turn down all kinds of Broadway offers. One time she turned down *Two for the Seesaw* and I just couldn't understand it. 'I can't do that and take care of a family at the same time,' she would say. Her family always came before her work. I'm sure she and Richard could easily have afforded a full-time housekeeper, but Mary always went home after the show and cooked for her family and took care of the house herself. I know how hard it must have been for her. But she was just that sort of woman."

Neither Mary Stuart nor her character have remained the same after twenty-three years. As Mary says, they both have grown up together. These days the show is a taped half-hour color show, and the characters deal with such sophisticated dilemmas as Women's Lib vs. old-fashioned marriage. Joanne, now a youngish-forty with a husband and an executive job, wears smart, expensive clothing. "Well, she has more money than when the show first started," says Mary. "And her lifestyle has changed. Back in the old days she was awfully homebound. Jo cooked and sewed a lot, and her clothing was no fun at all! Later she grew up and had more time for herself, and that helped her find out more about herself. And so did I. I remember I used to rush home from the studio to take my young children to the park. I spent a lot of time taking care of a family. Now my world has enlarged, just as Jo's has. We both reveal ourselves more now. Twenty years ago when someone was being a pain, Jo would just have been nice. Now she lets herself get angry when she has to. As for myself, I let the part reveal more of what's inside me."

In the beginning, when the show was done live from the Liederkrantz Hall, Roy Winsor was producing *Search* with a budget of $8,073.75 a week; that wouldn't even pay for a day's taping now. Many of the sets were merely suggested or improvised. Black backdrops, instead of walls, were employed, and rooms were only hinted at with door frames hung in thin air and paintings dangled from ceiling wires. One time, when Jo's mother-in-law, Irene Barron (played by Bess Johnson), had lost her custody suit to get Patti away from Joanne, the old lady went berserk and kidnapped Patti. A chase scene in the woods was aired using "just a little patch of woods no wider than a living room," and branches attached to music stands—with the director, Charles Irving, cutting from the branches, to a face going by, then to feet. "It was exciting to watch the way the whole thing was improvised," says Mary.

The actors on *Search* were forever getting into jams on the air when the show was still live; today, they can be rescued by stopping the tape and redoing the scene. Most of those jams were caused by technical problems. "Little Lynn was always saving me!" exclaims Mary. "Once I was in the kitchen of Joanne's Motor Haven and I was supposed to walk out onto the porch to say a few lines. The crew just didn't rig up the porch in time for the scene. Lynn knew, but I didn't. I started to walk out there, and would have walked out onto an empty stage, but Lynn said, 'Let's not go onto the porch, Mommy!' " Another time Mary was actually pregnant with her first child, Cynthia, and Joanne, who wasn't supposed to be pregnant, was getting ready to marry Arthur Tate. "I was as big as a house standing with Terry O'Sullivan in front of the preacher. Later little Lynn had to stand in front of me to hide my condition while I cut the wedding cake with a very long knife." Once, Melba Rae and Mary were supposed to do a scene in which they discovered that the soup was poisoned and had to pour it down the sink. "It happened that our sink that day wasn't connected with plumbing, and so the soup just lay there and began dripping—*clunk, clunk*—loudly into a pail throughout our whole scene. Melba and I had to fight to keep from breaking up. And then one day all the lights went out in the studio while I was doing a scene. I knew there'd be enough lights from the inkies, those little reflectors attached to the big lights, to keep the scene going—even if people saw only our outlines. Finally, a stagehand stood over me, just out of camera, and shone a flashlight on me. I had to look in his direction to say my lines, and his eyes looked right into mine and I don't think I've ever seen someone look so embarrassed! Of course I was still in character and the fact that he was only a few inches from my face didn't bother *me* at all."

We tend to think of Mary's Joanne as having always been the epitome of the idealized housewife, a sort of Olympian goddess with a dust mop. But Joanne has spent a surprising amount of time single and widowed, and she has had her goodly share of romance. Once, while the show was live, a hushed and moodily romantic scene between Mary and one of her between-husbands suitors was to take place in Joanne's home. Mary, on camera, came out and put a record on the player, which had been carefully placed on little blocks so that it would be in a close-up shot. The music began to play, Mary turned the lights down low, greeted her suitor, and began to dance with him. "We got into a lovely clinch, at which point the camera pulled in to get a nice, tight shot of us and, of course, hit the record player and knocked it right off its four sets of blocks! It brushed the back of my skirt, the crash came that close to me. I had to pull away to find out what had gone wrong; the noise was so loud. Well, we went right back into the love scene, as if nothing had happened, while four stagehands crawled around underneath the camera and put the record player back on its blocks.

There were a lot of blocks. It must have been the longest kiss on television!"

As the years have gone by, countless actors and characters have come and gone on *Search for Tomorrow*—each one adding his own contribution to the show's realism and depth. But Mary Stuart and Larry Haines alone have endured the test of time. Terry O'Sullivan was popular on the show for eight years as Arthur Tate, until, in 1966, the writers had him die of a heart attack, causing distressed viewers to write in many letters of grief and protest. Among the grievers was Terry O'Sullivan himself, since he rather liked his job on the show. (Today he's living in Minneapolis appearing in regional theater.) But the writers were really paving the way for a new, exciting romance between Mary and Bob Mandan, a handsome actor who had been on the show since 1965 playing Sam Reynolds. The on-screen love affair between these two attractive performers entranced millions of viewers and would probably have gone on for years, culminating in marriage, if Bob Mandan hadn't gotten bored with daytime serials. In 1969 he abruptly left the show to try to make a success for himself in Hollywood, and Sam was simultaneously sent off to Africa to work for the U.N. Again, viewers were dreadfully disappointed by Mandan's departure. Ironically, he never achieved the same sort of fame in Hollywood that he had had while working on *Search*.

Lynn Loring also left the show in 1961 for much the same reason. "I had just had it with soap work. I was sixteen, going through a difficult adolescence, and I wanted to do something else with my life. I remember one day Patti was supposed to be paralyzed from the waist down in a wheelchair and I just started laughing on air. We were live and somehow the whole thing just seemed so ridiculous to me. I couldn't stop laughing; it spoiled the whole show and I knew then that I had to quit." But Lynn says that she remembers her years on the show as especially happy ones. "I know you've heard this before, but it really was true on *Search*: we were all like a wonderfully happy family, for me especially while Charlie Irving was directing and producing. I never knew a more wonderful man. And Mary was wonderful for me, too."

Yet Mary never felt the same boredom that these others did, because of her interest in Jo and the sense of fulfillment she has always felt in creating something important over a long period of time. It seems inconceivable, but once some writers, Mary feels, were attempting to force her to quit the show by pulling things they hoped would infuriate her to the breaking point. It was probably then that Mary realized how much she wanted to stay on *Search,* even to the extent of paying the price that others had set down for her to remain. "It was also one of the few times that I remember becoming terribly emotionally involved in one of Joanne's problems, and you'll understand why when I tell you what happened. I had been married to Arthur on the show and discovered that I was pregnant myself with my own second child. We decided to play out the pregnancy on television, the very first time it had ever been done. Right after my son, Jeffrey, was born, they filmed both of us in the hospital bed and showed the scenes on *Search.* I only agreed to do that, of course, because they assured me that nothing bad would happen to the child in the story. The Friday before I came back on the show, I read ahead in the script and was shocked to discover that my new son in the story, Duncan Eric, was to wander out in the street and be killed by an automobile. I took violent exception. That was my own son they had filmed. They insisted they had to do it to increase the ratings." Instead of quitting, Mary ate the writers' bitter herbs and just went on.

Aside from this little squabble, which happened eighteen years ago, and an occasional tiff that she and Terry O'Sullivan would have as fellow actors, Mary has always gotten along famously with her fellow performers. New actors on the show, however, are usually terrified of her, because, after twenty-three years as the show's only real star, it is assumed that she possesses monarchical powers to fire and hire people at will. But as soon as actors begin to work with her they realize how ill-founded their fears were. "When I first came on the show six years ago," says Leigh Lassen, the current Patti Tate, "I was afraid of Mary. I had heard that she was some sort of great power on *Search*. Then after I started working with her, I realized that she was absolutely wonderful—a giving, generous person. As an actress, she relates so well to me in scenes that I feel more at ease with her than anyone else. She's always thinking of my welfare. She offered me some advice once and helped me over a difficult time with my family. She went to Greece recently and brought me back a gift that was very personal and meant only for me."

When Anthony George, who plays Jo's husband, Tony Vincente, first came on the show, he really didn't know what to expect from Mary. "Not only that, but I didn't know anything about soap work at that point, and was thoroughly worried about how well I'd do on the show. The technique is so different from other kinds of acting. Well, Mary was so sweet—she was marvelous from the first day. She helped me through the toughest crises in my work, but only because I wanted her to. I never saw her running the show. She just doesn't work like that. I find her an appealing person. In our scenes, I love to touch her, to kiss her. When we're on camera together, I'm more at ease than with other actors; I feel more confident, more attractive—I feel better."

Mary says she does not have the kind of power on *Search* that other people think she has. "I have no idea of what is going to happen in the story. I can influence the producers sometimes, but only when I feel strongly about something, and that doesn't happen often. I remember I didn't want to marry Sam Reynolds after the character came back from Africa, so I suggested that Jo go blind, psychosomatically, because she couldn't face the idea of marrying Sam. It was one of the few times I influenced a story-line."

Through the years, Mary has learned so much about the finer points of putting together a serial—lighting, directing, dialogue rewrite—that she is always being called on to help out when serious technical and creative problems arise. Once a director, in the middle of a taping, discovered he was five minutes short and became frantic. How could he invent five minutes of material that wasn't in the script? He asked Mary to help out, and in shorthand she wrote a five-minute scene between Dr. Rogers (Carl Low) and herself. In the conversation Dr. Rogers told Jo how happy he was about Janet Bergman's new marriage to Wade Collins and that he wished his own daughter, Emily, who had just died in a fire, could have had the same chance. It turned out to be one of the day's best scenes. Tony George says that when Mary, who often coached the lighting men on precisely the right setups for her scenes with Tony, was away on vacation for two weeks, his setups were just terrible. "With Mary around that would never have happened."

"Well, it's been a steady job and it's helped me make a nice home for myself," says Mary Stuart, underplaying, as always, whenever she is asked to sum up her long career on *Search for Tomorrow*. Obviously, from what has thus far been revealed, Mary has taken *Search* and Joanne as more than just a job. For Mary, Jo is a real person who must be reckoned with by other real people. For example, the writers occasionally forget who Joanne really is and make her too pushy or a shade too possessive, and it is always Mary who cares enough about the show and her viewers to stick up for Jo's true personality. She knows exactly how it has changed through the years and how it hasn't. It is a remarkable feat of self-control on Mary Stuart's part, for in recent years she and Jo have parted company on several distinct points of personality make-up.

Mary and Jo both raised families, and both were heroines in the way they conducted their affairs with other people. Both women spent a great deal of time dealing with the troubles and welfare of others and worrying far less about themselves. Mary won't say this about herself, but others will: she was the perfect housewife, the perfect mother and friend. She seemed not to possess any of the characteristics of the self-centered actress. But since her divorce six years ago, she has begun to veer away from a

oanne-like life and to acquire more of the traditional
haracteristics associated with an artistic temperament.
he spends her evenings at home writing songs, not worry-
g about other people; at the studio, she sometimes re-
eats into her own little world, while some people around
er begin to wonder if they aren't being turned away from
y Joanne and Mary. "These days," says Tony George,
some people think that she's aloof because she may not
in the other actors when they are socializing but goes off
to a corner and just thinks. But I know that at those
mes it's not that Mary has lost her warmth, but rather
at she's got her mind on a new lyric she's writing or
mething else creative that she's doing."

Mary convinces still others on the show, by her behav-
r in recent years, that the female part of her has grown
nely because, as one actress close to her on *Search* says,
It's hard to be a woman who has so much to offer with-
ut having a man to offer it to." Mary herself admits that
he's tended to use her work lately as a way of es-
aping—and, as Val Dufour (who plays John Wyatt) says,
'Mary *never* stops working . . . her attitude has made her
he most thoroughly professional person I've ever worked
vith."

Lonely or fulfilled? Her own person or the character
he has played for twenty-three years? Mary recently
nade a provocative statement on *The Mike Douglas
;how*, when she was cohosting with Douglas: "You know,
ny new album of songs represents the very first time that
've actually been able to present myself to the public as
ne. All my life I've always played other people. Now I
:an be myself." The new album she was discussing is just
:alled *Mary Stuart*, distributed by Bell Records, the only
other album of songs she's done since she sang Joanne's
ullabies (with Joanne's voice) on an album done years
ago called *Joanne Sings*. The singing on this new album
lidn't sound like Joanne *or* Mary, but like a third person.
The lyrics Mary wrote for the album were solid; they
:ommunicated; and the music—soft, balladic rock—and
he style of presentation were intriguing. Was this Mary

Stuart herself, or still another woman into whom Mary had evolved?

One can almost build a soap opera story out of the emotional and psychological behind-the-soap-scenes complexities of the brilliant Mary Stuart and her fascinating life. The mysteries her story weaves and the questions it poses go on forever. One would venture to say that Mary Stuart is certainly far more intelligent and dedicated than many of the movie stars who became famous on the big screen, while she was growing famous on a small one. Mary became Joanne; Joanne became Mary. Joanne goes on in our imaginations forever; and Mary Stuart, the artist, has sense and courage enough to allow that to happen, day after day.

❧ XI ☙

The Double Lives of Two Afternoon Favorites: Rosemary Prinz and Eileen Fulton

ON THE TV screen she was known as the impeccable Penny, nearly worshipped by the audience for her virtuousness, her even-temperedness, and, above all, for her ability to face constant hardship with a kind of simple nobility. Off the TV screen, during her twelve years on *As the World Turns,* Rosemary Prinz was playing out her own stormy, real life soap opera. In the latter she was not the lovable, simple Penny, but the complicated, explosive, often-temperamental Rosemary.

While Penny carried on a five-year romance with Jeff Baker, culminating in their marriage and then the tragedy of his sudden death, Rosemary was undergoing intensive psychoanalysis, suffering a nervous breakdown and divorcing the husband she had married at the time Penny Hughes was introduced to America. While Penny, a widow by 1960, was quietly picking up the pieces of her life in the semi-seclusion of her family, Rosemary, by her own account, was living a frantic and fast-paced single life. "I smoked and drank, went nightclubbing. I had a lot of catching up to do." Then, as heroic Penny Baker was trying to help Dr. Neil Wade regain his interest in life, Rosemary was living openly with her present husband without benefit of matrimony. Penny and Neil fell in love, were wed, and then Neil died in an auto accident. Meanwhile, Rosemary finally married Joe Patti one December, was separated from him the following May, divorced him in August, and remarried him in December. As one of Rosemary's friends said, "That must have been one hell of a fight!"

Penny, realizing she was barren, continued her fight for motherhood by marrying a man she didn't love in order to become the mother of his young son. Rosemary, realizing that she "was a crazy lady," continued her battle to keep her sanity through psychotherapy while engaging in endless imbroglios with the management of *As the World Turns* for time off to do stage work. Penny finally left Oakdale to find herself in England as the wife of a nobleman and the mother of an adopted Eurasian girl; Rosemary finally left Oakdale—and *As the World Turns*—following a dramatically successful period of psychoanalysis, in order to enjoy her new identity. These days we occasionally hear news of Penny from Nancy or Chris or Lisa. And occasionally we see Rosemary in one of her rare six-month appearances on other serials.

The drama in the lives of both the woman herself and the character she portrayed peaked and subsided in an event-crowded period of twelve years—1956 to 1968. Viewers, however, only saw the story of Penny and knew little of the real-life drama. To most people, Rosemary and Penny were one and the same woman. When viewers would occasionally get a glimpse of Rosemary as she was, their usual reaction was amazement. "People were shocked to discover that I smoked and drank and knew many men, used colorful language, that I was a sort of swinger and very liberal—liberal in the causes I would fight for, like my campaigning for Senator Eugene McCarthy. Some of those things about me made Proctor and Gamble's hair turn gray. You know, actors on soaps have morals clauses in their contracts, giving the producer the right to fire you if you violate their idea of what is moral—and some of the things I was doing were, shall we say, very un-Penny-like. But I never felt that they had any right to control my life with a clause. I was very open about everything. Joe and I weren't trying to hide the fact that we were living together. We even had both of our names on our door. My attitude was: if you don't like the way I live, you can always fire me."

Rosemary and Penny, Penny and Rosemary. That was a classic case of identity confusion—not so much on the part of the actress, but on the part of others. Penny was no ordinary soap character, one must realize. Because of Irna Phillips's excellent characterization of a lovable girl caught in the web of happenstance, and Miss Prinz's ability to project warmth into the character, Penny became an exceptional force on *As the World Turns*. She was the kind of daughter every mother longed to have—kind, generous, loving, honest. Unfortunately, to many people, including some closely connected to the show, Rosemary's individuality became secondary to Penny's.

"The producers never really told me that I had to behave more like Penny. Occasionally there were hints. I remember I was in a nightclub once—smoking and drinking and I guess smooching—and this lady writer, who was somehow a friend of someone on the program, came over to my table and pleaded, 'Rosemary, how could you? Penny would never behave the way you're behaving.'"

Rosemary Prinz eventually grew bitter. The role of Penny, per se, didn't annoy her, although she did find the character bothersomely two dimensional and unrealistic. What vexed her was the amount of time she was devoting to the role and her increasingly negative feelings toward the whole world of soap opera and, in particular, to her superiors, with whom she had many personal conflicts. "Let's face it," says Rosemary, "the advertising business is made up of Sammy Glicks, and the soaps are just a form of advertising, not art. There's a lack of loyalty to the actors—some incredible things were done to them while I was on the show that I will never forgive. There's a lack of integrity, and it's like Nixon—it starts way up high and goes down to the ranks. Television, anyway, is not rewarding acting. It's not immediate and spontaneous for the actor, the way working in a play is. The only reward I got from doing *As the World Turns* was from the other actors. As far as the rest of the show went, I just felt that no one cared about my professional integrity, who I was as an actress. I remember the fights I'd have with them to keep things truthful, when they'd give me the crap to say that wasn't truthful or when they'd forget what they had written a month ago because it was just convenient not to remember—like having me diagnosed as barren by the doctors after I had already had a miscarriage on the show. Now you can't have a miscarriage and be barren."

With so much ill feeling toward her program, why did Rosemary Prinz remain Penny for twelve years—an eternity for the hyperactive life of any actor? "Because I was a crazy lady and I needed the show to help me stay in New York and to pay for my analysis so that I could go get uncrazy. And I needed *World Turns* because I never had a real family life of my own; it became like an ersatz family for me. Well, I think it's easy for anyone to get trapped in a soap by the family structure the actors provide. We were all so very close . . . I had a lot of problems in those days, and I got emotional support from people like Don MacLaughlin, Helen Wagner, Santos Ortega, Wendy Drew, and Mark Rydell. Besides, I knew that I could never live the way I'm living now—going from one play to another, not knowing if I was going to be out of work for a few months. It's too much of an iffy life for someone who was the way I was—half dead. I mean, if your lying on the ground, integrity doesn't mean much. If my analysis had worked sooner—say if it had taken only five years instead of twelve—I would have left the show sooner."

Rosemary describes herself while she played Penny: "I was uncontrollably temperamental—explosive, high-strung, driven, and unhappy. It took me years of analysis to calm down—seven with a man who didn't help me, and then five with a woman who saved my life. I guess it is ironic—no one who followed Penny would have guessed that here was this crazy lady . . .

"You will never know what it was like to be brought up by an alcoholic. My father was a concert cellist—a marvelous, terrible, tyrannical, funny, dreadful, suicidal, manic-depressive, compulsive gambler. My life became a series of second-act curtains, a series of crises. I didn't know normal people. I lived at a pitch of hysteria. It caused problems—problems of man-woman relationships, oedipal problems, problems of loving life and wanting to destroy my life as he did his."

Two years after Rosemary originated the role of Penny, her father, Milton Prinz, died, and that precipitated her breakdown and her divorce from her first husband, in 1960. On *As the World Turns* Rosemary began showing temperament and became known as a difficult actress. All this was happening beyond the tube, beyond the shadow of Penny's own crises and troubles.

As the nation was clamoring for more and more of Penny, everything within Rosemary was clamoring to get away from this ready-made womb-world of the soap opera. She needed the show on one level and she despised it on another—simultaneous attraction and repulsion. "There was a part of me that never really wanted to stay on the show, and I didn't hide the feeling from the producers. They'd say, 'Get a short haircut—we want Penny to look different.' And I'd say, 'Get an actress with short hair.' Each time my contract period ended I made it quite clear that I'd only do it if they met all of my demands. I wanted more and more time off to do plays and more money, and each time I made my demands they'd meet them. They knew how little I wanted to stay on *World Turns*."

The producers also knew how important Rosemary was to the continued ratings success of the show. During her stay on *As the World Turns* she was able to bargain for enough time off to do at least fifty stock plays—each time, Penny would be sent off on a little trip—and to raise her final salary to an unheard of $750 a day, probably more money than any other daytime actor was receiving.

The end finally came early in June 1968 when, after five fruitful years with an Austrian woman psychoanalyst,

Rosemary proudly announced to the press—and only indirectly to *As the World Turns,* through her agent—that "I feel like I have come out of a crowded room and can take a breath of fresh air." She wasn't returning to *As the World Turns* and said she might only consider going back if her father were in a Nazi concentration camp and only her reappearance as Penny would get him out. The starkness of the imagery she used in describing her bitterness toward the world of soaps was matched only by the shock viewers felt and the emotional language they used in the maelstrom of mail-and-phone-call protest they hurled at the producers. Wisely, the show sent Penny off to England and didn't even attempt to replace Rosemary with another actress for two and a half years. In January 1971 *World Turns* tried out Phoebe Dorin in the part, trying their best to make her look just like Rosemary. The substitution only succeeded in making the audience mad. Penny quickly went back to England.

A little more than a year after Rosemary left the serial that brought her fame, Agnes Nixon, who once wrote *As the World Turns,* gingerly approached Rosemary about playing the lead in her new afternoon serial for ABC, *All My Children.* Rosemary said that she had had it with soaps where the heroine sat around drinking coffee and talking about miscarriages and whose husband was doing what with whom. But she might consider a six-month stay on the show if Agnes would make her an activist, much like Rosemary herself, who fought for important social causes. Mrs. Nixon agreed to make the necessary alterations on what she had originally conceived as a traditional soap story, and the result, when *All My Children* premiered on January 5, 1970, was a little strange. Viewers now saw Rosemary as a fortyish wife who spent a good deal of her time trying to hide the fact that her nephew was really her illegitimate son. She would have numerous Penny-like fainting spells and haunted dreams. But, a few times a week, she would make anti-Vietnam War posters and have heated conversations about social evils that sometimes lasted as long as two minutes. In effect, instead of being a sympathetic heroine with personal troubles, like Penny, who would sit around talking about who was doing what with whom, she became Amy Tyler, a sympathetic heroine with personal troubles who sat around talking about war protest. Says Rosemary Prinz today, "Oh, I know the problems of soap operas. I didn't expect a complete change. When I first talked with Agnes about the show I told her I didn't want to be a heroine who talked about sex as being an evil thing—the bad things are war, cruelty, raping of the environment, but not sex. Of course we ended up just talking about my activities. I really didn't expect them to film me in peace marches. But at least you saw me make a few posters now and then, and maybe I caused some of the viewers to think a little more about their world."

After her six-month stint on *All My Children*, Rosemary once again left the soaps for the straw-hat trail. Toward the end of 1973, she was approached once again to do another soap opera. NBC's *Return to Peyton Place* was failing dismally, and the network needed a new serial to take its place in the 3:30 EST spot. Lin Bolen, NBC's new vice-president in charge of daytime programing, called Rosemary and asked her to play one of the leads in the new replacement serial, *How to Survive a Marriage*— a contemporary, relevant, often psychoanalytic look at the problems of marriage and divorce. Lin Bolen, described later by Rosemary as young and vital, said on the phone to the actress she had never met: "Rosemary, we know we can't get you for very long, but would you consider coming on the show?" Rosemary, whose last play, *The Prisoner of Second Avenue*, had just closed, said she'd do it . . . provided (1) she got star billing, meaning the show would be advertised as "*How to Survive a Marriage* starring Rosemary Prinz"; (2) the money was right and that she got a good "guarantee"—i.e., the number of shows per week that the producers must pay her for, whether or not she actually appears on them; and (3) her contract on the show would be for no more than six months. As always, all of Rosemary Prinz's conditions were met. Rosemary's guarantee on *How to Survive a Marriage* was for three shows a week—only the biggest soap stars get that—with a salary, reportedly, of more than a thousand dollars per appearance.

"On the show I play your average, liberated, lady shrink, Julie Franklin. Julie doesn't really have a story of her own but helps the other characters iron out their problems, which are to be real ones. For example, in the scripts I'm studying now, I help the wife see that her husband was treating her more like a sexual object than like a real human being, and I also start helping the husband see that the marriage was not built on strength but weakness. Now that's pretty strong, relevant stuff. I don't know what will happen to the story later on, but I don't think Lin Bolen will let it become just another soap opera. I think she's sincerely involved in the issues at stake."

Interestingly, Rosemary Prinz has gone from the sweet, ne'er-do-wrong Penny to the guilt-ridden activist Amy Tyler, to the lady psychiatrist Julie Franklin, who has it all together and can now help other people with their problems. Rosemary's progress in her daytime serial roles seems almost a comment on her own life. After coming to terms with a chaotic childhood and an explosively self-destructive early-adult life, achieved partly through the liberating effect of twelve years of analysis, she's no longer on the couch, but sitting next to it. That "old Austrian broad" who helped her for five years became Rosemary's ego ideal, which she now transfers to the part she considers "probably the best I've ever had on a daytime serial." Unfortunately, since she refuses to do any television show for more than six months, she may very well be off the air once again by the time this book is in print.

In her next serial, Rosemary Prinz may show up as anything—can you imagine her as a senator fighting for legalized euthanasia? or a writer who proves that President Kennedy's assassination was part of a military plot to take over the country? But no matter what her lines are, no matter who she is supposed to be, for the vast majority of serial viewers she will always be Penny. The part was, despite her bitterness toward *As the World Turns,* a great achievement in art. Miss Prinz bared the real "Penny" that was in her and exposed to millions an extremely vulnerable nature. All the *relevance* in the world can't replace the very humanness of an exquisite, touching, long-term serial portrayal. Even Rosemary Prinz admits, in her occasional less-guarded moments, "Well, I liked Penny. She was a warm, nice, gentle human being. She brought me many friends."

Daytime serial actresses who make it big—like Rosemary Prinz and Mary Stuart—are alike in that they are all self-made women who became famous without the help of Hollywood studio publicity departments. As soap actresses they were isolated by afternoon exposure, and they lacked the prestige of film stars. They found a following among viewers by sheer talent and hard work. The same holds true for *As the World Turns'* Eileen Fulton, one of the more illustrious of that Olympian group of daytime serial players. But her rise to fame has been made all the more exceptional because she was the soap villainess, not the heroine. Now it is just as possible to have a following when you're a baddie as when you're a Joanne Tate or a Penny Hughes . . . but it's so much more difficult to build an entire career on a character that inspires the hate and venom of viewers. Eileen Fulton accomplished that seemingly impossible task with the help of no more than her wits, ability, and a certain charisma. During Eileen's long and wicked reign on *As the World Turns* as the scheming Lisa Hughes, the motto that was so often used in describing viewers' reactions to her on the show—"They love her and they hate her"—might have been hung on her dressing room door. It described Eileen Fulton's career on *World Turns* perfectly.

No one on the show really knew who Lisa Miller was supposed to be when Margaret McLarty, alias Eileen Fulton—the very proper daughter of an Asheville, North Carolina, Methodist minister—won an audition to try for the part along with at least two hundred other actresses. "It was 1960," says Eileen, "and I had to read and read and read before they finally gave me Lisa. This was my very first television role, and I really wasn't sure of anything—who I was supposed to be, how I was supposed to play the part. In the story I was dating Ronnie Welch, who was playing Bob Hughes as a high-school boy, and I seduced him. Then, through my conniving and scheming, I got him to marry me. But the scripts didn't really convey much more about Lisa—what her background was, why she did things. So I started making up a whole life for her myself to fill the gap. I had a sort of inner monologue going while I played out scenes. I pretended that I had come from a small town, that I was bored, that I needed to shake loose from my past but was having trouble doing it."

Lisa was quite an unimportant character in the story at first, but Eileen's way of suggesting the hidden motivations and reasons that the young girl was behaving so reprehensibly gave the character flesh and blood and supplied the story with the most haunting sort of villainess—the kind an audience feels it can understand. Here was a classic case of familiarity breeding contempt, for what Miss Fulton was really doing was using her own background as a Methodist minister's daughter for the character's psychology, a psychology that millions of viewers would comprehend instantly. The contempt and identification that the audience felt for Lisa was so exquisite that she not only soon became the focal point of the whole story, but eventually she was able to fill the emotional void felt by *World Turns'* devotees when Rosemary Prinz, as Penny, abruptly left the show.

Lisa's scheming and the *lieber-hasser*—Freudian love-hate—between viewers and Miss Fulton continued relentlessly. "Oh, I was just terrible. I had Bob's child and was living with Bob in Nancy and Chris's house, letting poor Nancy take care of little Tom while I just did as I damn pleased. I went galavanting all over town and then fell in love with a shoe salesman named Bruce Elliott—who was played by Jim Pritchett—because I thought he could give me a better life. You see, Lisa just felt that now, as a married lady with a child and living with her in-laws, she didn't have a life of her own. And she was really just a little girl at heart anyway. One day, while Nancy was away, instead of taking care of the house and

baby myself, I hired a maid and went on a picnic with
Bruce Elliott. And we had a mad love scene on a
beach—I always refer to that scene as 'The Daytime
From Here to Eternity.' When Nancy returned, she found
the house wonderfully shipshape and thought I had done
it all myself. She said, 'Why, Lisa, how wonderful you
were.' I had pulled the wool over everybody's eyes. That's
when people really started to hate me and I got all those
threatening letters."

It sounds amusing now, but the hate campaign
launched by viewers against Eileen Fulton grew to such a
fever pitch that it began to frighten even this cool and collected actress. On the one hand she realized that many people's reactions were simply a reflection of her own abilities
as an actress, but on the other hand she was only human,
and no amount of rationalizing would erase the very real
threat of all those dangerous-sounding letters.

In the mail, people referred to her by such sweet names
as "pig" and "southern bitch." Many of the mail hecklers
were men, and one man continued writing that if Eileen
wasn't taken off the show, he would fix it so that she
would never act again! At that point, Eileen had a guard
escort her from her apartment at Lincoln Towers to the
show, and then back again.

Her decision to get a guard also came after several actual physical assaults on the street. "The first time it happened," Eileen remembers, "I wasn't prepared for it. A
woman stopped me and asked if I was the Eileen Fulton
who played Lisa. I said I was, and was all set to pull out
my pen and sign an autograph when she said, 'Well, I
hate you. Take that!' And she upped and belted me with
her handbag right there on the street."

It was surprising to Eileen how many different kinds of
people reacted strongly to her character. "One preacher
even wrote to my father: 'How can you, a minister, lead
your flock when you have a daughter who's doing it in the
bushes with Bruce Elliott?' "

Those incidents were more common in the early days of
the show, when Lisa seemed purely selfish and immoral.
Eileen, however, remembers several later reigns of terror.

"Viewers really threatened me right after Michael Shea had been murdered and I had become more interested in Simon Gilby than in getting Bob back. An elderly lady smacked me in a store in Minneapolis, and then I got socked by another lady on the street. I had a dead fish sent to me."

Around 1965, Eileen began to feel what Rosemary Prinz often felt—that she was now trapped on daytime television and by the shabbiness of a character that was being kept one dimensional. And so she quit the show, hoping to make it in the sophisticated world of the legitimate theater or in nightclubs. The producers tried to keep the character of Lisa going without Eileen. They had her leave Oakdale, later being kidnapped by two men. "Lisa was raped repeatedly from California to Texas, and then lost her mind," Eileen remembers. For the first two weeks, producers made the actress who played the part keep her back to the audience for fear that too quick a transition to another actress would upset viewers. And it did, terribly. When Lisa finally looked straight into the cameras and announcer Dan McCullough said, "The part of Lisa is now being played by Pamela King," there was an immediate campaign of protest. Viewers wanted only Eileen Fulton, the girl they hated and the girl they loved all rolled into one. That was that. A few months later Irna Phillips talked to Eileen over the telephone and persuaded her to come back on the show by offering her the lead in a new nighttime television series called *Our Private World*. It was to be a spin-off of *As the World Turns*, with Lisa as the main character. A few months after she came back on *As the World Turns*, her story was wrapped up on the daytime show by having Lisa leave little Tom on the doorstep of the Hughes's house and run off to Chicago to seek a new life. On May 5, 1965, Lisa was in Chicago when *Our Private World* premiered. In the nighttime story, Lisa had moved in with the family of a kind lady, was meeting all sorts of attractive men and had her eyes on the son of a wealthy society matron, played by Geraldine Fitzgerald. References were made on the show to the characters of *As The World Turns*, where there was simultaneous conversation about what "Lisa was up to in Chicago."

"The show just never caught on," says Eileen. "It was only on twice a week, and at different times. People didn't know when to watch. I was supposed to be the central character, but after a while the story didn't seem to have very much to do with Lisa. And some of the actors from *As the World Turns* were supposed to come on the show, but none of them wanted to. *Our Private World* hardly made a splash. It played over the summer and was canceled in September."

Eileen then agreed to come back on *World Turns* for ten weeks to help wrap up the character of Lisa, since she was still determined to leave daytime. By the time Lisa left Oakdale for Chicago, for the second time, she was the wife of a wealthy Chicagoan by the name of John Eldridge. As far as Eileen and the producers of the show were concerned, Lisa was never to be heard from again.

What they didn't realize, naturally, is that daytime viewers hold on for dear life to actors and characters whom they love. Eileen received thousands of letters and phone calls from fans begging her to return to the show. At first Eileen resisted. Then, when her nightclub career seemed to peter out almost before it had started, Eileen began feeling a little like the wandering, homeless Lisa herself and she finally accepted *As the World Turns'* offer in 1967 for a return engagement as Lisa.

But Eileen was not to return as the old Lisa, but as a new, glamorous one complete with dyed hair and beautiful clothes. According to the developing plot, Lisa's rich husband had died in Chicago, making her an independently wealthy woman. This creature fit more into Eileen's changing image of herself as a vital and glittering woman in the entertainment world, rather than as the practical, hard-working, and self-conscious daughter of a southern minister. Eileen's fans loved this Lisa even more than the old one, for she was a more complicated and more mature woman. Somehow, with their uncanny instinct for knowing the truth that lies in the actor, beyond the character, the viewers sensed that the changes they were seeing on television were also happening in real life. Many of Eileen's fans wrote to say that they knew, without having to be told, that Eileen was a new person.

Unlike Rosemary Prinz, who had to completely leave her character, Penny, to find herself in real life, Eileen came to the realization that she could develop Eileen Fulton without having to give up Lisa. Eileen realized it would mean a great deal of hard work for her. She would have to keep Lisa going in the daytime while venturing forth in her spare time—weekends, vacations, and days off the show—to develop a nightclub career for herself.

Her nightclub career seemed to work much better this time. She was smart enough to incorporate the Lisa character into her club act. In a recent appearance, for example, she pretended to shoot the character with a gun, in a mock attempt to escape from her, and she would also hold dialogues about the serial with all the hundreds of people who had come to see "Lisa" perform. This time, Eileen also enjoyed the excellent promotional abilities of her new husband, Danny Fortunato. Most of all, Eileen was succeeding better in the nightclubs because she had become a more confident performer, with a fine voice range and singing style.

Over the past few years on *As the World Turns,* Lisa has been treated by the writers less like the superneurotic troublemaker and more like a well-liked member of the Hughes clan. She's still searching for love and has her share of problems, but at least she's settled enough now to spend some of her time worrying about the troubles of other people and not just her own. Yet it is a terrible shame that the show has lost such a wonderfully hated villainess—so many people tuned in regularly just to click their tongues over what that miserable but lovable Lisa was doing.

One night Van Cliburn, a friend of Eileen's and a close follower of the show, picked her up and took her to the Metropolitan Opera House to hear a performance featuring Eileen's most adored diva, Renata Tebaldi. After the performance, the pianist took Eileen backstage to meet her idol. Before he could introduce the two, Madame Tebaldi cried out, "Lisa! Lisa! You bad girl!" Eileen discovered that Tebaldi was a fan of hers and watched her every day.

Lillian Roth said that she wouldn't do *I Can Get it For You Wholesale* unless the management agreed to put a TV set in her dressing room so she could follow Lisa's antics. While Barbara Walters was interviewing Governor Connally of Texas and his wife, he suddenly said, "Excuse me, Miss Walters, but it's 12:30 and we have to watch *As the World Turns.* We've got to see what's happening to Lisa!" Governor Preston Smith, Mr. Connally's successor, called the producers of the show and said that he just had to meet Lisa. She flew out to have a talk with him, after which newspapers ran a photo of her with her head dreamily on his shoulders. "He was a wonderful man," says Eileen, "but he kept calling me Lisa. I told him, 'If you call me *Lisa* one more time I'll bop you one.'"

The universal fondness shown to Eileen Fulton these days is really a great tribute to the importance of daytime drama. "When I walk out in clubs, they want to touch me. 'I must touch her! I must touch her!' is what I hear. When I sang at *Diamond Jim's* in Minneapolis they nearly ripped my clothes off. I love to meet the audience because generally people are warm to me these days and are surprised to find out what I am like as a person. When I was working in Steubenville, Ohio, I had love marks from all the people kissing and hugging me. I remember CBS was trying to sell time on the daytime networks to some of the local stores. Well, they shrewdly got one Steubenville store to have me in to meet the customers. Seven hundred people showed up! High-school kids sneaked out of school to get my autograph. After that, CBS had no trouble selling local time in that town."

Any daytime fan can give you a dissertation on what he thinks of Lisa and of the development of the character through the years. What does Eileen herself think of Lisa? "She's a spunky lady who's completely misguided, who's wasting her life. She feels with her heart, not with her head. She's extreme. Lisa's a dreamer. It's because there are so many people like her that there are so many divorces in this country. I'll be glad when she finally kicks the bucket."

Eileen is also somewhat spunky, extreme, and theatrical herself. After she made an appearance on *The David Frost Show*, with five other daytime stars, she had half of soapland down on her for what various daytime actors referred to as her silliness, show-off nature, and pretended vivaciousness. One cannot exaggerate the intensity of her fellow daytime actors' criticism of her. "It was an awful showing of what the average daytime actor is like," said a coworker of Mary Stuart. On the Frost show, Eileen laughed about having been raped repeatedly as Lisa, and told one funny story after another, throwing her arms wildly about. In comparison, the other actors seemed rather subdued. Eileen defends herself: "Actors are supposed to be alive and spontaneous on talk shows, not act as if they were attending a funeral. Before the show we all sat down with David Frost for two and a half hours telling stories as a kind of warm-up for the actual show. But during the taping everyone just sat there like mummies, not saying a word. David Frost kept turning to me because I was the only one who was talking. I even had to tell stories that others had told during the warm-up but for some reason wouldn't tell on the air. After the show was all over, I heard comments from people: 'How dare you say all those things!' I dare say things because that's the only way to be—yourself."

Whoever was "right" in this minor dispute, it's a fact that few daytime actors make favorable impressions during their talk show appearances. While making a major concession to the importance of the soaps by having serial actors on their programs, hosts like David Frost and Mike Douglas generally act as if these actors were on exhibit. They are talked to as if what they do is strange and funny, even peculiar. Naturally they become self-conscious and come on as either stilted or awkwardly hyperactive. The fault is with the ignorance of the interviewers, not with the actors.

Eileen Fulton has spent fourteen successful years on *As*

the World Turns. She has recorded a song album (*Eileen Fulton Sings With You in Mind,* Nectar Records) and has had a number of single disks released (including the best-selling *Radio*). Her autobiography, *How My World Turns,* was recently published in paperback, and she has developed an enviable nightclub career for herself. Eileen has turned herself into a glamorous woman—she wears false eyelashes, bleaches her hair, seems vivacious to a fault, has a closet stuffed with clothes fit for a reigning princess—and wears most of those clothes on *As the World Turns.* All this grew out of Margaret McLarty, the practical and somewhat lackluster daughter of a Methodist minister. Eileen now is truly a living memorial to man's (and woman's) ability to mold himself *by* himself, simply because he wants to. To Eileen Fulton, it has meant fulfillment; to the public, sheer fascination.

How to Survive a Daytime Serial— As a Writer

THE AUTHORS OF the daytime serials have the largest audiences in the world. Every week an estimated fifty million viewers are exposed to the wares of a select handful of daytime scribes. Nighttime television writers don't have anywhere near the same kind of exposure; their scripts are only aired once a week, and many more nighttime writers are hired to work on a single series. The daytime writer, however, must pay dearly for the prestige of having such an enormous following.

"It's sort of a cross between being an F. Scott Fitzgerald and an Olympic athlete," says Agnes Nixon, who has had nearly twenty-five years' experience writing serials and currently heads *All My Children.* "It's grueling work. You know you have to finish a certain amount of writing every day, so you must always be in tip-top physical shape. You can't stay up late or let yourself get run-down. I remember during the fifties there was a period when I was only doing one-shot live TV plays, like *Philco,* and I could force the creativity by abusing my body—drinking a lot of black coffee, working till all hours of the night. But when you write a daytime serial you don't dare do that; you wouldn't be in any kind of condition to write tomorrow's show."

Writing a serial, just like acting on one, can begin to absorb one's whole life—especially for those writers who take their work seriously, and most do. Unlike writing a play or a novel, the characters and the town they live in do not just go away suddenly when the writing is finished. In the serials the same lives go on and on. Irna Phillips once said that when she wrote a serial she carried the whole town around in her head and thought of the fictional inhabitants as real people. Says Harding Lemay, the head writer of *Another World,* "It's almost like having another set of relatives. I live with them all day long. I have nightmares about them." One writer of a soap became so involved with his characters that he used to call up the actors on his show and refer to them by their character names.

Since soap writers must produce their shows on a daily basis—and so much of their time becomes absorbed in the creative process—it is not uncommon for some of them to use their own lives as models for their stories. George Reinholt said very recently, "You know, I always had the strangest feeling that the story of Steven Frame has something to do with Philadelphia, where I grew up. Maybe it's Frame's misguided sense of class status." What Reinholt didn't realize was that Agnes Nixon, who created his story on *Another World,* is a native of Philadelphia herself. Today, Steven Frame is being handled by Harding Lemay with subtle touches and changes that derive from Mr. Lemay's background. "When I was seventeen," says Mr. Lemay, "I ran away from home. I came from a poor family. When I started writing *Another World* two years ago, I discovered that Steven had almost no background at all—he was a sort of mystery. I started giving him a past very much like my own. I decided he had run away from his home on a farm when he was just a boy and that many of his difficulties today arise from having never been properly understood when he was younger." Interestingly enough, Alice (Jacquie Courtney) now talks a great deal about needing to understand Steven better.

Just before her recent death, Irna Phillips gave a rare insight into the development of a certain character on *As the World Turns*. In her characteristically raspy voice, Miss Phillips said, "Everyone asks me how I got the idea for Kim Reynolds on the show, because she certainly is an unusual character. She's really me—at a much younger age. She's fiercely independent, as I was, and she won't settle for second best. She looks in the mirror and refers to herself as 'The lady in the mirror.' Well, that was her other self, which no one knew about: the true me, the person that I always hid from the world. She's having a child out of wedlock, which will be only hers. I adopted two children—Kathy and Tommy—without having a husband. We're both the same. And she's going to have that child to prove that a woman can do it alone." (Unfortunately Kim never did. During the character's pregnancy, so many viewers wrote in disapproving of what she was doing that the producers decided to have Kim lose the baby. Even so, the character of Kim, played by beautiful Kathryn Hays, is probably the most poignant one Miss Phillips ever created for her daytime audiences.)

For genuine impact on their audiences, writers of daytime serials must take seriously the parallels between real life and the fictional stories they are creating. Otherwise, with the mounting pressure of having to create episodes week after week, daytime stories become unbelievable, full of worn-out clichés. However, one woman who has been writing serials for many years carries her concern for realism on her shows perhaps a bit too far. She calls her friends constantly to find out the intimate details of their lives—all the ins and outs of how they felt while they were bedridden with an illness, the pain of childbirth, what might have caused the depression they were going through. This woman's characteristic line: "Oh, isn't life so like the serials?"

Soap writing is by its very nature highly specialized. A typical head writer not only must invent story situations that should keep the audience enthralled, he must also worry about actors' guarantees and vacation periods. "It often becomes a problem of sheer logistics," says Henry

Slesar, who writes *The Edge of Night*. For example, in the middle of a heated quarrel between two rivals in a story, one of the actresses might suddenly decide to exercise an "out" option in her contract in order to do stock in Buffalo. Then the poor writer has to lose sleep in figuring out a logical way of sending one of the rivals out of town without interrupting story continuity. *As the World Turns'* writers were always thinking of new places to send Penny while Rosemary Prinz was in and out of the show.

But a greater difficulty is a purely creative one: maintaining the realism of day-to-day living in a soap town without (1) boring the viewer with realism that is too slow and uninteresting or (2) attempting to alleviate all the boredom of everyday life by becoming so melodramatic that the realism itself is shattered. The latter often happens, for instance, when writers, responding to their producers' pleas to get the ratings up with more story interest, start making all the available females in their stories pregnant, or decide to threaten the heroine with a murder rap. But these tactics would never be employed by the best soap writers.

There are other things that superior soap writers just won't do. They do not brush off the arduous but necessary process of recap work by just inserting excerpts of speeches used in the preceding episode. ("Re-cap" is when David Stewart on Tuesday must tell Bob Hughes that Ellen got angry with Lisa on Monday, for the benefit of viewers who missed the show.) "You have to get around recap," says Henry Slesar. "It should always be given a new dramatic form so that you're not throwing it in the audience's face that a character is simply saying something to convey information. It has to be logical for a character to be saying such-and-such a thing at such-and-such a time."

But even the most talented serial authors sometimes find themselves getting more involved with words than with the characters. It just happens because of the continual pressure of voluminous script writing. Clichés slip through. Actors are given wooden dialogue. Most writers realize this tendency toward occasional lapse ("I sometimes cringe when I watch a show I wrote," says Henry Slesar) and don't mind that actors often rewrite their lines to make them easier to say. If the actors didn't do this, some scenes would collapse in cardboard dialogue. On the ninety-minute opening episode of *How to Survive a Marriage*, the main characters Chris and Larry Kirby were throwing some pretty dreadful clichés back and forth. It marred a good show and seemed strangely out of place with the general tone of dramatic creativity. Finally, the producer, Allen Potter, cleared up the mystery when he said that none of the actors on *How to Survive a Marriage* were permitted to rewrite the lines of the author, Anne Howard Bailey. "She's just too fine and bright a writer," he said.

How are soap writers organized? Each of the fourteen daytime serials normally has only one head writer—although in a few instances there are two co-head writers—who is responsible for the whole story on his soap: from the general directions that it takes over a long period, to all the little details of day-to-day plotting. Every three to six months he submits to the producers and sponsors a story projection, some ten to thirty pages of intensive outlines of where a story is going. This is where the fun starts. The producer, assistant producer, sponsor, and advertising-agency representatives begin to pick at the poor devil's ideas like nervous birds attacking seed. Bruce Cox, who is Procter and Gamble's representative for *The Guiding Light* for Compton Advertising, says, "When we get the writer's story projection, we lock ourselves in a hotel room for days at a time and begin to go over every little detail of the story projection with the writer—what will work, what looks questionable. If someone objects to a story-line, the writer always has a chance to defend himself because he's right there. It's exhausting for him and for us." Irna Phillips used to describe these sessions with the executives as free-for-alls. After a second or possibly third draft, a story projection is finally approved. Then the writer begins to follow the outline, according to his own creative instincts, in his daily scripts. Says Henry

Slesar, "The whole process of working with story projection is like looking down a long tunnel. As you drive through the tunnel you begin to see more detail." The head writer may write the scripts himself, or employ his own dialogue writers to convert his script breakdowns (short synopses of what characters do and say on a particular day) into actual scenes with dialogue. The normal custom is for a head writer to write some of the scripts himself, and for his dialogue writer (or writers) to do the rest. The more subwriters a head writer employs, the less money he makes himself, for he is paid a set wage and then must pay his writers out of his own pocket. The minimum for subwriters is now $310 per script.

But however he accomplishes it, a serial head writer must come up with five half-hour episodes a week, fifty-two weeks a year. There are no reruns and no summer vacations. Despite the marathon routine, each of his scripts is supposed to be so compelling and filled with high drama that viewers cannot wait to see what he has in store for them next. How many writers can do this? Not many. That is principally why year after year the same people seem to be writing the serials. Such a long period of training is needed to learn to do this arduous and specialized work that once a writer makes it into the select ranks he becomes an invaluable commodity to soap sponsors and producers. He becomes a Brahman, earning a high salary (a minimum of twenty-five hundred dollars per week, but often much more) and attaining prestige in his field. He also enjoys such loyalty on the part of his employers that he can even slip up or have his creativity run dry—which frequently happens to overpushed soap writers—and the worst that will happen is that he is fired from one show and immediately hired by another.

Procter and Gamble Productions, which owns nearly half of all the soaps, seems to have refined the system even further. They engage a stable of writers in a unique system of rotation similar to the old writing factories run by the Hummerts of the radio soaps. The P & G system depends almost entirely on rating success and loyalty to its head writers. About a year and a half ago, when *As the*

World Turns' ratings were beginning to dive-bomb, Irna Phillips was called back from semi-retirement to rescue the show with her unique writing abilities; she did manage to bring the ratings back up, but soon had a disagreement with the producers over script policies and left the show for what seemed the umpteenth time. Meanwhile, Robert and Edith Soderberg, the brilliant team that was doing a fine job on *The Guiding Light,* was switched over to *As the World Turns,* which was still in trouble. Jim Gentile then filled their spot on *The Guiding Light.* At almost the same time, P & G was growing increasingly agitated with the failure of two major Women's Lib story-lines on *Search for Tomorrow,* and so they demoted its head writer, Ralph Ellis, to the position of dialogue writer under the Soderbergs—notice that he wasn't simply fired. P & G simultaneously took Theodore Apstein, who was writing dialogue for its *Another World* under the ingenious Harding Lemay—and therefore had had a fine apprenticeship—and put him in charge of *Search.*

Like so many soap producers, Procter and Gamble plays musical chairs with its writers. The system is effective. It propagates the special talents of its writers by giving them exposure on a number of different soap situations, makes them feel financially secure enough to want to stay in the field, and helps them over their dry spells by simply relocating instead of firing. The system also helps create new talent by making it clear to the less prestigious dialogue writers, the stage at which most soap writers start, that the frequent openings will make it possible for them to become head writers themselves . . . someday.

Agnes Nixon started this way. In 1949, three days after she graduated from Northwestern University, Mrs. Nixon (then Agnes Eckhardt) was hired by Irna Phillips—after Miss Phillips had read a half-hour original play she had written—as a dialogue writer. For years the two of them worked together on *The Guiding Light* and *Another World*—two shows which Mrs. Nixon eventually took over as head writer—and *As the World Turns.* Later, ABC asked Agnes Nixon to create her own serials: *One Life to Live* and *All My Children.*

Mrs. Nixon's development as a serial writer is a classic example: first a dialogue writer protégé of a more experienced writer, then a head writer, and finally a creator of her own shows. Occasionally head writers pop up without previous apprenticeship. Harding Lemay was hired by Paul Rauch, the new executive producer of *Another World*, after Rauch had read Lemay's autobiography *Inside, Looking Out* and decided to take a chance on fresh talent. But even Lemay wasn't really so fresh. He had written the last ten weeks of *Strange Paradise*, the Canadian version of *Dark Shadows*, and had thereby learned something about television serial writing.

Irna Phillips died at the age of seventy on December 23, 1973. Her secretary, Alice Shea, came into her bedroom in her Chicago apartment in the morning and found that the great writer had passed away in her sleep. There had been no illness, no signs of weakening. In fact, the secretary had left her the night before, sitting up in her bed, spryly working on her autobiography, which she had just started.

She had been the greatest of all daytime serial writers, often referred to in the press as "the queen of soap opera." Her contributions to radio serials have already been mentioned. Her television creations were among the most important: (in chronological order) *As the World Turns, Another World,* and *Days of Our Lives*. Now that she is gone, we will be seeing a new breed of daytime writers—writers who speak to young people, who speak to their comtemporaries, just as she spoke to hers. But all of them will have a debt to pay to Irna Phillips, who first gave life to the daytime serial and taught a generation of writers how to follow in her footsteps.

❧ XIII ❧

Where Are the Daytime Serials Heading?

A MIDDLE-AGED couple in Cincinnati are watching their favorite serial, *As the World Turns*. In today's episode, Bob Hughes, a retired doctor, is paid a visit by his son Tom, a successful, forty-five-year-old lawyer. Tom is asking the elder Hughes for some advice on what to do about his grown adopted daughter, who has run away to New York with a married man who will most likely hurt her terribly. The old man pauses a moment, shakes his head wistfully, and knits his brow. The scene is touching.

Meanwhile, a young girl, still living with her parents in a suburb of Los Angeles, is watching her favorite serial, *One Life to Live*, on another network. In the story she's watching, a young black man gives an engagement ring to a slightly older white woman and jokes about their "honey-colored children." Despite the seeming air of happiness, however, their eyes are giving away their apprehensions. After all, his family, only a generation removed from the ghetto, and her family, very middle class, are dead set against the union. The audience is torn between their concern for the feelings of the respective families and their desire to see the couple happy together.

Simultaneously, a Florida housewife is watching her favorite serial on yet another network. She's watching *How to Survive a Marriage* alone today because her husband, like most breadwinners in this country, must work three days a week. Both she and her husband have been having many discussions lately about Lori Kirby's insistence on having a child out of wedlock and raising it without a husband. In today's episode, Lori is in bed with a man, discussing the virtues of the simultaneous orgasm. The camera comes in for a close shot of her naked breasts as she says, "You know, I think I want you as one of the men in my life." Then the phone rings. It's Chris, Lori's mother, who wants to know whether Lori's pregnancy test was positive. The ratings on *How to Survive a Marriage* soared after Barbra Streisand took over the role of Chris Kirby, telling the press with her typical brashness, "Soap operas are where it's at. It's the only goddamn place where you can develop a character realistically without some phony ending. Life just isn't like that. Sure I'll be singing in it—the theme song, every day, at the beginning and at the end!" (Rock Hudson was reported to want the part of Larry, but from all indications it looked as if the younger Ryan O'Neal would get it.)

Absurd? Today, yes. These things could never happen, but tomorrow, maybe they could. One of the more obvious changes in daytime serials is that the audiences are becoming more and more segmented. Ever since the late sixties, expensive demographic studies have shown that different people watch different serials, and that no one serial satisfies everyone. Or perhaps one could put it a different way: as the audiences for daytime soaps have grown, the variances in the tastes of different groups in the audience—distinguished by age, social status, and economic factors—have also grown. In the above story projections for the future of certain serials some ten or twenty years hence, two distinct audience interests are apparent—one younger, one older. *As the World Turns,* for example, keeps the current status quo in the future because its audience has always been older and more conservative. Illegitimate births and extramarital affairs will most likely always be frowned upon on *World Turns*. Just recently, the show attempted to let Bob Hughes have an extramarital affair with his wife's sister. The viewers simply wouldn't have it and wrote bushels of protesting letters, so the producers thought it best to have Bob pay for his sin by suffering an almost fatal auto accident, and by having his sister-in-law, Kim, lose his baby. On another show, with younger demographics—*The Doctors, All My Children,* or *The Young and the Restless*—such a story-line might have succeeded.

In the other two examples of future soaps the status quo is not kept but grows considerably from already existing trends. The people who watch these shows will be different from the people who watch *World Turns*. A certain kind of person—the very young or the very socially aware—will prefer to watch serials that relate to overall social problems. *One Life to Live* is already exploring boundaries that were never before broached by daytime serials—or nighttime shows, for that matter—and is being successful in its efforts. One of the interesting things about *One Life to Live* is that it speaks to young people as well as to older people who are filled with social prejudices but who, consciously or unconsciously, are trying to get rid of them. In one of its story-lines a light-pigmented black girl, Carla Gray, tries to pass for white. She was engaged to a white doctor but fell in love with a black intern. One Texas station canceled immediately, and several other southern stations threatened the same. Mrs. Nixon's show was swamped with letters of complaint. A viewer wrote in to say that if the actress playing Carla (Ellen Holly, who *is* black) were white, she shouldn't be kissing a black man; and if she were black, she shouldn't be engaged to a white man. However, what was rather obvious about the whole turmoil is that the show didn't lose viewers. Despite their shock, people watched. Something in them made them feel they needed this sort of medicine.

A much more specialized group of people is expected to watch NBC's new serial, *How to Survive a Marriage*. They are people in their early thirties who have had enough experience with marriage and sexuality to want to see a serial that focuses specifically on the social and psychological problems of divorce. In this serial a couple, Larry and Chris Kirby, are now divorcing after twelve years because of a psychosexual maladjustment in their marriage. They both have to adjust to becoming single people again and living the swinging singles life, even though their values remain with the generation that frowned upon such living. But an even greater urgency for them is to reexplore their own mental states and sexualities, in order to discover, after so many years of living a "mistake" with the other person, what courses their lives should take. On *How to Survive a Marriage,* the frankness and contemporaneity of the subject matter is equally matched by explicit scenes involving sexual relations. In the opening ninety-minute episode, for example, Larry Kirby was shown in bed making satisfying love to Sandra. Later on, Larry was shown with his wife, Chris, trying to make love but suffering from impotency, which was suggested when Chris said, "I'm sorry," after an obviously failed attempt at intercourse. *How to Survive a Marriage* is going further in both showing and discussing sexuality than any other TV show before it, nighttime or daytime. So far the serial has gotten past the censors because of the network's absolute faith that the show will attract a strong group of viewers who will see not only the explicitness, but who will also appreciate the detailed discussions, in dramatic form, of all the sexual and psychological ramifications of marriage and divorce. Said Allen Potter, then *Marriage*'s producer, "Other shows deal with these problems, but not with the same sort of depth that we do. We think we'll attract a large audience of women who are in the age bracket of thirty-two or thereabout. By then many of the problems that we're discussing will become important. In this country, one out of every 2.7 marriages ends in divorce."

Should *How to Survive a Marriage* succeed, it may change the whole future of daytime programing. It will once and for all show that all those millions of dollars poured into demographic studies on what young people watch vs. what older people watch (vs. what that special-

ized middle ground of thirty- to thirty-five-year-old young
marrieds or divorcees watch) was not for nothing. Serials
of the future should be aimed at special groups within the
audience rather than attempting to reach everyone. Perhaps the exceptional success of CBS's *The Young and the
Restless* has already proved this adequately to the ad
agencies and sponsors. Its demographics are extraordinarily young and there's a strong chance that current studies
will prove that it has even drawn in young viewers who
might not have otherwise watched any soap opera. Like
How to Survive a Marriage, The Young and the Restless
has explicit sex scenes; its audience would not necessarily
object to sexual intercourse between people who are not
married or perhaps not even in love. On this serial, unlike
As the World Turns, characters do not have to pay (with
accidents or still births) for what they do in bed with
other people.

Incidentally, CBS and the producers of *The Young and
the Restless* have devised a sort of story which attracts not
only young people but also a certain number (although a
smaller group) of older people. This is important for overall ratings. How did they do this? The writers show their
young characters against a backdrop of family relationships rather than on some protest-ridden campus, making
it easy for older people to identify with the parents of the
young ones. Although this does interfere with the contemporary trend of the story—young people tend to leave
their families earlier these days—at the same time it satisfies a larger portion of the audience.

What all this amounts to is that the look and feel of the
serials is becoming increasingly heterogeneous. When, in
the late sixties, it was obvious that enormous profits were
to be had in daytime serial programing, a number of new
approaches were tried in order to attract either totally new
serial watchers or at least to steal some of the habitués
away from the other shows. Invariably, most of these new
approaches were tied in with a growing awareness on the
part of the ad agencies that soap operas should start
reaching young people (they weren't up until then) for the

simple reason that young people have greater consumer needs than older people and buy more products. Think of how much more soap a young housewife with three children consumes than an older woman whose children are all grown up. Viewers started seeing shows like *Dark Shadows*, which proved that soaps could have an appeal for school children. *Love is a Many Splendored Thing* likewise proved that young, talented stars in a youth-oriented story-line will attract a young audience. Other youth-oriented shows, such as ABC's *All My Children,* soon arrived on the scene with one further addition to the rapidly changing soap world—relevance. Although often abused by old-fashioned writers who simply did not know how to handle the stories of Women's Lib or drug addiction that they were pressured into injecting into their plots, relevance by and large has done great good for the soap world. It has not only upgraded the consciousness of many viewers, but it has helped cause an atmosphere of publicity and excitement around the daytime dramas.

Publicity means attention is being paid, and when attention is being paid sponsors purses begin to open up. Starting in the late sixties, many millions of dollars were poured into the serials. Procter and Gamble alone poured $120 million into its serials in 1971. ABC spent a bundle launching its three serials in 1970—only *All My Children* survived, but then all the network needed was one more success—and is still pouring fortunes into new daytime projects, such as its ninety-minute plays. CBS, during the same period, went on a campaign to increase the budgets of all of its shows. The result of all of this recent expenditure has been bedazzlingly lavish sets, better acting, and increased use of on-location filming when certain episodes require an outdoor setting. Now, with the addition of a new sort of sexual permissiveness in the afternoon, which viewers don't enjoy on nighttime TV, the only logical prediction for the near future of daytime television would be that the audiences will grow bigger still.

More audience means bigger budgets and higher salaries for actors. The effect of higher salaries combined with the new prestige that the daytime world is receiving will most likely mean famous Hollywood actors, suddenly seeing the possibilities of a new form of art, will begin to vie for parts. Joan Bennett, Macdonald Carey, and even Joan Crawford—filling in for her daughter, Christina Crawford, one day on *The Secret Storm*—have already started a trend. It doesn't really seem so unlikely that Rock Hudson and Ryan O'Neal will one day vie for the part of Larry Kirby on *How to Survive a Marriage,* or that Barbra Streisand will give it a whirl, especially since daytime may also become prime time when and if our society eventually adopts a three-day work week and the nighttime hours are no longer strictly thought of as family viewing time.

All this is speculation. But we learn from the past, and the past seems to be adding up to an even more exciting future for the world of the serials.

❦ XIV ❧

Complete Plot Directory for Viewers

TUNING INTO A continuing daytime drama for the first time can be a perplexing experience for a viewer; it's a little like walking into a strange living room filled with people who have known one another for years, and although they are quite willing to confide in you, the newcomer, you haven't the foggiest idea of what they're talking about. You hear dialogue like, "Well, David, I did as you asked and went over to Lisa to warn her about Jay Stallings, even though she *is* having trouble renting Penny's apartment in the store to a woman. But I had to tell her that I liked Jay when he was a boy, even though he got into all kinds of trouble with the authorities. I know that you and Carol don't agree with me." The kind of background required to comprehend this "recap" information (what sort of woman is Lisa? Who is Carol? Why isn't Penny in the story anymore?) might take a new viewer ages to acquire—and some of the necessary background information might *never* be acquired by new viewers.

This extended section is meant as a briefing for serial viewers—new or old—on the stories of the various current daytime serials. But first, be forewarned: a serial drama, especially one that has been on the air for a number of years, is not like a movie or a nighttime TV installment of a series—for example, *Medical Center* or *Bonanza*. The serial has a definite beginning, but it has no middle and no end. Instead, a string of events are woven into a complicated fabric of subplots, which concern core characters—the ones who have been with the story for a long time—and cause them to interact with characters who have just been introduced into the story. So, over a number of years a small number of characters are involved in numerous melodramatic "substories," or events, have intermarried, divorced, borne legitimate or illegitimate children, and have generally been part of the kind of fictional plot that, if read all at once, might seem ridiculously complicated and overwrought. But then, the story of anyone's life, intertwined with the lives of others, might also seem absurd when boiled down to its melodramatic essence.

Of course, there are certain conventions that serial writers do use excessively—such as murder and the inevitable murder trial in which the hero or heroine is tortured until the miraculous denouement brings exoneration to him or her, and relief to the viewers. Amnesia victims stumble around as if the condition were as epidemic as the Hong Kong flu. And there are more evil bitches breaking up marriages than one can count. In reading the following plot summaries of the serials, be aware of the difference between the extraordinary fictional devices, which can rightly be criticized for their excessive use and their clichéd character, and the day-to-day *realistic* dilemmas that the characters face.

In any single volume about daytime serials it would be a physical impossibility to boil down, in detail, the entire plot of a serial like *Search for Tomorrow*, which has been on the air some twenty-three years, or *Love of Life*, which has had more minor characters and subplots than our galaxy has suns. For a reasonably good understanding of a particular serial it is important to learn, in general terms, how present characters have developed through the years, the details of the plot in recent years, and—in a broad overview—what happened in years past. In some instances the original theme of a show—if it is an old one—is followed to see how well the theme has been adhered to over the years. So often a viewer gets caught up in a daytime drama without really knowing what the story is all about, or what it originally was supposed to be all about.

Using these plot summaries (up to date as of July 1974), you should be able to unravel the existing complex relationships that are the basis of each and every daytime drama: how Steve Frame came to Bay City on *Another World* and had an illegitimate child with Rachel while courting Alice Matthews; how Julie Anderson Olson's unhappy early years made her the kind of unpredictable, grasping woman she has become on *Days of Our Lives*; how romance led to the original marriage of Nick and Althea on *The Doctors*; how Mike Bauer's first marriage on *The Guiding Light* produced his daughter, Hope; how Lisa became wealthy on *As the World Turns* and why she is always talking about feeling "lost" even though she's loved by so many of her friends. In other words, after reading this section, you will be able to walk into that living room filled with all those strange people telling you all their problems, and you will feel as comfortable and as "knowing" as you do in your own home.

1. ALL MY CHILDREN

"The actors are always asking me, 'How are all your children?'" said Agnes Eckhardt Nixon, phenomenally successful owner and creator of the relatively new ABC series, *All My Children.*

"It's just a joke, because I have four children of my own. But a lot of people do talk as if *All My Children* were my autobiography, which is not true. It has prototypes of people I knew in my childhood and know today, and, yes, I feel very close to it because I wrote it for myself years ago; it was an extremely personal piece of writing."

Mrs. Nixon went on to say that the first year's plot-line for the serial was put to rest in her files ages ago, until one day about five years ago ABC network heads called her and asked if she could put together a new serial for them in a hurry. "I was busy with *One Life to Live* and writing *Another World* and couldn't take time out to write another serial—so I thought, 'There's that one in my drawer . . .'"

The one in her drawer proved to be one of the better-rated serials and a boon to ABC's afternoon lineup. The resulting show was somewhat different, however, from the one Agnes Nixon conceived before she filed it away. There were the illegitimate births, concealed romances, thwarted marriages, and tortured young lovers of her own story; but there was also—as if someone had inadvertently crosswired a weekday soap opera with Sunday's *Face the Nation* and *Meet the Press*—much talk of peace marches to Washington, anti–Vietnam War protests, programs to clean up the air, and other important social causes. Viewers were, in turn, perplexed and delighted by this new breed of daytime fare. How did all this social consciousness get stuck onto that piece of personal writing in Mrs. Nixon's drawer?

Before the show premiered, Mrs. Nixon shrewdly asked her old friend, Rosemary Prinz, to lunch. Would Rosemary play the part of the central character, Amy Tyler? Rosemary, who swore after her twelve-year stint as Penny on *As the World Turns* that she would never return to soap opera, said that she would only consider playing Amy if she could leave the role after six months and if there was social relevance in the role. The two famous women shook hands on the deal, and a new, "relevant" soap opera was born.

Rosemary Prinz, as per her agreement with Mrs. Nixon, left the show six months after the premiere and the character of Amy was written out. Gone too were all the anti–Vietnam War peace marches and other bits of social relevance—aside from a stirring anti-war speech made by Ruth Brent after her stepson Phillip was presumed killed in Vietnam. The show's ratings have been growing ever since it started. The high point of its success came recently when Mary Fickett, who delivered that powerful polemic against war, was given an Emmy Award in 1972 for The Most Important Contribution to Daytime Drama.

All My Children premiered on January 5, 1970, and featured:

ROSEMARY PRINZ (Amy Tyler)
LARRY KEITH (Nick Davis)
RUTH WARRICK (Phoebe Tyler)
DIANA DE VEGH (Ann Tyler)
HUGH FRANKLIN (Dr. Charles Tyler)
JACK STAUFFER (Chuck Tyler)
PAUL DUMONT (Lincoln Tyler)
MARK FICKETT (Ruth Brent)
MARK DAWSON (Ted Brent)
RICHARD HATCH (Phillip Brent)
RAY MacDONNELL (Dr. Joseph Martin)

KAREN GORNEY (Tara Martin)
FRANCES HEFLIN (Mona Kane)
SUSAN LUCCI (Erica Kane)

Overview

Despite all the social relevance that was injected into
the first months of *All My Children*, the show's important
theme has always been Thwarted Young Love. Interfering
adults are forever making it difficult for young people to
find romantic happiness. These young people come mostly
from two important families in the fictional town of Pine
Valley: the Tylers and the Martins.

The Story

PHOEBE TYLER (Ruth Warrick) is the prime matriarch,
wed to the town's leading physician, DR. CHARLES TYLER
(Hugh Franklin). She's a snobbish, wealthy, and often
overbearing woman who is always worrying needlessly
about appearances, especially where her children's conduct is concerned. Phoebe, nonetheless, always means
well. Their children are ANN (Judith Barcroft) and LIN-
COLN (Paul Dumont); Charles's grandson, CHUCK (Chris
Hubbell), has been living with them ever since he was
orphaned in infancy.

The other important family in Pine Valley has DR.
JOSEPH MARTIN (Ray MacDonnell) at its head. His wife
Helen had died and left Dr. Martin a widower and their
children, JEFF (Charles Frank) and TARA (Stephanie
Braxton), motherless.

AMY TYLER (originally played by Rosemary Prinz and
now out of the story), the serial's first real protagonist,
was described in a network press release as a "liberal political activist dedicated to the peace movement, who marries into a conservative family with considerable wealth
and stature in the community." Amy married Lincoln Tyler. Phoebe, however, did not approve of Lincoln's marriage to Amy because she was beneath him socially.

Everyone thought that young PHILLIP BRENT (Nicholas

Benedict) was the son of Amy's sister, nurse RUTH BRENT (Mary Fickett), and her husband TED BRENT (Mark Dawson). However—unknown to the Tylers, to Phillip, or to anyone else in Pine Valley—it was revealed, when NICK DAVIS (Larry Keith) first came to town, that Amy was Phillip's real mother. Years before, Amy had had an affair with Nick Davis, now a dancing instructor, and Phillip was born illegitimately. In secret, Amy asked her sister, Ruth, and her brother-in-law, Ted, to adopt Phillip, who grew up believing that the Brents were his real parents.

Of course, the newly wealthy Amy displayed great fondness for her "nephew," but would let no one know that Nick was the father and she the mother, nor that there had been a secret adoption by the Brents. ERICA KANE (Susan Lucci), a young and beautiful troublemaker in Pine Valley, learned the whole story and made sure everyone else in the town found out including Phillip. Ted, not knowing that the story had come from Erica, and believing Nick to have gone back on his word never to tell Phillip who his real mother and father were, drove toward Nick Davis's place, intending to have it out with him. But it was a rainy night and Ted's car went out of control on the slippery streets, and he was killed, leaving Ruth Brent a widow.

Phillip was horrified by the accident and by the knowledge that "Aunt" Amy and Nick Davis were his real mother and father. As self-protection against all this unhappiness, Phillip's mind rebelled, and he developed amnesia. He wandered off to New York, completely forgetting his vow of love to his high-school sweetheart, Tara Martin, a wonderful girl who had always been full of zest for life. Now she became broken-hearted and uninterested in everything.

Everyone's finding out about Phillip so humiliated Amy that she left her husband, Lincoln, and Pine Valley. Of course Phoebe, who always wanted her children to marry on their own level, was pleased by Amy's sudden departure. At the same time, Phoebe learned that her daughter,

Ann, was returning from New York, where she had been working.

Ann came back to Pine Valley and together with a girl friend, SYDNEY, opened a chic boutique, which became an instant success. Lincoln, now alone, fell in love with Ann's friend, but Sydney wasn't sure how she felt about him. When she returned to New York to try to think things over, Lincoln left Pine Valley and followed her to New York.

Ruth Brent, however, didn't have to think twice about accepting Joe Martin's proposal of marriage. Ruth, who had never been happy with her now-dead husband, Ted Brent, finally found happiness with Joe. Tara and Jeff Martin became her stepchildren.

Beautiful but dangerous Erica Kane, who helped to destroy Amy's marriage and Phillip's mental well-being, set her designing sights on naive but hard-working Jeff Martin, a fine young doctor. Unable to cope with the wiles of such a seductress, Jeff succumbed and they later eloped. Although motherhood was not what Erica was aiming for, she became pregnant. Against Jeff's objections, Erica had an abortion, which nearly killed her because she did not consult her doctor afterward when dangerous symptoms appeared.

By now, Phillip's psychosomatic amnesia had lifted, and he remembered that he had once been in love with Tara. But Tara was still in a state of shock because of the way Phillip had treated her before his amnesia, and she decided to spurn his affections for those of Chuck Tyler. Tara accepted Chuck's engagement ring—but she didn't love Chuck; she loved Phillip.

Ann Tyler, meanwhile, was falling in love with Nick Davis despite her mother's predictable objections. Phoebe couldn't stand the idea of a bottom-of-the-social-ladder dance instructor marrying into her family. Ann and Nick eloped behind her back. Their happiness, however, was marred by Nick's obsession that he was sterile and could never father Ann's children. Fearing that Ann would discover his inadequacy and lose all love and respect for him, he asked her for a divorce. Ann—horrified and feeling that Nick had simply stopped loving her—gave him the divorce. Shortly afterward, Ann learned she was pregnant by Nick; Nick, of course, wasn't sterile, and by the time he found out about Ann's pregnancy, she had already married Joe Martin's younger brother, PAUL MARTIN (William Mooney), a brilliant lawyer. She was fond of Paul, but she didn't love him.

On the day of Tara's wedding to Chuck Tyler—a grand, elaborate affair, in the best tradition of the wealthy Tyler family—there was a melodramatic turn. Before the couple could say "I do," Nick shouted out from the audience that the marriage couldn't take place because Tara still loved his son. Chuck keeled over—not from shock of the announcement, as everyone suspected, but from a grave kidney affliction.

Chuck went into the hospital, leaving Phillip and Tara to reestablish their old relationship. Because of Chuck, however, they restrained themselves physically until Phillip was drafted and learned that he was going off to Vietnam. No longer willing to keep their relationship platonic, they eloped just two days before Phillip was to leave for the war. A violent snowstorm prevented them from getting to a justice of the peace, so they stopped at a roadside chapel and got "married" by exchanging vows by themselves.

Tara couldn't bring herself to tell Chuck about her union with Phillip because she was afraid the shock would worsen his condition. And by the time Chuck was recovered enough to hear the news, Phillip was reported missing in action.

The grief was almost unbearable for the Martin family—for Tara, Phillip's "wife," and for Ruth, his adoptive mother, who had, until this terrible news, finally found happiness by marrying Dr. Joe Martin. Dr. Martin and his son Jeff, also saddened, tried to console Ruth and Tara, but by now Jeff had enough problems of his own with Erica, who was told by a New York modeling agent, JASON MAXWELL (John Devlin), that she could become a glamorous, successful model in New York. She began making forays from Pine Valley to New York for modeling assignments, and in so doing was slowly destroying her marriage to Jeff, who objected to her new career. But obstinate Erica refused to let go of her New York job, and in addition she found herself falling in love with Jason Maxwell and the way of life he represented. For comforting, Jeff turned to MARY KENNICOTT (Susan Blanchard), an attractive nurse who had loved Jeff from afar while working in the hospital with him.

Tara found out that she was pregnant with Phillip's baby and told Chuck, who said he didn't care and still wanted her to marry him. She later gave birth to a baby boy, whom she called Little Phillip.

Nick Davis, believing he had lost Ann for good, turned to a fellow dancing instructor, KITTY SHEA (Francesca James), for solace. They had a brief affair, which ended in Kitty's becoming pregnant. Not wanting to father another illegitimate child, Nick agreed to marry Kitty—especially since Kitty, a self-pitying, neurotic woman, had tried to commit suicide when she discovered that Nick was still in love with Ann, despite Ann's marriage to Paul Martin. Kitty lost the baby and was put under the care of a psychiatrist. Nick vowed that after she was cured he would divorce her and try to get Ann back.

Meanwhile, Erica had asked Jeff for a divorce and she continued to see Jason Maxwell in New York. Jason, one day, came to Pine Valley, registered in a hotel, and then phoned Jeff, asking him to come visit him there that night. Before he arrived, someone unknown had gotten to Jason and murdered him. Jeff, an innocent bystander, was then accused of the murder. The motive: jealousy.

Jeff stood trial for Jason Maxwell's murder and was defended expertly by his uncle, Paul Martin. Destructive Erica again made Jeff's situation worse by asking to be "paid off" by Joe Martin, Jeff's father, in return for telling the jury the truth—that Jeff harbored no hostility against Jason Maxwell. Erica's mother, MONA KANE (Frances Heflin), and MARGO FLAX (Eileen Letchworth), Erica's friend from New York now living in Pine Valley with Erica and Mona, were both skeptical of Erica's real motives.

In fact, *everyone* soon became suspicious that conniving Erica was the real murderess.

During all this, Tara was dumbfounded on learning that Phillip, presumed killed in Vietnam, was really alive. When he returned home, he was shocked to learn that his "wife" had married his best friend, Chuck Tyler. Although still deeply in love with her high-school sweetheart, Tara decided that, for the good of her baby and for Chuck's sake, she would keep her marriage intact and not tell Phillip that her son was really his son, too. Phillip, however, would not accept her decision, and tried everything he knew to win her back. Eventually, out of loneliness, he allowed himself to be seduced into a minor romance with Erica, who—now that she was losing Jeff to Mary Kennicott—found him irresistible.

After many agonizing months of a murder trial, Jeff was freed when the true circumstances surrounding the murder of Jason Maxwell were revealed. Under the influence of sodium pentathol, Mona Kane—Erica's mother—revealed that it was *she* who had killed Jason Maxwell! It had been an accident. On the night of his death, Mona had come to his hotel room to ask him to stop seeing Erica. Jason said that Margo had already been there and threatened him with a gun for having jilted her for Erica, and then left the gun behind; Jason then tried to get Mona to take the gun with her; she resisted and the gun fired in the ensuing struggle. After Jason received the fatal wound, Mona had blocked the whole incident from her mind—until the truth serum brought it all flooding back. All the residents of Pine Valley were relieved at the exoneration of gentle Dr. Jeff Martin.

When Ann Martin finally learned the truth of why Nick had divorced her—because he thought himself to be sterile—she grew haunted by a mirage of the happiness that they could have had together, but for a misunderstanding; soon she was torn between Paul, her new husband, and Nick. For his part, Nick tried his best to get Ann to divorce Paul and re-marry him. When Ann went to New

York on a buying trip for her boutique, he saw his opportunity and pursued her there. Although Ann responded to him momentarily, she told him—while they were driving home in the midst of a violent snowstorm—that she realized that it was Paul she loved, and not him. Seconds later the car went out of control, crashed, and its passengers brought home to Pine Valley in critical condition. Nick, who regained consciousness first, lied and led everyone to believe that Ann fully intended to divorce Paul to marry him. Crushed, Paul began seeking comfort in the arms of Margo Flax. Meanwhile, Ann—who was now recovering and thought Paul knew it was he, not Nick, she loved— was appalled and dazed by her husband's apparent lack of fidelity, and simply got up from her hospital bed and wandered out of the hospital to parts unknown. Naturally her family and friends were agonized by her disappearance.

2. ANOTHER WORLD

The daily episodes of *Another World* used to begin with the announcer briefly telling the philosophy of its creator, Irna Phillips: "We do not live in this world alone, but in a thousand other worlds." Since the show premiered in 1964, that philosophy has been interpreted in several different ways by the show's writers. Irna herself said recently that the story was meant to represent the difference between "the world of events we live in, and the world of feelings and dreams that we strive for."

Miss Phillips brilliantly illustrated this difference by, first, creating—and writing—a story about one big family (the Matthews) that was realistic in terms of the behavior of individual family members, showing how they dealt with marital discord, ambition, or with other family members who were either neurotic, dishonest, or both. Unlike other serials of the time, she seldom had husbands suddenly reappear from the dead, nor did she have people stumbling around with amnesia just to suit the story. Second, she suggested that "other world" of longing and heartfelt need by portraying all her characters as neither moral nor immoral, but rather trapped by the emotional insecurities caused by their backgrounds. Each person sought a well-justified happiness, but because of the "world of events," that happiness often could only be obtained at the expense of someone else's.

After Irna left the show, Robert Cenedella and Agnes Nixon both perpetuated Miss Phillips's philosophy in their writing of *Another World*—especially with Mrs. Nixon's ingenious creation of the characters of Steven Frame and

Rachel Davis, and her idea of involving the vulnerable, oversensitive, and childlike Alice Matthews in a deeply emotional story with these two selfish, other-side-of-the-tracks people. As Mrs. Nixon says, "I envisioned Steven Frame as a young Cash McCall. I may have been thinking of a football hero here in Philadelphia who would have attracted the beautiful Alices and the beautiful Rachels. I patterned Rachel after Erica Kane, since I wrote the original story of *All My Children* years before. Rachel is a character with doom potential—meaning that she is destructive but is ultimately a greater threat to herself than to other people." By introducing a love triangle—involving a selfish and handsome *nouveau riche* bachelor, a destructive young girl with an equally knockabout background who appealed to the young man's baser sexual feelings, and another young girl with "good" upbringing who appealed to the young man's better nature—Mrs. Nixon fired the imaginations of viewers with an *inward* drama that brought the daytime serial to a new level of excellence.

It took Harding Lemay, however, a skilled playwright who thoroughly believed in the heretofore unexplored psychological potential of the daytime serial, to transform Mrs. Nixon's love-triangle subplot into a balanced story contrasting realistic human behavior and that "other world" of fantasy and striving. He found story devices no longer necessary. "For example," Lemay said, "I didn't feel it was necessary to keep Rachel a black-and-white character. I didn't see her as a villainess . . . I saw her instead as a human being who had always had bad breaks and who defeats herself because she is so used to failure. When she lost Steve this last time, I wanted the audience to feel her pain as I felt it. I wanted them to feel her tears."

Mr. Lemay, along with his producer, Paul Rauch, should be given an award for the Greatest Contribution to Daytime Serials for completely eliminating melodramatic clichés in a daytime drama, and for their invaluable demonstration that what viewers really want is drama that is soundly based on psychology rather than on escapist melodrama. Under Lemay and Rauch, *Another World,* which had previously used many tried-and-true soap-opera devices (although fewer than most other shows), got rid of them, employed "inward" writing, and became one of the top two or three daytime television shows.

The show premiered on May 4, 1964, and had the following cast:

VIRGINIA DWYER (Mary Matthews)
JOHN BEAL (Jim Matthews)
JACQUELINE COURTNEY (Alice Matthews)
SUSAN TRUSTMAN (Pat Matthews)
JOEY TRENT (Russ Matthews)
VERA ALLEN (Grandma Matthews)
SARA CUNNINGHAM (Liz Matthews)
LIZA CHAPMAN (Janet Matthews)
FRAN SHARON (Susan Matthews)
JOE GALLISON (Bill Matthews)
CAROL ROUX (Melissa Palmer)
WILLIAM PRINCE (Ken Baxter)
NICHOLAS PRYOR (Tom Baxter)

Overview

When the Matthews family of Bay City was introduced to viewers in 1964, it seemed much larger; for there were more immediate blood relatives involved in the story. Actually, there were two separate branches, headed by two brothers: James and William Matthews. William's side of the family had money and were high society; James's were more middle class—even though both brothers were partners in the same accounting firm. Over the years, the wealthy branch of the Matthews family has disappeared from the story, and now only Jim and Mary Matthews, their three children—Alice, Russ, and Pat—the people their children marry or become involved with, and the various friends of the Matthewses, dominate the story.

Most central to the show are the weaknesses and strengths of Jim and Mary's children. Both Pat and Alice are dependent, vulnerable women who often cannot weather crises without the intervention of family and friends. In other ways, however, they are extremely attractive people—both still love and are loved by the men they originally married, despite many marital mishaps. The men are lawyer John Randolph, Pat's husband, and Steven Frame, Alice's great love. Russ, on the other hand, is perpetually mismatched. His pattern is to fall in love with the wrong women.

Other characters include: Lenore Delaney, who has always been Pat's best friend and has through the years become a confidante of the rest of the Matthews family; and Ada Downs, a simple and poor woman who has had to raise her beautiful daughter, Rachel, alone (her husband, Gerald Davis, left her years before and she has recently married a police lieutenant, Gil McGowan, following the death of Ernie Downs, her second husband). New characters introduced are Robert Delaney, a widower who works for Steven Frame and has recently married Lenore; Janice Frame, Steven Frame's sister; and Iris Carrington, a wealthy woman recently divorced from writer Eliot Carrington.

The Story

Two deaths in succession caused turmoil for the huge Matthews family. William Matthews, wealthy brother of JIM MATTHEWS (Hugh Marlowe), had just died, leaving his widow, LIZ MATTHEWS (for many years Audra Lindley, later Nancy Wickwire, and currently Irene Dailey), and their two children. Then Jim and his wife, MARY MATTHEWS (Virginia Dwyer), were horrified when their daughter PAT (Beverly Penberthy) was accused of murdering the boy who caused her pregnancy and talked her into having an illegal abortion, which Pat thought had left her sterile. Jim and Mary hired the best lawyer they could afford, JOHN RANDOLPH (Michael Ryan), who not only got her off with a plea of temporary insanity (it was proved that the murder was accidental), but managed to fall in love with her.

Pat and John's marriage should have been happy, but there were snags. LEE RANDOLPH (Barbara Rodell), John's grown-up daughter from a previous marriage, resented Pat for taking her place as the lady of the house. However, when John was struck by a car and wound up paralyzed, Lee and Pat called a temporary truce. Then handsome lawyer MIKE BAUER (Gary Pillar) showed up in Bay City with his daughter, Hope, after his wife had committed suicide. Trying to start a new life, he was helping the crippled John Randolph with his cases when, despite himself, he fell in love with Pat, who one day had to admit that she also returned his love. Lee, however, was desperately in love with Mike. When she overheard Pat and Mike talking about their mutual love, she lost control of herself and ran away from home. She fell in with a bunch of hippies who introduced her to LSD. Meanwhile, realizing he was causing trouble in Bay City, Mike Bauer returned with Hope to Springfield.

ADA DOWNS (Constance Ford) and her second husband, ERNIE DOWNS (Harry Bellaver), were simple, hardworking people. Ernie owned a garage, where Ada's brother, SAM LUCAS (Jordan Charney) was employed while studying for his law degree. Sam fell in love with Lee Randolph and wanted to marry her, but Lee was terrified because she believed her bouts with LSD would cause any children she bore to be genetically damaged. Finally, under the influence of LSD, Lee crashed her car and was killed. Sam married model LAHOMA VANE (Anne Wedgeworth) and they moved to Somerset when he got his law degree. Pat and John (now fully recovered and able to walk), settled down to a happy life together and eventually became the parents of twins.

While all this was happening to Jim Matthews's clan, the family of his dead brother were having problems of their own. Lawyer BILL MATTHEWS (Joe Gallison), son of William and Liz Matthews, fell in love with MELISSA (MISSY) PALMER (created by Carol Roux), a beautiful, sensitive girl who was tormented by the fact that she had spent her life in foster homes. To add to her misery, she discovered, just before she was to become Bill's bride, that

she was illegitimate. Too ashamed to marry Bill, she ra
away to Chicago.

Missy—alone, distraught, and wandering the streets c
a big, frightening city—soon became involved with
small-time crook named DANNY FARGO (Antony Ponzini)
After convincing her to enter into a platonic marriag
with him—only for protection—he raped her, and she be
came pregnant. Later, Danny's old girlfriend, hystericall
jealous over his marriage to Missy, killed him with a knif
during a tussle. Since Missy had mistakenly picked up th
knife and left her fingerprints on it, she was put on tria
for Danny Fargo's murder.

Bill had been searching furiously for her, but by th
time he located Missy she was already being tried fo
first-degree homicide. Defending her himself during th
emotional trial, Bill was able to track down the real kille
and Missy was set free. Bill and Missy married—despit
the objections of his mother, Liz, who thought no woma
was good enough for him—and the two of them moved t
California with Ricky, her baby by Danny Fargo. Thei
happiness, however, didn't last long. Bill Matthew
drowned in a terrible accident.

While rich Bill Matthews was courting Missy, RUS
MATTHEWS (David Bailey, but for years played by Sa
Groom), scion of the poorer Jim Matthews clan, fell unde
the spell of RACHEL DAVIS (Victoria Wyndham, earlie
Robin Strasser), a beautiful and calculating young gir
who was a patient at the hospital where he was an intern
Rachel, who had known poverty all her life with he
mother, Ada Downs, felt this was her chance to marr
into a respectable, well-off family. Ambition, not love
made her marry Russ.

But young interns' wives must economize and live sim
ply, which was not Rachel's cup of tea. Bored with Russ
bored with having to make ends meet with a man sh
didn't love, Rachel's eyes began to wander in the directio
of handsome, virile STEVEN FRAME (George Reinholt)
who had come into his own after a lifetime of povert
quite like Rachel's. In fact, it was as much their similarit

n backgrounds as his great, self-made wealth (his "Steven
Frame Enterprises," for example, was becoming phenom-
nally successful) that lured her to him. It was her one
chance in life, she felt, to become a woman of means. At
very possible juncture she would arrange on-purpose
chance meetings with him.

Steven wasn't at all interested in Rachel, but one night
he threw herself at him in his penthouse and he took advantage of the opportunity. He regretted the mistake later,
for Rachel became pregnant. He realized that it was even
more of a mistake on his part because he had fallen in
love with ALICE MATTHEWS (Jacqueline Courtney), the sister-in-law of the woman he had impregnated. He knew
he Matthews's middle-class mores would have prevented
im from marrying Alice if the truth ever got out.

It did—Rachel made sure of that. It was a moment of
ntense drama. An engagement party was being held in
onor of Steven and Alice, and a vituperative Rachel got
Alice alone in a room and told her who was really the father of the child she was carrying. Alice, hurt beyond be-
lef but too considerate of the feelings of her brother,
Russ, to tell him the truth, canceled her engagement to
Steven and took an extended tour to Europe. When she
eturned to Bay City, she forgave Steven his transgression
with Rachel, and became Mrs. Steven Frame.

The problems of selfish and tempermental Liz Mat-
news were exacerbated when her daughter, SUSAN MAT-
HEWS (last played by Lisa Cameron), began competing
with her for the affections of handsome FRED DOUGLAS.

After the confrontation between mother and daughter
nded in the younger woman marrying Fred Douglas—
hen divorcing him, and finally finding happiness by mar-
ying Dr. Dan Shearer—wealthy Liz turned to corrupt
layboy WAYNE ADDISON (Robert Milli) for her new ro-
nance. At the time, Addison was involved in dishonest
lealings with Bay City's once greatly respected district at-
orney, WALTER CURTIN (Val Dufour). Fortyish and inse-
ure, Walter felt he needed more money than he could
arn as D.A. to provide for his new young bride, the

former LENORE MOORE (Susan Sullivan, previously played
by Judith Barcroft). So he quit his job as D.A. to become
Wayne Addison's partner in shady deals, all the while
putting up a good front as a partner in John Randolph's
law firm.

Liz Matthews began to secretly hate Lenore Curtin,
whose mother, HELEN MOORE (Murial Williams), was her
good friend. Wayne Addison, to rid himself of Liz, had
lied and said he was having an affair with Lenore behind
Walter Curtin's back. Then Walter killed Wayne Addison
in a fit of rage. Lenore, seen leaving Wayne Addison's
apartment on the night of his death, was accused of his
murder. With the help of the vindictive Liz Matthews, the
state was able to get an indictment. Ironically, Walter
Curtin himself defended his wife and Lenore was acquitted. Some time later, Walter confessed the murder to her
and she was shattered. Walter promised to tell the authorities, but on his way to his lawyer's office he was killed in
an auto accident, leaving Lenore a widow and his little
son WALLY (now Scott Firestone) fatherless. To protect
her husband's memory, Lenore vowed that she would never
reveal Walter's crime.

Rachel called her new infant baby boy Jamie, and for a
time Russ was a proud father and husband—until he
learned that Steven was the real father. After the stunned
and unhappy Russ divorced his unfaithful wife, he became
interested in CINDY CLARK (Leonie Norton), a young nurse
at the hospital where he worked. Her brother, TED CLARK
(Steven Bolster), was simultaneously falling in love with
the forlorn and husbandless new mother, Rachel. Again
Rachel married a man for her convenience, rather than
for love. Ted, who was involved in a drug ring, was later
sent to prison. Meanwhile, Rachel's father, GERALD DAVIS
(Walter Matthews), came to Bay City from Somerset to
help her run the Fireside Inn, which Ted had been managing for Steven. When Ted was released, he, Rachel, and
Gerald ran it together.

Rachel, however, was still scheming to get Steven for
herself, despite the fact that they were both married to

other people. She was getting Steven to see her, without Alice's knowledge, by making her presence a condition of his seeing his son, Jamie. Gerald Davis, even more of a schemer than his daughter, left a message one day for Alice to meet Steven at his apartment over his office, knowing that she would discover Steven and Rachel together. Gerald was after Steven's money, through his daughter.

The meeting was quite innocent, but Alice overheard Rachel saying that Steven and she were "together" the day that Alice lost her own baby, and she imagined the worst. Instead of confronting Steven with her suspicions, she left him flat and ran off to New York.

Meanwhile, Pat Randolph discovered that her husband, John, was seeing another woman. She began drinking out of self-pity, as do so many suburban housewives. But Pat quickly turned into a complete alcoholic. She was so devoted to the bottle that none of the Matthewses would tell her that Russ's fiance, Cindy, was dying of a heart ailment. When she learned that Russ had married Cindy only hours before she died in the hospital—believing to the end that she and Russ would live a happy, full life together— Pat began to realize that her own problem was cutting her off from others. John's extramarital affair ended when his paramour, Bernice, was accidentally pushed off a terrace and killed by a second lover, and he and Pat came together again.

Steven was mystified and hurt by Alice's running off suddenly. After waiting months for her to return, he finally allowed Rachel (now divorced from Ted Clark) to re-enter his life, for the sake of his son, Jamie. From New York, where she was working for writer ELIOT CARRINGTON (James Douglas) as his son's governess, Alice granted Steven a divorce so he could marry Rachel. But when Eliot Carrington convinced Alice to return to Bay City because her brother, Russ, was now treating his invalid son, she and Steven finally confronted each other and realized that their divorce had been a mistake. Steven vowed

that he would find some way to free himself from Rachel
so he could remarry Alice.

Eliot's wealthy, estranged wife, IRIS CARRINGTON (Beverlee McKinsey), was all too happy to see Steven and Alice marry—she even had Eliot's suite "bugged" to discover their true feelings for each other—because she still
loved Eliot and feared he would marry Alice.

On the verge of being arrested for bugging her husband
Eliot's suite, Iris Carrington had a nervous breakdown
and had to be confined to a hospital. Realizing how vulnerable Iris really was, Eliot dropped all charges against
her and even asked her for a reconciliation. But Iris, wishing to sever all ties with the past, chose instead to divorce
Eliot and take up life in Bay City with her son, DENNIS
CARRINGTON (Mike Hammett). Eliot decided to take a job
as a correspondent in London. Iris was now torn between
her attraction for her philandering neurologist, DR. KURT
LANDIS (Donald Madden), and her affection for kind and
gentle Russ Matthews.

Meanwhile, Lenore Curtin and ROBERT DELANEY (Nick
Coster), an architect working for Steven, had fallen in
love. Lenore, however, couldn't face the possibility of
being hurt in a second marriage; and so, temporarily
spurned, Robert allowed his attentions to wander to
JANICE FRAME (Victoria Thompson), Steven Frame's
sister and a newcomer to Bay City. Robert had been the
first man Janice had ever loved, and she wasn't about to
let the on-again-off-again Lenore get him without a fight.
Janice, however, eventually saw how futile it was to try to
win a man who didn't really love her. So, perceiving that
Robert would only be happy with Lenore, Janice encouraged a reconciliation between them. Lenore and Robert
soon married.

When Steven finally discovered why Alice had left him
(Alice had received a phonecall from Gerald Davis that
caused her to discover Steven and Rachel together in his
apartment), he seized the opportunity to sue Rachel for
divorce on the grounds that their marriage was based on a
fraud. To insure the success of his suit, and because he

was so desperate to remarry Alice, he bribed Gerald Davis to falsely testify at the divorce hearing that he made the call at Rachel's urging. The divorce was granted, but John Randolph, Steve's lawyer, found out about his client's obstruction of justice and felt compelled to tell the court— over the frantic objections of his wife, Pat. Steve remarried Alice only days before being sentenced to prison for six months. John Randolph—blamed by Pat for Steve's "betrayal" and deprived of Steve's legal business—quickly took to drink. Divorce seemed likely, especially with Pat now taking up with Dr. Kurt Landis, a cad always willing to wine and dine beautiful but unhappy women. About the only really *happy* event happening in Bay City now was the brand new infant Ada and Gil McGowen were shortly expecting.

3. AS THE WORLD TURNS

People sitting around a coffee table discussing domestic problems—that's always been the way critics have described and ridiculed the soaps. Interestingly enough, the first show to bring "coffee-table talk" to everyone's attention (including the critics') was *As the World Turns,* which had such a unique style of presenting slowly evolving discussions of personal problems. If its creators—head writer Irna Phillips and producer Ted Corday—hadn't possessed such a fabulous talent for "mere talk," twenty million people wouldn't have been sitting spellbound in front of their sets every day at 1:30 P.M. EST for nearly two decades, and the critics would never have used the "coffee-table-talk" example as the reason why the serials were so slow and static. Irony, *n'est-ce pas?*

As the World Turns, through its core characters, Nancy and Chris Hughes—ordinary American people of good midwestern stock—made a point of a day-to-day pace. *Only* Irna Phillips, veteran serial writer, would have realized when she originated this first half-hour TV serial that the extra fifteen minutes every day did not mean she had to have more action, or more characters running around on-screen. Instead, she knew what her viewers really wanted. She used Nancy and Chris Hughes to let people get a good look at other people—let them savor their talk and their feelings—and not worry so much about plot. People never tire of watching Nancy and Chris sitting in the kitchen, discussing with great concern their children and friends—whether Bob, or Lisa, or the Stewarts—because

234

Nancy and Chris care deeply for each other, and because they are, by now, much beloved characters.

As the World Turns' style breaks all the rules of drama; it abides by its own rules, by the rules that govern real life itself. And, judging by the acquiescence of millions upon millions of steady viewers, who are the only critics that really count, it succeeds.

The serial premiered April 12, 1956. It was live then and, except for occasional emergency taping, it is still live today. When the show premiered it had the following cast:

DON MacLAUGHLIN (Chris Hughes)
HELEN WAGNER (Nancy Hughes)
ROSEMARY PRINZ (Penny Hughes)
HAL STUDER (Donald Hughes)
RUTH WARRICK (Edith Hughes)
SANTOS ORTEGA (Grandpa Hughes)
BOBBY ALFORD (Bob Hughes as a boy)
LES DAMON (Jim Lowell)
ANNE BURR (Claire Lowell)
WENDY DREW (Ellen Lowell)
WILLIAM JOHNSTONE (Judge Lowell)

Overveiw

As the World Turns is today the same snail-paced drama of deep interpersonal relationships in midwestern Oakdale, U.S.A., as it was back in 1956 when it began. However, the serial no longer needs to contrast a family of wealth with one of modest means as a main story element—probably as a result of how we Americans have changed our attitudes toward wealth and power. When the story started, Chris and Nancy Hughes were the middle-class people of good character; and their rich friends, Jim and Claire Lowell, had all sorts of unwholesome problems. Today Nancy and Chris are family heads of some means. Jim and Claire Lowell died long ago, and all that is left of that once-prominent family are their daughter, Ellen, now married to Dr. David Stewart, and her grandfather, Judge Lowell, who's retired.

Nancy and Chris have three children: Bob Hughes, a

doctor currently married to the former Jennifer Ryan;
Penny Hughes, who lives in England now; and Donald
Hughes, who moved to San Francisco. Susan, a fourth
child, died years before. Tom Hughes, married to the
former Carol Demming, is their grandson, son of Bob and
his former wife, Lisa, who is now a family friend.
Grandpa Hughes, Chris's father and a retired farmer, lives
permanently with Nancy and Chris.

Chris is senior partner (and the only real practical
head) of the law firm started years ago by Judge Lowell
and his son, Jim Lowell: Lowell, Barnes, Lowell, and
Hughes.

The Story

Wealthy JIM LOWELL kept after his good friend CHRIS
HUGHES (Don MacLaughlin) to join the town country
club with his wife NANCY HUGHES (Helen Wagner), but
Nancy and Chris were much too down-to-earth to want
that sort of thing. Unlike the well-fixed Lowells, they believed in the old-fashioned virtues; so they were under-
standably upset when they discovered that Chris's sister,
EDITH HUGHES (Ruth Warrick), was having an affair with
Jim, who was already married to CLAIRE LOWELL (played
by Anne Burr, and later by Nancy Wickwire and Barbara
Berjer).

Chris always worried about his sister Edith because of
his guilt feelings toward her. His parents had worked a
farm in Illinois and put Chris through law school, with
the provision that he would pay his parents back by helping to send Edie to college. But Chris didn't. He had fall-
en in love with Nancy, a former schoolteacher, and had
to start supporting his own family. When the show started
Nancy and Chris had already been married more than a
decade and a half. Grandpa was already a widower.

Nancy and Chris's teen-aged daughter, PENNY HUGHES
(Rosemary Prinz), and her friend, Jim and Claire's daughter, ELLEN LOWELL (Wendy Drew, and later Patricia
Bruder) were both deeply disturbed by the relationship
between Edith Hughes (Penny's aunt) and Jim Lowell. El-

len was further haunted by the lack of love her parents felt for one another; and Penny, by the feeling that her mother, Nancy, loved her sister, Susan, more than she.

Confused, Ellen became infatuated with DR. TIM COLE (William Redfield), by whom she became pregnant. After she had her child out of wedlock, she gave it up for adoption. After her son was adopted by DR. DAVID STEWART (Henderson Forsythe) and his wife, BETTY (Pat Benoit)— and named Dan Stewart—Ellen became desperate to have her son back and took the matter to the courts. After a long, drawn-out battle, Ellen realized that it would be best for her son's happiness if she let him stay with his new parents. However, by a twist of fate, Betty Stewart died, and David, now all alone, came to Ellen for advice on how to take care of Dan and his natural son, Paul. Before long they fell in love. A wedding would have taken place quickly but for the troublemaking of David Stewart's insanely jealous housekeeper, FRANNY BRENNAN (Toni Darnay), who threatened to tell young Dan of his illegitimacy if Ellen went through with her plans to marry David. In an ensuing struggle with Ellen, Franny was accidentally killed. Ellen was sent to prison. Upon her release, she and David finally married.

Penny also had a string of problems. Her disillusionment with her family pushed her into a relationship with wild JEFF BAKER (Mark Rydell), with whom she eloped. A stunned Nancy and Chris were fortunately able to have the marriage annulled. With the passage of time, Jeff straightened himself out, and this time Nancy and Chris gave glowing approval to the marriage of Jeff and their daughter. Penny was shocked to discover that she could never have children; but nonetheless, she and Jeff were happy—until he was tragically killed in a car crash. Distraught, Penny tried to pick up the pieces of her life, and fell in love with handsome NEIL WADE (Michael Lipton), a doctor who for personal reasons could no longer face practicing medicine. Together they started the Wade Bookshop and were going to adopt a child when again Penny's hopes were dashed. Neil, going blind, was hit by a car and killed. Shattered, Penny vowed she'd never marry again and, later, left Oakdale for England. When last heard from, she had married a European racing champion and had finally succeeded in adopting a little Eurasian girl by the name of Amy.

While Penny's brother BOB HUGHES (Don Hastings) was attending college, he was ensnared by a designing young girl named LISA MILLER (Eileen Fulton) from Rockford, Illinois. Nancy and Chris were stunned when they learned from Lisa that Bob and she had eloped, but this time they could not annul the marriage because Lisa had become pregnant. So Nancy and Chris offered to let the couple live in Bob's old bedroom. This was kind of them, but at the same time it caused a strained domestic situation when Lisa became pregnant and especially when newborn infant TOM HUGHES (played by various boy actors, and as adults by Paul O'Keefe, Peter Galman, and currently David Colson) joined the family.

Lisa was a poor wife and a neglectful mother; she would let Nancy do all the work of taking care of her child while she tried to end her own boredom by continuing school, and later having an extramarital affair with a shoe tycoon named BRUCE ELLIOTT (James Pritchett). She saw a chance to become the well-to-do Mrs. Elliott and divorced Bob Hughes. Though she tried to put on airs, Lisa could not hide the fact that she was just a lost and confused farm girl at heart, and Elliott would have no more to do with her. At the same time, little Tom became seriously ill and almost died. Ashamed, the once self-confident Lisa begged Bob to take her back, and when he refused, she begged Nancy to get him to remarry her. Finally, after much self-pity, Lisa left young Tom with the Hugheses and fled to Chicago.

After Jim Lowell's death, Claire, a rather elegant woman, married DR. DOUG CASSEN (Nat Polen), who eventually died. Later, she became interested in a much younger man, DR. MICHAEL SHEA (the late Roy Schuman), who was full of charm but really only interested in himself and in gaining money and power. Claire, blinded by love and upset by her own oncoming middle age, married him, not realizing that he didn't love her in return.

After some months, Lisa returned from Chicago a totally changed woman. In Chicago she had married a wealthy man, whom she later divorced with a good settlement. The newly glamorous Lisa and Michael Shea were immediately attracted to one another, and an affair between them took place behind Claire's back. When Lisa got pregnant, Michael Shea became furious. A social climber, he was worried that Claire would find out and ruin his glorious plans. He turned a deaf ear to Lisa, who begged him to divorce Claire and marry her. Eventually Claire did find out, and she divorced him. She was later hit by a car and killed. As his and Lisa's son, CHUCK, grew older, Shea became fond of the boy and offered to marry Lisa, but this time she turned *him* down.

Lisa's other son, Tom Hughes, was growing up quickly in the story and had already returned from the war in Vietnam—an experience which had shaken him up. He began to seek refuge in drugs, and one day even tried to steal some from Dr. Shea's cabinet. The unscrupulous Shea caught Tom and forced a written confession from him. He used the confession to blackmail Lisa into marrying him.

Back at the Hughes household, Bob Hughes hadn't been sitting on his hands all this while. After his marriage to Lisa had ended, he married SANDY MCGUIRE (Dagne Crane), a beautiful girl whom Ellen had met in prison. It turned out that she had been sent up because she was an unwitting accomplice to a crime her husband, ROY MCGUIRE (Konrad Matthaei), committed. When she was paroled, Ellen introduced her to Bob. Sandy married him mostly because she wanted security for herself and her son, Jimmy. The basis of the marriage was shaky, and it soon collapsed. Sandy went off to New York to try to become a professional model.

Lisa and Michael Shea's marriage was a farce—with Lisa prancing before him in sexy nightgowns and then locking her door just to torment him. Angered, Shea announced that he was going to prove her an unfit mother in court. Frightened by the possibility of losing her son, Lisa fled with Charles to Mexico.

Hearing that her mother, ALMA MILLER (Ethel Remey), was ill, Lisa secretly returned to Oakdale, only to discover that her son Tom was on trial for the murder of Michael Shea. She rushed to the courtroom in a panic just in time to hear her son confess to Shea's murder—to protect her. Lisa fainted on the spot and developed amnesia; she couldn't remember if she was the murderess. It was soon revealed, however, that a former paramour of Shea's had snuffed out his life. Lisa and Tom—and everything else in Oakdale—returned to normal.

Like Tom, the two Stewart boys had grown up, and all three had problematic love affairs. DAN STEWART (John Colenback, currently John Reilly)—Ellen's son by the late Dr. Tim Cole—had become a fine doctor and was already married to SUSAN STEWART (Marie Masters) when he fell in love with an English girl by the name of ELIZABETH TALBOT (Jane House). Susan refused to give him a divorce; later both she and her rival, Liz, became pregnant at the same time. Susan had a miscarriage, but Liz's baby girl lived and was named Betsy. Also in love with Liz, PAUL STEWART (Dean Santoro)—Dan's adopted brother and David Stewart's natural son from his former marriage—offered marriage, and Liz accepted in order to give her baby a name. That marriage, however, broke up; Paul later died of a brain tumor. When Susan at long last divorced Dan to marry another doctor, Liz and Dan wed and were able to find happiness—if for only a few days. Right after their wedding, Liz fell down a flight of stairs and fatally ruptured her liver. Feeling that his life in Oakdale was wrecked by all this tragedy, Dan took his daughters Betsy and Emily and went to live in England, hoping to find himself again.

Tom Hughes fell in love with a beautiful and rich runaway named MEREDITH HALIDAY when he should have been paying more attention to the call of true love, in the person of pretty, down-to-earth CAROL DEMMING (Rita Mc-

Laughlin). Meredith's wealthy guardian, SIMON GILBEY, stormed into Oakdale, where he had learned his daughter was hiding. After a brief but passionate romantic interlude with Tom's mother, Lisa, Gilbey took Meredith away, leaving the path clear for a healthier romance to develop between Tom and Carol Demming, who were soon married.

After a number of disastrous marriages and affairs, the now-worldly Lisa Shea began to realize what a wonderful man her first husband, Bob Hughes, had been in comparison with the men she had known. So she again set her sights for him; but Bob's own sights were set on JEN-NIFER RYAN (Gillian Spencer), the widow of a brilliant surgeon who had gone through school with Bob.

Lisa was blocked with Bob, but not with Bob's older brother, DONALD HUGHES (Peter Brandon), a man with almost as many marital mishaps and romantic false starts as Lisa. Lisa fell in love with Don, who was fascinated by Lisa but in the end refused to marry her. The result of that affair was a pregnancy, which Lisa tried to have secretly aborted—but it turned out to be only a false pregnancy.

Bob Hughes married Jennifer Ryan, but trouble started immediately when her son, DR. RICK RYAN (Con Roche), who worshipped his father, openly displayed his resentment toward Bob. When Jennifer, torn between her son and her new husband, left Bob, he and Jennifer's sister, KIM REYNOLDS (Kathryn Hays)—beautiful, utterly independent, and totally sympathetic—fell in love and had a brief affair in Florida. Jennifer returned to Bob when she learned that she was pregnant. Ironically, Kim also learned that she was pregnant from her affair with Bob. DR. JOHN DIXON (Larry Bryggman), a devious man who wanted Kim—and always got what he wanted—eventually convinced her to marry him for the sake of the baby, even though she had vowed, in Woman's Lib fashion, to have her baby out of wedlock. Jennifer eventually discovered whose baby Kim was really carrying when Bob, delirious after being struck by a car, confessed all. But Jennifer

confronted neither her sister nor her husband and forgave
them. Kim lost Bob's baby and bravely tried to make a go
of a marriage with a man she didn't love; but it was
hopeless. When she asked John Dixon for a divorce, he
"blackmailed" her into staying with him by threatening to
reveal her affair with Bob to Jen—who, of course, already
knew. Further tragedy threatened Kim and Bob's lives
when Bob alone discovered that Jennifer had a terminal
neurological disease. At first he kept the awful secret to
himself.

Meanwhile, Lisa Shea was, as usual, being pursued by
a number of suitors. One, a minister-turned-doctor, WALLY
MATTHEWS (Charles Siebert), attracted Lisa's eye for a
while; then a mysterious, handsome young man by the
name of JAY STALLINGS (Dennis Cooney) appeared in
Oakdale and took the empty apartment next to the Wade
Bookshop—managed by Lisa for her ex-sister-in-law,
Penny Hughes, still living in England. When mysterious
attacks were made on Lisa's life, everyone was worried
and many thought Jay responsible because of his moodi-
ness and shady past. Among those who tried to save Lisa
from her unseen assailant was GRANT COLMAN (Konrad
Matthaei, now James Douglas), a new lawyer in Chris
Hughes's firm. He, as well as young Jay Stallings, found
the temperamental Lisa irresistible. Lisa's pursuer was discovered to be Jay Stallings's stepfather, who eventually
tried to murder his stepson and Lisa together as part of a
plot to acquire Jay's inheritance, and to make it look as if
Jay had killed Lisa himself after numerous attempts on her
life. Fortunately, Grant Colman arrived at the Wade Book-
shop just in time to save Lisa and Jay. Jay's stepfather was
killed by the police. Now safe from harm, Lisa could turn
her attention to her two ardent suitors, Grant and Jay.

Storm clouds were again forming over the Stewart
family. Dr. Susan Stewart began to work at the hospital
with David Stewart, her ex-husband Dan's stepfather.
The relationship between David and Susan was uneasy because of past events, and because David and Ellen consid-

ered Dan an "exile," since his return to Oakdale would mean that he would lose Emily to Susan, who had legal custody. When Dan finally did return to Oakdale, Susan—still in love with him, despite everything—started scheming ways of getting him back again; she wasn't above using even their little girl, Emily, as a pawn in her plan to reconquer Dan.

4. DAYS OF OUR LIVES

Days of Our Lives is the sleeper of daytime serials. For the first year of its existence viewers paid so little attention to it that the show was rated 32nd out of a possible 34 daytime network programs. Possibly, to the casual dial-turning observer, its stories appeared to be exaggerated melodrama, with the familiar theme of a family with lots of doctors plagued by infidelity, a brother-against-brother feud, and the like. But *Days* caught on like a flashfire one year after it started, and it now jockeys with *Another World* and *As the World Turns* for top ratings. What suddenly happened? We can only guess that viewers took a closer look at *Days of Our Lives'* unique style of strong dramatic confrontations between characters and at its greater emphasis on action than other daytime serials. Also, the show's persistent use of psychiatric problems has always been compelling.

Days of Our Lives has a real, live movie star—MacDonald (Mac) Carey as Dr. Tom Horton, the "tent-pole" character who tells viewers at the start of each and every program: "Like sands through the hour glass, so are the days of our lives." The simultaneous and intriguing full-screen view of an emptying hourglass almost seems a reminder of this program's potential enduring quality.

NBC premiered *Days of Our Lives* on November 8, 1965, with the following cast:

MACDONALD CAREY (Dr. Tom Horton)
FRANCES REID (Alice Horton)
JOHN CLARKE (Mickey Horton)

PAT HUSTON (Addie Horton Olson)
CHARLA DOHERTY (Julie Olson)
ROBERT KNAPP (Ben Olson)
DAVID MCLEAN (Craig Merritt)
FLIP MARK (Steve Olson)
BURT DOUGLAS (Jim Fisk)

Overview

Dr. Tom Horton and his wife, Alice, head a large, old-fashioned family in Salem, U.S.A., where Tom is Chief of Internal Medicine at University Hospital. The problem-plagued Horton brood originally consisted of five children: Addie (recently deceased) and Tommy (twins, in their mid-forties), Mickey (late thirties), Bill (mid-thirties), and Marie (late twenties). Addie, who married singer Doug Williams before her death is the mother of Julie (mid-twenties) and Steve (late teens), who was raised in Europe and now lives in Paris. Mickey is a successful attorney wed to psychiatrist Laura Horton, and they have a son, Michael, Jr. (mid-teens). Bill is still the bachelor. Tommy, now a widower, lives in the Horton household with his daughter, Sandy. Marie is a nun. Julie, Addie's daughter with the late Ben Olson, has recently made Tom and Alice great-grandparents with the birth of her son, David.

The Story

Sixteen years ago (in terms of the story) the Hortons were a happy family, all still living together—with the exception of the oldest son, TOMMY HORTON (later played by John Lupton), who was missing in action in Korea. Then ADDIE HORTON OLSON (Pat Huston, and now Patricia Barry) married to wealthy banker BEN OLSON (Robert Knapp), moved to Europe with him. DR. TOM HORTON (Macdonald Carey) and his wife, ALICE HORTON (Frances Reid), felt little joy at their daughter's sudden departure. But they did have a consolation in that Addie and Ben left their daughter, JULIE OLSON (now Susan Seaforth), to be raised by her grandparents. Young Julie, however never forgave her mother for deserting her.

Julie became the tortured and motherless young girl searching for love and friendship wherever she could find them. Unfortunately she tended to find both in all the wrong places.

Her one-time best chum from high-school days, SUSAN MARTIN (Denise Alexander, and now Bennye Gatteys) eventually became her bitter rival and the cause of many of her heartaches. The friendship was first severely strained when Julie found out that Susan was carrying the child of DAVID MARTIN, to whom Julie was then secretly engaged. Julie, however, stepped aside and let the two marry, even stoically agreeing to become Susan's maid of honor, but bitterness raged between the two women when Susan, after the birth of her child, refused to divorce David so that Julie could marry him.

While the two rivals steamed, DR. BILL HORTON (Edward Mallory), a brilliant young surgeon attempting to follow in his father Tom's footsteps at University Hospital, met and fell in love with a fellow intern, DR. LAURA SPENCER (Susan Flannery), who was specializing in psychiatry. They became engaged, but when Bill discovered that he could no longer operate because of an infirmity in his hands, he suddenly left Salem.

As if fate were punishing Susan and David for their sins, tragedy engulfed them. Shortly after their son, Richard Martin, was born, his father, David, was playing with him on a swing and the child was killed accidentally Susan went out of her mind and shot David Martin!

Susan was put on trial for his murder. Since she was a patient of Laura Spencer's and was being defended by MICKEY HORTON (John Clarke), Bill's brother, Laura and Mickey had to spend a great deal of time together. Laura distraught over Bill's continued absence from Salem, began to return Mickey's affections. The outcome of Mickey's defense was Susan's acquittal on the charge of murder on the basis of temporary insanity—established during the trial by Laura's expert psychiatrist testimony. Laura married Mickey, and Bill returned to Salem—heartbroken to find that his brother and fiancée had wed.

Shattered though he was, Bill had to turn his attentions to a young doctor (played by John Lupton) whom he had brought home with him. Burned and tortured during the Korean war, the young doctor had undergone extensive plastic surgery, which completely changed his appearance, and was still suffering from the amnesia inflicted by shell shock. MARIE HORTON (Marie Cheatham), the Horton's youngest daughter, was instantly attracted to the handsome doctor and fell in love with him. Later, when the young man was revealed to be her missing brother, Tommy Horton, Marie was able to retain her sanity only by becoming a nun. KITTY HORTON (Regina Gleason), to whom Tommy was married before leaving for Korea, had returned to Salem with their daughter, SANDY HORTON (Heather North), and she immediately began causing trouble for everyone.

Meanwhile, Bill couldn't forget Laura. The thought of the woman he loved being married to his own brother haunted him day and night. Having to work with her every day at the hospital made it even worse for him. One night at the hospital the pressure became too much for him, and he raped her. Soon after, she became pregnant and knew that it had to be Bill's child. By then Tom Horton knew that Mickey was sterile and could never father his own child, and so confronted Laura with this knowledge. She was forced to admit that Bill had raped her. Tom was beside himself but dared not say anything for fear someone would tell Mickey the truth about himself.

After Bill's son, MICHAEL HORTON (now Stuart Lee) was born, the interfering Kitty Horton got hold of a tape recording of a conversation between Laura and Tom Horton that proved Michael's true parentage. She threatened Bill with revealing the truth to the whole world. A struggle between the two of them took place, and Kitty, who already had a heart condition, died on the spot. During Bill's trial for supposedly killing her, he repeatedly re-

fused to say what caused the struggle in order to protect
Mickey from the truth, and was finally sentenced to six
months in prison for manslaughter.

Julie Olson, pregnant with the murdered David
Martin's baby, gave birth to an infant boy, and on the advice of the family and against her better judgment, Julie
put him up for adoption. SCOTT BANNING (Ryan McDon-
ald) and his wife, Janet, adopted the baby, calling him
Brad Banning. Soon, however, fate began to weave a sin-
ister web. Susan became the Bannings' next-door neighbor, never suspecting that their adopted baby was really
the son of her old nemesis, Julie Olson. After Scott's wife
died of a brain tumor, Susan began helping him raise his
little boy and the two started falling in love.
Tormented by the loss of her baby and also by the
thought that her hated rival, Susan, might soon become
her son's mother, Julie sued to win back custody of the
boy. Since Scott was no longer married, the court gave the
baby back to Julie, who renamed him "DAVID" BANNING
(Jeffrey Williams), after his father. But Scott, meanwhile,
had grown so attached to the child that he agreed to
marry Julie in order to remain the boy's father. Julie's
only interest in marrying Scott, however, was to settle the
score with Susan, who she knew loved Scott.

While still in prison, Bill Horton met a singer named
DOUG WILLIAMS (Bill Hayes). An adventuresome con man,
Doug was excited by Bill's revelation that Salem's Susan
Martin had inherited $250,000 after the death of husband
David Martin. When Doug was released from prison he
immediately came to Salem in order to win over Susan
and her money. Not a bit interested in his love-patter,
Susan tried to get Doug interested in Julie in an effort to
destroy her marriage to Scott. Susan even offered Doug
money for his trouble. It was indeed little trouble on
Doug's part, for he and Julie fell madly in love almost at
once.
Julie's happiness with Doug was interrupted by the sudden reappearance in Salem of her mother, Addie Olson

Her husband (and Julie's father), Ben Olson, had died of a heart attack while they were living in Paris, where she decided to leave her second child, STEVE OLSON, to finish his education. From the very start, Julie did not attempt to hide her hostility toward her mother. After all, not only had Julie been abandoned by Addie as a child, but she was rejected by her a second time when the young girl, pregnant with David Martin's child, had gone to Paris to seek her mother's help. With Addie, Julie became secretive about all her affairs, including the one with Doug Williams.

Addie, however, found out about Julie's involvement with Doug through a private investigator. Although she despised Doug at first for the bon-vivant small-time opportunist he seemed to be, as time went by Addie became unexplainably attracted by Doug's charm and easy-going manner. Doug seemed to make Addie realize that her life with her dead husband, Ben Olson, had been a shell, a facade for his business life. In a desperate maneuver to discover the true meaning of life and love, Addie suddenly asked Doug to marry her—on the very night he and Julie had had a bitter quarrel. Doug, also acting on a mad impulse, agreed and eloped with Addie. Later, although happy with his new wife, he suffered many months of soul searching, realizing that Julie, who blamed herself for causing her break with Doug, was willing to make amends with him at any cost—even the happiness of her mother or that of her husband, Scott Banning.

Addie, despite the ever-present threat of Julie, was able to strengthen her marriage to Doug by buying the club in which he was singing, "Sergio's," and renaming it "Doug's Place." She then offered it to him. Later she became pregnant with his child.

Julie, realizing that her heart belonged only to Doug and that her life was becoming a sham, began to make secret preparations to divorce Scott Banning. On the day she was filing divorce papers, Scott was tragically killed at the construction site where he was designing a structure for architect BOB ANDERSON (Mark Tapscott). He died without realizing that his wife belonged to another. Mean-

while, Bob Anderson and his wife, PHYLLIS ANDERSON
(Corinne Conley), an older couple, were shocked by
Scott's death and allowed Julie, torn by guilt over Scott, to
lean on them and make them substitute parents. However,
Bob, feeling the pangs of middle-age, began to have
mixed emotions about the luscious young Julie. Added to
Bob's secret affections for her, Julie's laywer, DON CRAIG
(Jed Allen) also began falling in love with her. But Julie
continued loving only one man—who belonged to her
mother.

Susan Martin's own melodrama hadn't subsided one bit.
The night that Scott Banning had left her for Julie, Susan
had relations in a park with a young stranger. Later she
convinced herself that it was rape. After a few weeks of
emotional shock, Susan finally snapped out of it by involving herself in running the free clinic she had bought
with her inheritance. After handsome DR. GREG PETERS
(Peter Brown) began to help her run the clinic, Susan began to fall in love with Greg. But, to her horror, she discovered that she was pregnant from her encounter in the
park. Considering having an abortion, Susan was told by
Dr. Tom Horton that she had cancer of the uterus and the
child she was carrying would be her last. Susan, realizing
that she had to keep the baby, forced herself to tell Greg
the truth—or what she believed to be the truth—that she
had been raped one night. Although shocked, Greg still
agreed to marry Susan, since he believed her story.
When Susan Martin met Greg's younger brother, a novelist by the name of ERIC PETERS (Stanley Kamel), it was
her turn to be shocked. He was the man in the park! Suffering from a near breakdown, Susan was made to realize,
in therapy sessions with Laura Horton, that what had
happened in the park was a willing act on her part as a result of losing Scott and young David all at the same time.
However, Greg soon learned that Eric was the father of
Susan's child. An episode in Eric's new novel, *In His
Brother's Shadow,* told the whole story of Eric, Susan, and
Greg in thinly veiled terms. Greg, furious at Eric, assaulted his brother so badly that he had to be put in the hos-

pital. Susan, shocked by Greg's unjust treatment of his brother, told Greg the truth she had learned in therapy with Laura. After an apology to his brother and much soul-searching, Greg realized that, despite everything, he still loved Susan and soon made her Mrs. Greg Peters. The memory of her night with Eric, however, along with his constant presence, began to haunt Susan and cause trouble in her marriage.

The lives of Bill, Laura, and Mickey continued to sink deeper into a morass of trouble and confusion. After Bill returned from prison and Laura learned why he had refused to tell the court the real reason for his struggle with Kitty Horton, Laura was filled with compassion and love for him; she made sure that his medical license was reinstated by testifying in his favor at a formal board hearing.

Laura and Bill were in love, but both had too much regard for Mickey Horton, who still believed himself to be the father of Michael, to carry on behind his back. But Mickey began to unjustly suspect Bill and Laura of having an affair, and to pay them back he had an affair with LINDA PETERSON (Margaret Mason), his secretary. Finding out, Laura threatened divorce, but eventually decided against it when young Michael, hearing his distraught mother and "uncle" Bill declare their love, rushed out into the street in a panic and was hit by a car. After his recovery, Laura tried to make a go of it again with Mickey, who by now had developed a serious heart condition and needed her more than ever.

After this storm had seemingly passed, another one developed. Young Michael found out about Mickey's affair with Linda Peterson and turned against the man whom he believed to be his father. Mickey, in the ensuing struggle with his son, suffered a serious heart attack. It was his brother, Bill, who then performed a brilliant piece of surgery on Mickey—a triple multiple bypass—and returned him to near normal. However, his despondency over his health, over Laura and Bill and young Michael, and his fear of never again being a complete man because of his heart condition, caused him to have a stroke, resulting in total amnesia. Alone in the hospital while everyone was attending Greg and Susan's wedding, Mickey quietly dressed, left the hospital, and disappeared. Later he began working on a small farm, some distance from Salem, owned by a lovely young girl, MAGGIE SIMMONS (Suzanne Rodgers), who was crippled by a car accident which had resulted in the death of her parents. All the Hortons and the police back in Salem frantically began following every lead in an attempt to find him. However, Laura and Bill, although worried sick about Mickey's whereabouts, were also falling more and more in love each day that Mickey was gone, and finding it increasingly difficult to keep from living together. Mickey himself seemed to have found happiness with Maggie Simmons, whom he finally married—still remembering nothing of his past life. When Laura and Bill, meanwhile, were also marrying, since everyone assumed Mickey to be dead. Only Maggie knew who her "Marty" really was in his former life—but she vowed never to reveal the truth lest she lose him for good.

Addie and Doug, happy in their marriage and excitedly awaiting the birth of their child, were both stricken by the news that Addie had leukemia. Although she vowed not to tell anyone that she was dying until the birth of the child, the whole family eventually found out—with the exception of Julie—and began giving the moribund Addie all of their support.

Julie, ignorant of her real mother's distress, was finding mother-love elsewhere in the form of Phyllis Anderson. Phyllis herself was beginning to need Julie's friendship more than ever now, for her husband, Bob Anderson, had left her. Little did Phyllis suspect that it was Julie herself who unwittingly caused the breakup of her marriage.

After Addie gave birth to HOPE, Julie found out that her mother was dying and rushed to her bedside. Addie made Julie promise to take care of Doug and Hope when she was gone. Julie, still in love with Doug, broke off her forthcoming marriage to Don Craig, believing that she and Doug and Hope would soon become a family. But Addie didn't die; instead she had a miraculous remission which enabled her to resume her life with her husband and new-born daughter. Poor Julie—torn between happiness over her mother's recovery and despair at losing Doug once again—suddenly became cynical, deciding that love wasn't important, only material wealth. She married Bob Ander-son after he impulsively asked her to be his bride. Phyllis Anderson was shattered that her best friend would do such a thing to her. Already emotionally disturbed by her divorce from Bob, Phyllis grew even sicker and tried to murder Julie. But she mistook Julie for her daughter MARY ANDERSON (Karin Wolfe), and to her dread realized that she had shot her own flesh and blood! Mary recovered, but another tragedy soon followed: Addie was struck by a car and killed while bravely saving her daughter Hope's life from its wheels. Once again Julie, married to Bob, and Doug, now a widower, had to confront the possibility of finally finding happiness together as the ironical outcome of Addie's sad fate.

5. THE DOCTORS

So real is the medical atmosphere of *The Doctors* that a great many viewers are convinced that the show is done in an actual hospital. It may as well be. There are enough surgical props in the taping studio at 30 Rockefeller Plaza for real doctors to perform any operation from a frontal lobe lobotomy to a double kidney transplant. Of course, one may wonder how the actors learn what to do with all those clamps and plasma bottles once the show's many delicate operations (especially the extraordinarily large number of brain surgeries) get underway. Producer Joseph Stuart, a stickler for authenticity, and the writers, Mr. and Mrs. Robert Pollock, often visit hospitals, talk to doctors, and observe operations before attempting major operations on the show. Some of the nurses seen on the program during critical surgeries are not actors at all, but real registered nurses hired to make sure that the prop table is laid out correctly and the instruments handled right. The regular actors have developed incredible facility in properly pronouncing all the polysyllabic disease names.

About the *only* technical problem this show doesn't have is clothing. You don't have to go to Bergdorf's to buy hospital uniforms.

Although *The Doctors* is not primarily about diseases or the patients who suffer from them—but rather about the personal problems of doctors and nurses who work in a hospital—the show does perform a public service by accurately dramatizing operations, and sometimes even promoting important causes. Once, in 1964, the producers

wove Van Johnson, Arlene Francis, and Johnny Carson
into the story-line in order to plug the National Associa-
tion for Mental Health.

The Doctors, which premiered on April 1, 1963, is
unique in two ways: it is the only current daytime serial
which did not begin as a continuing story but, rather, had
a one-story-a-week format about hospital doctors (written
by *Ma Perkins'* head writer, Orin Tovrov) similar to the
old *Modern Romances* on NBC; and it is also the first
daytime serial to win, in 1971, the Emmy Award. (In
1973 it won the award a second time—with Elizabeth
Hubbard winning also as Best Actress in a Daytime Series.) *The Doctors* became a regular serial in 1964 and
featured in its cast:

ANN WILLIAMS (Dr. Maggie Fielding)
JIM PRITCHETT (Dr. Matt Powers)
ELIZABETH HUBBARD (Dr. Althea Davis)
ADAM KENNEDY (Brock Hayden)
GERALD O'LOUGHLIN (Pete Banas)
ELLEN MCRAE (Dr. Kate Bartok)
DOROTHY BLACKBURN (Nurse Brown)
KARL LIGHT (Dave Davis)
KATHERINE MESKILL (Faith Collins)
COURT BENSON (Willard Walling)

Overview

Hope Memorial Hospital is run by Dr. Matt Powers,
whose family consists of his wife, Dr. Maggie Powers,
Maggie's daughter, Greta, and Matt's son, Dr. Mike Powers. Both Maggie and Mike practice at Hope Memorial.
Matt and Maggie Powers are solid, sensible people who
have had an exemplary marriage, despite a few rough
spots. Other important doctors at the hospital are: hot-
tempered but brilliant neurosurgeon Nick Bellini; strong-
minded Althea Davis, mother of Penny; pediatrician Steve
Aldrich, who works closely with his wife, nurse Carolee.
Hope Memorial has one black doctor (in the story, at
least), resident neurosurgeon Hank Iverson, whose wife
is nurse Lauri James, an ex-singer. Laboratory technician

Matha Allen is regularly on hand to give advice to whomever will listen.

The Story

People at Hope Memorial always felt comfortable coming to DR. MATT POWERS (Jim Pritchett) with their troubles because of his easy, armchair manner and his solid character. So did a new doctor at the hospital, DR. MAGGIE FIELDING (first played by Ann Williams, then by Bethel Leslie, and currently by Lydia Bruce), who was having trouble in her marriage to KURT VAN ALLEN. More and more, Matt became Maggie's confidant and constant companion. After Van Allen's murder, Maggie gave birth to GRETA (Jennifer Houlton) and married Matt, a widower with a sixteen-year-old son, MIKE (Peter Burnell). Matt hoped Mike would follow in his footsteps someday—perhaps he pushed the boy too hard.

DR. ALTHEA DAVIS (Elizabeth Hubbard), nee Althea Hamilton, had already been divorced from DAVE DAVIS, with whom she had two children, PENNY (Julia Duffy now playing the young adult) and BUDDY, by the time she came to Hope Memorial as Head of the Outpatient Clinic. For a while the refined, bright Althea Davis dedicated her life to her career as doctor and mother—until a certain brain surgeon found his way to the doors of Hope Memorial.

That was DR. NICK BELLINI (Gerald Gordon), who was just about ready to give up medicine and wind up on skid row when Maggie Powers, his old medical-school chum, talked him into coming to the hospital. Nick had been obsessed with guilt. He and his gangster brother were first-generation Italian-Americans raised in a Chicago ghetto. One night his brother, who had put Nick through medical school, was brought into a Chicago hospital riddled with gun wounds, and Nick couldn't save his life. He saw himself as a failed doctor. But his success as a surgeon at Hope Memorial slowly revived his self-confidence. Then he met Althea.

Their difference in backgrounds—she of proud, puritanical, New England stock, and he rough and earthy, a brilliant but unmannered product of the Chicago ghettos—once again proved the old axiom: opposites attract. Their stormy romance came to an abrupt end when Althea's son, Buddy, died suddenly of spinal meningitis while Nick and she were spending an illicit weekend together. Although they were reunited and eventually married, it was inevitable that their love couldn't overcome their individual temperaments and pride. After a Mexican divorce, Althea took a leave from the hospital in hopes of straightening out her life. During this period she was swept into a new romance with a debonair English psychiatrist, DR. JOHN MORRISON (Patrick Horgan), who later came to the hospital and married her.

A bright, brash and devil-may-care girl-chasing intern by the name of STEVE ALDRICH (David O'Brien) came to Hope Memorial and instantly started creating havoc. Handsome but immature, Dr. Steve seduced DR. KAREN WERNER (Laryssa Lauret) just to prove he could; but when she became pregnant and attempted suicide, he suddenly realized the error of his ways and married her. But the marriage couldn't work. Shortly after their child was born, Karen attempted to return to Germany with their son, ERICH (Keith Blanchard), but the plane crashed and Karen was killed, although Erich survived and later began living with his father.

Through all this, a happy-go-lucky, self-effacing gal Friday to Matt Powers, nurse CAROLEE SIMPSON (Carolee Campbell), watched Steve from a distance. The young doctor wouldn't give her a tumble, which she didn't find surprising. Although liked by everyone, she didn't imagine she could be loved by anyone. She was proved wrong when Dr. Steve, now wanting to settle down with a woman he could love, began to pay serious attention to her. A love affair started. Carolee found herself pregnant, but because of jealousy and misunderstandings—mostly instigated by nurse KATHY RYKER (Holly Peters)—she didn't tell Steve. Instead, Carolee accepted the marriage proposal of DR. DAN ALLISON, who was, in fact, a psychopath. Dan knew that he was dying of a heart condition and, taking revenge against Steve for the love Carolee bore him, took his own life, making it appear that Steve had murdered him. Steve was tried and found guilty, but before he was sentenced Carolee came up with Dan's old diary and the evidence to acquit Steve. By then she was in labor with Steve's child. But instead of going to the hospital, she risked her unborn baby's life and went to the courthouse with the new evidence. Steve was exonerated, and STEPHANIE ALDRICH was born, and the two were married at last.

When Steve's ever-scheming mother, MONA ALDRICH (Meg Mundy), arrived on the scene, she did everything she could to break up the marriage. But Steve and Carolee's marriage survived that, as well as the kidnapping of baby Stephanie by Nurse Ryker, who turned psychopathic when she lost her own baby. In one dramatic moment, John Morrison, who himself had been responsible for many of Kathy's wild acts, caught the Aldrich baby from Kathy's hands only seconds before Kathy committed suicide by throwing herself off a cliff.

At this point, Dr. Morrison's sole interest in life was in holding on to Althea, who had never really loved anyone but Nick Bellini. Dr. Morrison would use every means he could think of to keep Althea—faking a wheelchair paralysis to get Althea's sympathy; trying to get Nick Bellini married off to other women; convincing Althea that only he, a psychiatrist, could help her daughter Penny, who was suffering psychological damage because of a brain tumor. Althea became particularly vulnerable to John's efforts because of a lack of communication between herself and her daughter.

Penny's problems and her loneliness caused her to try to seduce Dr. Mike Powers, Matt's son, who was happily married to a pretty lab technician, TONI FERRA POWERS (Anna Stuart)—happily that is, until the fear of not knowing whether he could live up to his father's high expectations caused him to turn to dangerous pep pills—amphetamines—for courage. Unable to practice medicine properly and with his marriage endangered, Mike ran away to work as a ship's doctor. Soon after, Toni found herself pregnant.

New romantic mix-ups came to Hope Memorial when DR. ANN LARIMER (Geraldine Court), one of Steve Aldrich's ex-wives, came to the hospital and became engaged to Nick Bellini. Mona, Steve's mother, first tried to get her son to set up private practice with Ann—hoping that a new romance between them would break up Steve's marriage to Carolee—and then tried to get him to set up private practice in Boston, where he was raised and where Carolee would feel out of place. Naturally, Mona believed she was doing all this scheming out of pure motherly love. Steve and Carolee were far too happy a couple, however, for any of her efforts to succeed. So Mona married a doctor and moved to Boston. With Mona out of their hair, Steve and Carolee turned their attention to consolidating their family. By now their three children were: Stephanie (theirs), Billy Allison (Carolee's by the late Dan Allison), and Erich (Steve's by the late Karen Werner). Carolee decided that to be a real mother to her husband's son, Erich, she had to legally adopt him.

Nick Bellini never believed John Morrison's story that the suicide of Kathy Ryker was all her own doing. Nick felt that John, as her psychiatrist, had used psychology to get her to kill herself—since, had she lived, she might have revealed all the tricks John had played in order to keep Althea from divorcing him. Nick confronted John with his suspicions, and John admitted the truth, adding that no one would believe it. John, after all, was considered a hero for saving little Stephanie Aldrich's life. John didn't realize that Penny Davis's tape recorder had been turned on when he made the confession. When Althea heard the tape she was in shock. After telling John that she would reveal the truth to Matt Powers, she took the tape and began driving toward his house during a violent snowstorm. The car cracked up and Althea not only lost her memory, but nearly lost her life.

Of course, no one but John and Althea knew about the

tape, which was flung out of the car during the crash impact and was found by an old schoolteacher, who eventually returned the tape to Penny. Now, with the tape as proof, everyone knew that Nick's accusations against John Morrison were true, and Matt Powers immediately fired him from the staff. Distraught, John came to Nick's apartment one night and pulled a gun on him. A struggle ensued, and Nick was knocked unconscious. Then Penny suddenly walked in the door, and a gunshot was heard. John Morrison was dead. Did Penny kill John? "I guess I killed him," she said, not really remembering anything that happened because of emotional shock. She was charged with first-degree murder.

DR. ALAN STEWART (Gil Gerard), Matt Powers nephew, joined the staff of Hope Memorial after spending three years in a P.O.W. camp in Vietnam. His beautiful but selfish wife, MARGO STEWART (Mary Denham), had been living near her father in Hawaii while Alan was in Vietnam, and she hoped, after his return, that they could continue living there. But Alan insisted on becoming a resident at Hope Memorial and came to the hospital without her. Later she joined him and, hoping to save her marriage, insisted on having a baby immediately. Alan, however, refused, since he wasn't sure the marriage was solid enough to last.

While Penny was on trial for murder, Althea depended a great deal on Nick. By now their bond was strong, though strictly one of friendship. Nick's fiancée, Ann Larimer—who had long ago been hurt by a romance turned sour—misinterpreted Nick's attention to his ex-wife and began to feel cheated. Ann was unaware—at first—that a new romantic interest was growing between Althea and LUKE MCALISTER (Alex Sheafe), the lawyer who was defending Penny.

6. THE EDGE OF NIGHT

The Edge of Night's title made a lot of sense when it was a late-afternoon show (just *edging* into nighttime television), but when Procter and Gamble changed the time of the show to early afternoon, one would think that they were stuck with a vague poetic title that didn't seem to mean very much. In any case, meaningful title or not, the show has been a winner ever since it started in 1956.

At that point it was supposed to have been television's serialized answer to radio's *Perry Mason*—in fact, the show was to have been called that, but the new producers couldn't work out a deal with the owners of the old show, so they did the next best thing. They invented a new courtroom-crime melodrama similar to *Perry Mason* and made sure viewers noticed the parallels by starring John Larkin, radio's old Perry, as the main character, Assistant D.A. Mike Karr.

The Edge of Night's writers, producers, and actors have often boasted that it is the only daytime serial that doesn't have a lot of "coffee-table" talk, emphasis on marriage and children, or the like. *Edge* cannot afford to be so snippy about its differences from other soaps these days, however, since, in order to keep housewives watching at an earlier hour, writer Henry Slesar has had to replace much of the old courtroom-oriented plotline with stories of marital discord, romantic mishaps, and other domestic crises. "I strike a compromise," says Slesar. "It can't be all crime these days."

Compromise or no, *Edge* still packs a wallop when it

comes to suspense. Slesar, a master of subplot mystery, manages to tear housewives away from their chores long enough to find out who'll get it in the back next, and if that marriage will somehow be saved. The popular serial was the second to receive—in 1972—the coveted Emmy for Outstanding Achievement in Daytime Drama.

The Edge of Night has always been aired live. It premiered on CBS on April 2, 1956, with the following cast:

> JOHN LARKIN (Mike Karr)
> TEAL AMES (Sarah Lane)
> DON HASTINGS (Jack Lane)
> MARY MOOR (Betty Jean Lane)
> IAN MARTIN (Det. Sergeant)
> MAXINE STUART (Police Dept. Secretary)
> BETTY GARDE (Mattie Lane)
> WALTER GREASEA (Winston Grimsley)
> LAUREN GILBERT (Uncle Harry Lane)
> SARAH BURTON (Uncle Harry's wife)
> MARY ALICE MOORE (Uncle Harry's secretary)

Overview

Since *The Edge of Night* is a cross between a daytime soap and a nighttime detective series, major plotlines change yearly, involving a whole new batch of criminals, and there is a turnover of a good third of the characters. Most of the core characters—people who stay on in the story and are familiar to viewers—came on the show originally via the same yearly crime-story route. More and more on *The Edge of Night*, these characters are providing a story of personal conflicts within the larger framework of a detective drama.

Among the central characters are lawyers Mike Karr and Adam Drake, the two Perry Masons of the town of Monticello, whose chief of police, Bill Marceau, aids them in foiling criminals. Nancy Karr is Mike's wife, and Laurie Ann Lamont is his daughter, wed to lawyer Vic Lamont, an associate of Mike and Adam's. Martha Marceau is Bill Marceau's good-natured, ever-concerned wife. They are the legal guardians of Phoebe Smith. Heiress Liz

illyer Fields and her psychiatrist husband, Dr. Jim
...elds, are also prominent in the story.

he Story

The gentleness and quiet simplicity of SARAH LANE
(Teal Ames) immediately attracted Assistant D.A. MIKE
KARR (originated by John Larkin, later played by Larry
...ugo, and currently by Forrest Compton). His gang-
...sting work was tough. When she became Mrs. Mike
...arr, Sarah's sympathetic, understanding nature always
...lped ease the emotional burdens of his work. With the
...rth of their daughter, LAURIE ANN KARR (played longest
... an adult by Emily Prager, and now by Jeannie Rus-
...n), Mike became the happiest crook-catcher alive. But
...hen Laurie was only two, tragedy, with one of its
...uelest blows, struck the Karrs. Sarah, rushing into the
...reet to shove Laurie Ann away from the wheels of an
...nrushing car, was killed.

Mike thought he would never recover, but he had little
...aurie to think about; so two years later he married a
...ung reporter named NANCY POLLOCK (Ann Flood) in a
...ig, elaborate wedding. Nancy has always been a fine
...other to Laurie and a great help to Mike in his work.

When Mike Karr quit being D.A. to go into law prac-
...ce for himself, his main link with the police department
...as its chief of police, BILL MARCEAU (Carl Frank, and
...ow Mandel Kramer). Widowed Bill Marceau—he had a
...eurotic daughter, JUDY (Joan Harvey), who later left
...onticello after causing everyone much grief—began
...orking with an efficient police secretary, MARTHA (Teri
...eane), and slowly the two fell in love and were married
... few years later. They weren't young enough to have a
...hild of their own, so they adopted fifteen-year-old
...HOEBE SMITH (originated by Heidi Vaughn, and cur-
...ntly played by Johanna Leister). At first Phoebe was a
..."bad seed" type, causing all sorts of trouble for Monticello
...esidents, but she later straightened out.

Tall, attractive lawyer ADAM DRAKE (Donald May) ar-
...ved in town just in time to give Mike Karr some badly

needed help in catching some elusive murderers, and
simultaneously frustrate all the ladies by his perpetu
bachelor's standoffishness. One of those ladies was Nan
Karr's young sister, COOKIE (Fran Sharon), who, unab
to get anywhere with Mike, fell in love with New Yo
public relations man RON CHRISTOPHER (Burt Dougla
and later married him.

Beautiful, wealthy and spoiled NICOLE TRAVIS (Mae
McGuire) arrived in Monticello from Capital City aft
being forced into a divorce by her ex-husband, DWAYN
STEWART (Richard Clarke). Embittered by the loss
Dwayne, Nicole tried to "get even" with the world by a
tempting to seduce happily married Mike Karr, and,
course, she failed. Meanwhile, she opened a dress sho
with her friend, SUSAN FORBES (Bibi Besch), who had he
own sights set for Adam Drake. Adam, however, foun
Nicole much more interesting than Susan Forbes, but-
c'est la vie—Nicole simply found Adam boring.

Nicole's father, BEN TRAVIS (Bill Prince, later Cec Lir
der), was a corrupt senator, who headed a vicious loar
shark ring. Among the victims of Ben Travis' organiza
tion were the husband and daughter of STEPHANI
MARTIN (Alice Hirson), both of whom were killed in a
auto "accident" arranged by the mob. Both Stephani
and her other remaining daughter, Debbie, consequentl
became mentally ill, but in different ways: Debbie becam
autistic, and Stephanie swore a secret vendetta agains
Nicole Travis, because, with twisted logic, Stephani
saw Nicole as just as evil as her father (who was ar
rested and sent to prison). Stephanie began to sen
Nicole poison chocolates, spiders, quotes from Macbet
dealing with blood and murder, and would creep aroun
in man's clothing with a stocking over her face, jus
to try to scare Nicole out of her wits. At the same time
Stephanie was pretending to be Nicole's friend, and eve
got a job in her dress shop. Adam Drake, who by nov
had gained Nicole's affections somewhat, became suspi
cious of Stephanie. Yet Nicole refused to believe that he
friend was trying to do her in.

Adam finally gathered evidence to prove to Nicole tha

Stephanie was the culprit. Before Adam could warn Nicole about it, though, Dwayne Stewart showed up in Monticello, intent on winning her back. In a jealous fury, his new wife, PAMELA STEWART (Irene Dailey), tried to kill Nicole, but instead mistakenly murdered Stephanie Martin! When Nicole walked onto the scene and saw Stephanie lying on the ground with a knife sticking out of her back, she was horrified—and so was Stephanie's daughter, Debbie, who happened to be there. "Take the knife out!" Debbie screamed. Shocked because autistic Debbie Martin had uttered her first words, Nicole didn't stop to think and pulled the knife out of Stephanie's back, of course leaving her fingerprints on it. Nicole was charged and tried for the murder. Adam pled and won her case, causing Nicole to fall more deeply in love with him, but in the end Adam wouldn't give up his bachelorhood to marry her as everyone expected. However, the experience of being tried for murder caused a dramatic personality change in Nicole Travis. Her spoiled, haughty nature had been knocked out of her.

Then began the bizarre saga of the wealthy but tragic Whitney family. Though influential and powerful himself, ex-Senator GORDON WHITNEY (Allan Gifford) always seemed to stand in the shadow of his domineering wife, GERALDINE WHITNEY (Lois Kibbee). They had two sons: one, a hard-working junior senator, COLLIN WHITNEY (Anthony Call), and the other, a devilishly handsome but schizophrenic young man, KEITH WHITNEY (Bruce Martin). Collin Whitney was so dedicated a politician that his wife, TIFFANY WHITNEY (Lucy Martin), felt perpetually neglected and was driven to having affairs. One of her extramarital flings was with Ron Christopher, the husband of Nancy Karr's sister, Cookie. When Cookie found out about the affair, she had a complete breakdown and had to go into a mental institution, of course causing Nancy and Mike much grief. The Karrs' lives were also deeply affected by the Whitneys in another way. Their daughter Laurie became infatuated with a bearded hippie-type by the name of JONAH LOCKWOOD—who was really Keith

Whitney in disguise! A classic psychotic "split personality," the "Jonah" part of him seemed simple and appealing and truly loved Laurie; but the "Keith" part was a vicious multiple-murderer. Adam Drake, growing suspicious of Jonah's true identity and of Keith's shady past, visited a tropical island where Keith had lived and discovered that he had murdered his native-girl wife. Adam then rushed back to Monticello to warn Laurie. But by then the murderous "Keith" personality had already emerged. Keith was about to push Laurie off a high turret, but fortunately, in the last few moments of high melodrama, Keith slipped and fell to his death and Laurie was saved. Much later, both Gordon and his son, Collin Whitney, were killed in a tragic accident. Geraldine and Tiffany, the sole survivors of the ill-fated family, were left to live with their haunted memories. Cookie, recovered from her breakdown, and Ron Christopher were eventually reunited, and they left Monticello.

LIZ HILLYER (Alberta Grant), who first came on the scene as the daughter of wealthy ORIN HILLYER (Lester Rawlins), fell in love with DR. JIM FIELDS (Alan Feinstein), a resident psychiatrist in the home for disturbed children where she was doing volunteer work. After their marriage, her lonely father, Orin, recently injured in a plane crash and confined to a wheelchair, convinced Liz and Jim to move into the family mansion, Claybank, with him. Liz became pregnant, and the conniving ELLY JO JAMISON (Dorothy Lyman), a relative of Orin's dead wife, arrived at Claybank to "help out," but what she really was interested in furthering was the demise of Orin and Liz so that she would get his money. Orin died. But when Elly Jo tried to kill Liz and her unborn child in a speeding automobile, she fell out and was killed herself in a dramatic finale. Liz and Jim then had a beautiful baby boy, the new Hillyer heir.

Liz's former boyfriend, lawyer VIC LAMONT (Ted Tinling) joined the Mike Karr–Adam Drake team and fell in love with Mike's daughter, Laurie Ann Karr. After Vic risked his life by letting himself get sent to prison to ge evidence to break up a Monticello narcotics ring, Laurie Ann and Vic were married in an elaborate wedding. Although the two were in love, their marriage did not go smoothly. Vic, ambitious to do well as a lawyer, worked hard and long hours, and he had little energy to devote to his bride when he got home. Laurie Ann, bored, insisted on taking a job despite Vic's male-chauvinist objections and began working at the New Moon Cafe, owned by ex-convict JOHNNY DALLAS (John La Gioa), who started falling in love with her.

Meanwhile trouble was brewing for Adam Drake and Nicole Travis. Adam made his long-awaited proposal of marriage to Nicole, which infuriated lawyer JAKE BERMAN (played by Ward Costello), Nicole's new employer who had fallen in love with her himself. To get Adam convicted on an attempted murder charge, Jake Bergman arranged for young KEVIN JAMISON (Dick Schoberg) to wound him in the arm and make it look as if Adam had done it. Instead, JOEL GANTRY (Nick Pryor), Jake's stepson posing as a private detective, murdered Jake himself with Adam's gun, saying, when the shot was fired, "This is for mother!"

Just before Adam was to be tried for murder, Adam and Nicole were married in a big ceremony at Mike and Nancy Karr's home. All of their well-wishing friends were present, knowing that at any second Adam would be taken away. Later the prosecution would try to prove in court that Adam married Nicole just to keep her from testifying that Adam had been "insanely jealous of Jake Berman's interest in Nicole," since a wife cannot testify against her husband! Things looked dark indeed for Adam Drake and his new bride until Kevin Jameson, attempting to atone for the part he played (inadvertently) in the murder-indictment of Adam, found Joel Gantry and forced a confession out of him. Adam and Nicole's "honeymoon" of horror was over and at last they were able to settle into a quiet married life.

Vic and Laurie Lamont were not so fortunate. Their marital troubles were worsened when it was revealed at the trial that Laurie had had a brief extramarital affair with her boss, Johnny Dallas. Vic sued Laurie for divorce, and he soon became involved with one of his clients, a wealthy divorcee named KAYE REYNOLDS (Elizabeth Farley). The rejected Laurie took up again with Johnny Dallas, despite the disapproval of her parents, Mike and Nancy, who suspected that, in some way, Johnny was involved with "the mob." They had, in fact, infiltrated Johnny's New Moon Cafe.

The mob was Monticello's huge crime syndicate, which little by little seemed to be invading the lives of not only Nancy and Mike, through their daughter's involvement with Johnny Dallas, but also Bill and Martha Marceau, and Adam and Nicole.

Martha, who had never had a child of her own, became obsessed with the idea of adopting an infant. Eventually she and Bill adopted little JENNIFER, but unknown to them, the child came through a black-market baby-adoption ring—one of the mob's "franchises." With the town's leading law enforcement officer in their vise, the syndicate began to tighten the screws. Bill now had to choose between blackmail payoffs or losing the little girl who was giving Martha the first real happiness she had known in many months. Bill's whole career seemed on the brink of disaster.

Adam was delighted when wealthy Geraldine Whitney—morbidly seeing in Adam the image of her dead son, Collin Whitney—offered to back his campaign if he ran for state senator. Little did he suspect when he accepted Geraldine's generous offer that the mob was already devising means for keeping him out of the election race. The syndicate made arrangements for Ben Travis—now dying of cancer—to be released from prison in the custody of his daughter, Nicole Drake. The plan was for Ben to try to dissuade Adam from running for senator by convincing Nicole that she'd be unhappy as the wife of a politician. "Convincing," however, often meant deceiving and concocting plots to cause marital dissension between his daughter and son-in-law during Adam's campaign. Ben's male nurse, MORLOCK (Jay Gregory), planted by the mob in Adam's house, was to make sure that Ben kept

Adam out of the race. When it looked as if Ben was failing with his task, Morlock arranged for Adam's murder. Adam was devastated when the mob tried to sink the boat that he and Nicole were on during a Caribbean cruise— and Nicole was reported drowned.

Meanwhile, Geraldine Whitney had made of Kevin Jamison a permanent houseguest. Just as Adam reminded her of Collin Whitney, Kevin reminded her of her other dead son, Keith. The woman's unhealthy motivations added to Adam's troubles and portended only unhappiness for Kevin in the long run, despite her seeming generosity.

7. GENERAL HOSPITAL

General Hospital's cast has been almost as loyal to the show as its viewers. A surprising number of the major characters on the serial are still being played by the actors who originated them—and most were originated in the show's first few years.

General Hospital premiered April 1, 1963, with Emily McLaughlin as nurse Jessie Brewer and John Beradino as Dr. Steve Hardy. A few months later, in July, Lucille Wall—radio's memorable heroine on *Portia Faces Life*—moved to California to become the tough-but-with-a-heart-of-gold senior nurse, Lucille March. And in September 1964, Rachel Ames came on as Dr. Hardy's love interest, Audrey March. Peter Hansen, the now deceased Meg Baldwin's long-suffering husband Lee Baldwin, came on in July 1965.

What has caused this incredible longevity of characters and actors on the same series? Cynics explain that Hollywood has only a few daytime serials—and actors, if they want to eat, had better stay on their soaps. The *General Hospital* cast uniformly explains it a different way: their backstage life is so satisfying, with friendships growing as strong among the actors as the relationships among their doctor/nurse characters, that to leave the program would be heartbreaking.

Whatever the reason, actor-and-character longevity on *General Hospital* has certainly been one important factor in this show's great success. Even more so than with other daytime dramas, viewers feel that their relationship with the major actors on this show will continue indefinitely—

and that feeling offers a special security for watchers, as well as for ABC. *Hospital,* the network's first great success in the daytime hours, gave it the shot of confidence it needed to originate other long-lived, high-rated daytime dramas.

On the premiere of *General Hospital,* cast members included:

JOHN BERADINO (Dr. Steve Hardy)
EMILY MCLAUGHLIN (Jessie Brewer, R.N.)
ROY THINNES (Dr. Phil Brewer)
DOUG LAMBERT (Eddie Weeks)
ED PLATT (Dr. Miller)
K. T. STEVENS (Peggy)

Overview

Unlike most daytime dramas, *General Hospital* does not have "tent-pole" characters per se—that is, very stable, righteous people (like Jim and Mary Matthews of *Another World*) who help others with their problems but never seem to have personal conflicts of their own. Nurse Jessie Brewer, everyone's friend and confidante on the seventh floor (Internal Medicine Division) of General Hospital, has always been at the center of a number of stormy love stories. Attractive but not glamorous, she possesses a quiet strength and inner goodness that have caused numerous handsome men to fall in love with her, although it's been Dr. Phil Brewer whom she's always loved. That love, however, has brought her nothing but pain. Dr. Steve Hardy, Director of Internal Medicine at the Hospital, is also a source of strength to all who know him; and just like Jessie Brewer, he's had but one long-standing and tragic love—for nurse Audrey March. Nurse JANE DAWSON (Shelby Hiatt), who is always ready with advice and sympathy for her coworkers, is herself problem-ridden with a weak-willed husband, HOWIE DAWSON (Ray Girardin). The "mother figure," senior nurse LUCILLE MARCH (Lucille Wall) recently became childlike in her romance and marriage to AL WEEKS (Tom Brown).

All the other doctors and nurses whose lives intertwine

work in, or are closely associated with, the Department of Internal Medicine on the seventh floor of General Hospital.

The Story

JESSIE BREWER, R.N. (Emily McLaughlin), met and married DR. PHIL BREWER (originally Roy Thinnes, then Rick Falk, Bob Hogan, and most recently, Martin West), a handsome young intern seven years younger than she, and sacrificed to help him become a practicing cardiologist. Phil returned Jessie's love, but, having a willful, less than noble character, he also sought the excitement of an illicit romance. Jessie found out and sued for divorce. While she awaited the final papers, Phil, drunk and frustrated, assaulted her one night and she became pregnant. The child was born with a serious heart ailment, and cardiologist Phil Brewer was helpless to prevent his own baby's death. The tragedy ended when Phil and Jessie were finally divorced.

Trouble didn't stop there for the two of them. Feeling pity for the dying DR. PRENTICE, Jessie married him, and when he finally died of an overdose of drugs by his own hand, Jessie had to stand trial for his murder. Phil and Jessie were reunited during that terrible episode, ending with her acquittal and their remarriage. But the reunion was short-lived. Phil, now himself accused of murdering Jessie's stepdaughter, ran away and was later reported killed in a plane crash.

Jessie's closest friend and ally in the daily encounters with death, despair, and hope at the hospital was, and has always been, DR. STEVE HARDY (John Beradino). Reserved and wise, Steve, the son of a missionary family and born and raised in China, was devoted to his work at the hospital. But he also needed love. That need was fulfilled, for a while, in his marriage to one-time swinging airline stewardess AUDREY MARCH (Rachel Ames), sister of LUCILLE MARCH (Lucille Wall), the good-hearted senior nurse. Audrey had gotten tired of all the men and all the parties and had wanted children with Steve. When she failed to become pregnant, Audrey mistakenly believed Steve to be sterile and became pregnant through artificial insemination. But the unborn child died in an auto accident when Steve was at the wheel, and their marriage subsequently ended in divorce. Audrey, ever-obsessed with motherhood, went to Vietnam to care for orphans.

With Phil out of the picture, Jessie found temporary happiness in a marriage to psychiatrist DR. PETER TAYLOR (Craig Huebing), a quiet and undemanding type, about as different from Phil Brewer as imaginable. But unwittingly, Jessie was committing bigamy, for Phil was still alive. To be near Jessie, whom he still loved, Phil assumed a new identity—HAROLD WILLIAMSON—and began working as a dishwasher in a restaurant near General Hospital. Afraid to tell Jessie he was still alive, Phil—as Harold—soon was diverted by an involvement with beautiful DIANA MAYNARD (Valerie Starrett) who worked at the restaurant as a waitress. However, when Jessie and Phil finally confronted each other one day when he was brought into the hospital after an auto accident, Jessie was forced to annul her marriage to Dr. Peter Taylor and try to find happiness again with Phil. Diana Maynard faded into the background.

Meanwhile, Audrey March returned from Vietnam to become a nurse at General Hospital and marry DR. TOM BALDWIN (Paul Savior), whom she married just to prove to herself that she didn't love Steve. Audrey realized she didn't love Tom, a self-destructive loser type, and wouldn't have relations with him, but he forced himself on her anyway, and she became pregnant. When Audrey realized that she still loved Steve Hardy, she sued Tom Baldwin for a divorce and left town to have her child. When she returned to the hospital she told everyone that the baby had died, in order to keep Tom from invalidating their divorce. After Audrey and Steve decided to remarry, Audrey had to keep spinning a bigger web of deceit, hurting their relationship. The remarriage between Steve and Audrey never took place because Tom did find out about his son, whom Audrey was secretly hiding at home; and Audrey had to return to him to keep her child.

But of course a loveless marriage can't work; so Tom
threatened himself this time with the loss of his son in ⅎ
divorce action, kidnapped young Tommy—with the helⱷ
of an adult babysitter—and ran away, leaving Audrey iⱵ
a state of shock.

Tom Baldwin's handsome, fortyish attorney brother
LEE BALDWIN (Peter Hansen), had once fallen in love witᚺ
Jessie Brewer, but after losing her to Phil, he married MEᒑ
BALDWIN (originally Pat Breslin, later Elizabeth MacRae)
a nurse with a young son and a problem stepdaughter
BROOKE CLINTON (Indus Arthur). After her mastectom
(breast removal) Meg had a mental breakdown and waⱵ
committed to a sanitarium. Later, she was cured but de
veloped high blood pressure, for which beautiful and inde
pendently single DR. LESLIE WILLIAMS (Denise Alexander
began treating her. Meg finally died, leaving Lee a wid
ower with a stepson, SCOTTY BALDWIN (Don Clarke), tⱷ
care for.

Again, Jessie and Phil Brewer's reunion for the ump
teenth time turned into utter disaster, especially when Phⅈ
found out that Diana Maynard, with whom he had beeⱵ
living before coming back to Jessie, had married Dr. Peteⱺ
Taylor in order to give her unborn son (Phil's) a name
However, after Phil's breakup with Jessie, Diana informeⅆ
Phil that she was now in love with Dr. Taylor. Diana gavⅇ
birth to Phil's child while still married to Peter, who kneᵂ
that it wasn't his. But Phil, who previously thought he waⱾ
permanently impotent, forced himself on Diana in heⱵ
apartment and raped her, which caused another preg
nancy. Diana became frantic with worry that her husbanⅆ
Peter would discover that this child, too, wasn't his.

Jessie, meanwhile, found herself another young "Phil"
by the name of TEDDY HOLMES (John Gabriel). Teddy, a
recklessly handsome newspaperman and an adventurer in
the worst sense of the word, first came to General Hospital as a hepatitis patient. He immediately saw a way to ex-
ploit Jessie and her money and to give him the independence he needed to get to the top of the literary world.

Lonely and vulnerable, unsuspecting Jessie invited Teddy to stay at her home during his recovery.

With the death of Jessie's widowed brother, she became the guardian of his two children, CAROL MURRAY (Anne Wyndham) and KENT MURRAY (Mark Hammil). Teddy, learning that Jessie's niece, Carol, was to come into a large inheritance on her eighteenth birthday—and his eyes now burning with dollar bills—told Carol he was in love with her and not Jessie; and Carol took the bait. When they ran away together Jessie was in shock, especially since she had cosigned a $25,000 loan for Teddy, supposedly for an investment for a motorcycle shop, and was stuck for the money. She turned to Lee Baldwin for help in paying off the burdensome loan.

Audrey Baldwin was also dangling by a string waiting for her husband to bring back their son, whom he kidnapped just before the boy was to have vital heart surgery by DR. JAMES HOBART (James Sikking). While Audrey worried for her son's safety, Dr. Hobart obviously attracted to her, was relieving her anxiety somewhat by his attention.

Diana Taylor soon gave birth to MARTHA, still concealing the fact from husband Peter that Phil Brewer was the real father. With Phil trying to coerce Diana into leaving her husband for him, Peter inevitably discovered the child's parentage. He refused to have further relations with his wife, whom he felt he could no longer trust. Even after Phil realized his pursuit of Diana was hopeless and once again left General Hospital, Peter was not to be appeased. Depressed over his prolonged rejection of her, Diana reluctantly sued for divorce. Ironically, Peter admitted to friends that he was still in love with his wife.

Dr. Leslie Williams was now treating an ulcer patient by the name of FLORENCE GRAY (Anne Collings), the daughter of a wealthy and influential businessman, WYATT CHAMBERLAIN (Ed Platt), and wife of an ex-college professor, GORDON GRAY (Howard Sherman). Florence's ulcers, it turned out, were caused by her feeling that her husband didn't love her. She revealed to psychiatrist Peter Taylor

that she was disturbed over the fact that her husband ha
left her years before to have an affair with one of his stu
dents: he only returned to her when the girl left him. Un
known to Florence, the woman was Dr. Leslie William
herself! When Gordon and Leslie met again after so man
years, he said he would leave his wife and begged her t
marry him. The old feelings were still there. Leslie wa
filled with guilt because of her patient and asked Stev
Hardy to take her off the case. But Steve, feeling Lesli
the best doctor for the woman, refused.

At first it was Audrey Baldwin who needed comforting
later, it was Audrey's suitor, Dr. James Hobart, who
needed support. An automobile accident left his hand
damaged and the possibility existed that he would neve
be able to operate again. He slowly turned to alcoholism
To rescue him, Audrey became his wife—more out of pity
than love. After they married, Audrey was uneasy abou
their love-making. The marriage seemed destined for trou
ble.

Jane and Howie Dawson, who were very much in love
were also having their problems. Howie, not wanting the
responsibility of children, had had a vasectomy withou
Jane's consent. After many arguments over Jane's insis
tence that they adopt a child, Howie moved into a hotel
Later, after being promoted to assistant to the head of
General Hospital, Howie asked to come home again. Jane
took him back, despite her suspicions that he came back
to her only because his new job necessitated the appear
ance of marital stability. The vasectomy, however, was
constantly on Jane's mind, and it was beginning to make
her intimate relations with Howie an ordeal.

Another unhappy husband was DR. HENRY PINKHAM
(Peter Kilman), whose wife, nurse SHARON PINKHAM
(Sharon DeBord), left him temporarily to return to her
home to nurse her ill mother. There she started dating her
old boyfriend and finally wrote to Henry that she had
fallen in love with someone else and was suing for divorce.

Upset, Henry was comforted by another nurse, LINDA COOPER (Linda Cooper, the character's name simply taken from the actress's own name!). It looked as if Linda might soon fill the emptiness in Peter's life.

8. THE GUIDING LIGHT

On the air for more than thirty-seven years, and the only daytime serial to successfully make the transition from radio to television, *The Guiding Light* has had an utterly spellbinding history. Chapter III of this book takes a good look at the show's many years of broadcasting— the old radio story and early plotline on television, as well as the actors, writers, and producers who gave the breath of life to those original situations. Here we shall confine ourselves to more current developments in the plot.

The Story in Recent Years

As always, BERT BAUER (Charita Bauer) was powerless to help when the demon of alcoholism once again struck her family. Her deceased husband BILL BAUER (Ed Bryce), had been an alcoholic, and now she feared that the same thing would happen to her son, ED BAUER (played as an adult by Bob Gentry and now Mart Hulswit), a gifted surgeon practicing at Cedars Hospital in their town of Springfield.

Ed was the protégé of DR. STEPHEN JACKSON (Stefan Schnabel), head of Cedars Hospital. Dr. Jackson, a widower (or so everyone thought), was frightened that his only daughter, LESLIE (Lynne Adams), would marry the wrong man; and so, fond of Ed, the well-meaning Dr. Jackson encouraged them to marry. After a time, Ed and Leslie did marry, but it wasn't a good union. Ed was not emotionally mature enough to be a husband. He began to drink heavily and beat up Leslie in alcoholic rages.

Meanwhile, handsome lawyer MICHAEL BAUER (Don Stewart), Bert and Bill's only other son, returned to Springfield with his small daughter, Hope. Mike's first wife and Hope's mother, JULIE BAUER, had been unbalanced and committed suicide, after which Mike had gone to Bay City to start fresh, only to become involved in a destructive romance with PAT RANDOLPH, the wife of another attorney. Now, back in Springfield, Mike was again falling in love with another married woman. But this time it was far worse for Mike, for the woman was Leslie Bauer—the wife of his brother Ed.

Both Mike and Leslie were torn by guilt feelings and tried to keep their love for each other a secret. But with Ed's drinking problem destroying what little was left of her marriage to him, Leslie was finding it harder and harder to keep Mike out of her life and thoughts.

When Cedars Hospital could no longer keep Ed on staff because of his drinking, he ran off to Tarrywood where he had an affair with an attractive secretary, JANET MASON (Caroline McWilliams). Leslie found out, and finally this persuaded her to openly admit her love for Mike. But Ed's sudden return from Tarrywood and his begging her forgiveness—saying that both the affair with Janet Mason and his drinking were finished—made her break off with Mike and resume her life as Ed's wife. She intended to divorce Ed later on, when he was better rehabilitated.

Mike was distraught when he learned that Leslie was pregnant with Ed's child, and he turned for comfort to CHARLOTTE WARING (originally Victoria Wyndham, and lastly played by Melinda Fee). Circumstance led Mike into misjudging Charlotte, whose character was not at all as fine as it appeared. She had helped Mike gain the acquittal of PEGGY DILLMAN (Fran Meyers), an old friend of the Bauer family who was accused of murdering her husband. Mike, depressed over Leslie's temporary reconciliation with Ed, married Charlotte on the rebound.

Leslie, devastated by Mike's marriage to Charlotte, left Ed for good this time and got a divorce. When their son was born she named him FREDERICK, after Ed and Mike's wonderful, good-hearted grandfather, PAPA BAUER (Theo

Goetz). Leslie, now alone and quite vulnerable without Mike to turn to, met handsome millionaire, STANLEY NORRIS (William Smithers) and allowed herself to become entranced by him and his glittery life-style. Against her father's objections, she became Mrs. Stanley Norris.

At this point the elaborate saga of the Norris family began to unfold. Stanley's insecure and immature daughter, HOLLY NORRIS (Lynn Deerfield), attempted to revive her relationship with her wealthy, power-lusting father, who had been alienated from her and from his son, KEN NORRIS (Roger Newman), a lawyer, and from his (Stanley's) ex-wife, BARBARA NORRIS (Barbara Berjer), who wrote a syndicated cooking column.

Ken fell in love with Janet Mason (Ed Bauer's old affair). She returned his love and—despite her misgivings about their relationship because of his fanatically jealous temperament—finally married him. His sister, Holly met ROGER THORPE (Mike Zaslow), an employee of her rich father, and had an affair with him, convinced that Roger would marry her. But Roger, a lascivious type, only had eyes for Janet Norris, Ken's wife. Meanwhile, Barbara Norris met and fell in love with Roger's father, ADAM THORPE (Robert Milli), as good and decent as his son was irresponsible.

Within a short period of time, all the Norrises were touched by tragedy and mishap. Stanley Norris was murdered in cold blood, and Leslie was accused of the murder when her fingerprints were found on the murder weapon. Holly Norris was struck by a car after running into the street in a daze on seeing her lover, Roger Thorpe, leave the apartment of her sister-in-law, Janet Norris, wiping lipstick off. And, to complete this tragedy of errors, Ken left Janet when his hospitalized sister told him about seeing Roger Thorpe leaving Janet's apartment. However, what really happened was that Roger had forced his way into her apartment and Janet had successfully repelled his advances.

With Leslie accused of murdering her husband, Stanley Norris, none other than Mike Bauer defended her in court. Mike had by now realized what a conniving, hard-hearted schemer Charlotte really was—interested only in being the wife of a prominent attorney rather than in being a real wife and mother. Her treatment of Mike's daughter, Hope, of whom she was jealous, was despicable. After it was proved that Stanley Norris was murdered by his secretary's mother, Leslie was acquitted. In love with Mike more than ever before, Leslie now had to leave town—for the man she loved was married to another woman.

But Mike had already taken Hope and moved away from Charlotte. One night, Charlotte's ex-husband, Flip Malone, once sent to prison with her help, tried to shoot her. But he mistakenly shot Mike, who just happened to be walking into the house. Leslie, hearing that Mike had been seriously wounded, rushed to be with him at the hospital. At long last, they decided to marry.

But Charlotte wouldn't have it. She thought of every scheme she could to keep the court from granting Mike a divorce so that he could marry Leslie—even telling the court the outright lie that she was carrying Mike's child. The court wouldn't buy it and granted the divorce.

But Leslie's father, Dr. Jackson, *did* buy it—or at least the idea that the adverse publicity Charlotte and Mike's divorce was creating would sour a marriage between Mike and his daughter. When Leslie and Mike both told him that they would marry despite his objections, he suffered a heart attack and kept on suffering at each and every suggestion of a marriage between his daughter and her ex-husband's brother. Eventually Mike and Leslie had to call off their wedding once again.

A rejected Charlotte began to seek other hunting grounds for prey—this time it was DR. JOE WERNER (originally Ed Zimmermann, then Anthony Call), Chief of Staff at Cedars Hospital and married to DR. SARAH MCINTYRE (Millette Alexander). Joe, in love with his wife but temporarily fascinated by Charlotte, had a brief, guilt-ridden affair with her. However, the mentally disturbed KIT VESTED (Nancy Addison), a hospital volunteer working with Joe, had already become infatuated with him. When she discovered that Charlotte, whom Kit believed to be her friend and confidante, was seeing Joe on the side, she felt betrayed by Joe *and* Charlotte and so invented a scheme to get even. One night she slipped a number of sleeping pills into Charlotte's drink and then called Joe Werner to come over to the house, saying merely that Charlotte had passed out after a fall. Joe proceeded to treat her simply for a concussion, and, when Charlotte died of an overdose instead, an investigation was held and he was asked to leave his post as Chief of Staff. His peers felt that he should have recognized the symptoms of an overdose of barbiturates. Joe himself felt even more responsible for Charlotte's death than his peers felt he was—because she had once threatened to commit suicide unless he came back to her, and he had totally forgotten her previous threat when he found her unconscious that night. So Joe, a broken man suffering from guilt and self-castigation, ran away and took to the bottle. Kit had her revenge.

While young, overwrought Holly Norris was being treated at Cedars by the handsome Ed Bauer, she began to forget she was betrayed by Roger Thorpe and fell in love with her doctor instead. And Ed—feeling sorry for himself because he was a thirty-year-old man living alone with his mother while his ex-wife Leslie was about to marry Mike, and Janet, with whom he had fallen in love again, was now reconciled with her husband, Ken—began to see a lot of Holly. One night he got drunk and married her; they spent the night in a motel. The next morning Holly claimed, falsely, that they had consummated the marriage, and so he was forced to accept her as his wife. Ed's mother, Bert Bauer, and everyone else in Springfield was shocked to learn of the elopement.

A happier event was the marriage between his brother Mike and Leslie. Her father, Dr. Jackson, finally relented and gave his consent to their marriage, and an elaborate wedding was held in Bert's house. The waiting all these years was finally over for Mike and Leslie.

But the surprises for them weren't over. It suddenly turned out that her father hadn't been a widower at all, as everyone believed. Her mother, MRS. BALLENGER (Carol Teitel) showed up in Springfield, having deserted Dr. Jackson years before when Leslie was just a baby. A cunning woman, Mrs. Ballenger appealed to her daughter Leslie's sympathies and wormed her way into living with Leslie and Mike. She was even able to make a pretense of love for Steve Jackson—who had lived for years with the great hurt she caused him in the past—and she seemed to be winning him over too. However, Mrs. Ballenger, a born troublemaker, failed in her attempt to cause a rift between Mike and Leslie, and ran off with an old lover—but only after telling Leslie that Steve was not her real father! Leslie believed the story and it caused serious problems between her and Steve.

Ken Norris's old neurotic jealousies were revived when he began to suspect Janet of harboring a secret love for Ed Bauer. Ken's suspicions were created by mere circumstances. Ed just happened to be around when Janet suddenly went into labor. He saved the life of her baby and became her constant visitor when she showed signs of severe back troubles. Holly Bauer also began to resent Ed's self-appointment as Janet's Good Samaritan. After Janet's back was operated on, she and Ken again reconciled their differences; but Ken's latent jealousies seemed destined to cause continual problems for the couple. Holly and Ed's marriage, too, seemed headed for trouble. Holly seemed far too immature to be a responsible wife.

The disturbed Kit Vested's fantasies of a love affair with Joe Werner were, strangely, becoming fulfilled when Kit found him sick with pneumonia in a hotel and brought him to her brother's cabin in the woods. While he recuperated, Kit viciously intercepted all the letters he sent to his deeply worried wife, Sarah, to reassure her. When Joe heard from Kit the lie that Sarah was happy and not in the least interested in hearing from him, he had a law-

yer ask her for a divorce on his behalf. Sarah said she'd
only consent if a face-to-face meeting with Joe were set
up. Kit, realizing that all her lies were about to be uncov-
ered, prepared to murder Sarah the same way she had
murdered Charlotte. She failed when Joe found the drugged
Sarah in the nick of time. Then, to take revenge on Joe
for his inevitable reconciliation with Sarah, Kit shot him
and was in turn shot and killed herself while she and the
wounded Joe struggled with the gun. After the ordeal, Joe
recuperated from the bullet wound, and he and Sarah were
at last happy again.

9. HOW TO SURVIVE A MARRIAGE

The trend today is toward highly specialized, contemporary, and extravagantly expensive daytime dramas. *How to Survive a Marriage* is the "most" in all these categories. Aimed primarily at young marrieds (and divorcées) in their early thirties, this most recent continuing daytime serial incorporates many of the new interests of modern Americans: psychiatric therapy and psychiatric jargon, sexual liberation, the merits of the single life vs. the married, how to divorce, feminism, and improving one's life-style through improving one's interpersonal relationships (including interfamilial) by extremely concrete, practical methods. The same strain in American life that gave birth to numerous magazines and books devoted solely to single people—including the newly divorced, separated, or widowed—has also given rise to this serial. It is really the very first daytime drama to suggest that marriage and childbearing are not worth any sacrifice. The people in *How to Survive a Marriage* slowly realize how untrue that dictum is.

The show is the brainchild of NBC's new vice-president in charge of daytime programing, Lin Bolen—in her mid-thirties herself, vital, and, as one observer puts it, "a woman who knows and believes in all the modern jargon concerning sexual liberation. She speaks it like a native."

Ms. Bolen describes *How to Survive A Marriage*: "It's a very contemporary dramatization of a problem which confronts so many couples in today's society—separation and impending divorce. The heroine of the story, Chris Kirby, is a thirty-two-year-old woman who has separated

285

from her husband, Larry, after twelve years of marriage. She finds herself faced with the challenge of making a new life for herself, and she must cope with situations she has never before faced—job hunting, apartment hunting, and serving as both mother and father to her young daughter. Both husband and wife must adjust to their new life-styles as they try to learn to live apart from each other. In the process, they begin the search for new single friends while trying to retain their married friends; they must learn to date again in a singles society which is dramatically different from the one they knew twelve years ago; and they face the possibility of staying together solely for the sake of their child."

How to Survive a Marriage sounds, from that description, as if it will be of interest only to married people on the verge of divorce, or to the already divorced (and that group alone is probably large enough to make the show worth doing), but the show's fascinating first few weeks demonstrated a much broader interest on the part of its creator—Anne Howard Bailey—in all forms of psychsexuality, whether of the happily married, the liberated, the unliberated, the unhappily married, the swingers or the nonswingers. Ethnic sexuality also seemed to be creeping in. In the show, for example, a Jewish couple with a healthy marriage, Fran and David Bachman, have frequent discussions in which their own individual approach to marital sex betrays a certain liberated, modern American-Jewish flavor. As we were going to press, it was beginning to look as if *How to Survive a Marriage* would become not only the most startlingly fresh daytime serial ever presented, but perhaps the most startlingly fresh television show period.

The first episode, on January 7, 1974, ran ninety minutes in order to introduce the major characters and dilemmas all at once to the audience, and the show preempted both *The Doctors* and *Another World*. It was the first time a half-hour daytime drama had ever been introduced in this manner. The first few weeks featured elaborate sets, a large cast (including Rosemary Prinz as the therapist who helps liberate the Kirbys), and a number of outdoor action sequences, accomplished through the use of Metromedia's PCP-90 mobile videotape camera. Many of the actors in the opening cast, which follows, have never before appeared on a daytime serial.

JENNIFER HARMON (Chris Kirby)

MICHAEL LANDRUM (Larry Kirby, her husband)

SUZANNE DAVIDSON (Lori Kirby, their daughter)

ROSEMARY PRINZ (Dr. Julie Franklin, the Kirbys' friend and therapist)

GEORGE WELBES (Dr. Tony DeAngelo, Dr. Julie Franklin's lover)

JOAN COPELAND (Monica Courtland, Lori's three-times married mother, who's in public relations)

PETER BRANDON (Terry Courtland, her husband)

LYNN LOWRY (Sandra Henderson, Larry's "affair")

FRAN BRILL (Fran Bachman, best friend of Chris Kirby)

ALLAN MILLER (David Bachman, her husband)

STEVE ELMORE (Peter Willis, a friend of the Kirbys')

TRICIA O'NEIL (Joan Willis, his wife)

PAUL VINCENT (Dr. Charles Maynard, a colleague of Dr. Julie Franklin)

GEORGE SHANNON (Neal Abbott)

10. LOVE OF LIFE

Love of Life, which holds the rare distinction of being the second oldest afternoon serial drama on television, has undergone drastic thematic and story-line changes since it premiered on September 24, 1951. *Love of Life* started out as a story of conflict between two sisters: one, Vanessa Dale, who believed fully in the old maxim, "To thine own self be true"; and the other, Meg Harper, who thought happiness could be achieved without that belief and at the expense of the happiness of others. In fact, the theme of threatened integrity was so clear cut that the producers had the announcer tell it at the start of each new episode: "VANESSA DALE'S SEARCH FOR HUMAN DIGNITY."

After ten years of pursuing this strong story of the Dale sisters in conflict over personal life-styles, the producers dropped most of the Dale family and their friends and introduced a whole new cast of characters, with the exception of Vanessa and her mother. Along with the original characters, the original theme of a search for human dignity also went out the window. The show now centers around Vanessa and Bruce Sterling and their problem-harassed friends in Rosehill, New York, and no longer dwells on one particular dilemma or philosophy of human conduct. However, on December 18, 1973, Meg was reintroduced into the story, along with the original theme contrasting the lifestyles and moral outlooks of the two sisters.

An interesting observation: the story, which first took place in the town of Barrowsville (Anywhere, U.S.A.), a rural community, was eventually moved to Rosehill, New York—a *real* state—in order to give the characters more of an urban environment. This is really symbolic of what has happened to *Love of Life* itself: it has attempted to become more generalized, urbanized, modernized—to smack less of the old single-theme radio serials. Is the show better off for the complete changeover? Only those viewers who have been watching *Love of Life* for more than ten years can say with any certainty.

When *Love of Life* premiered on CBS in 1951 it had the following cast:

PEGGY MCCAY (Vanessa Dale)
JEAN MCBRIDE (Meg Dale Harper)
DENNIS PARNELL (Beanie Harper)
PAUL POTTER (Charles Harper)
JANE ROSE (Mrs. Sarah Dale)
ED JEROME (Will Dale)

The Story

When the first episodes aired, the unmarried VANESSA DALE (played first by Peggy McCay, then Bonnie Bartlett, and most recently by Audrey Peters) was trying to get her sister, MEG DALE HARPER (Jean McBride, most recently Tudi Wiggins) to be a more concerned mother to her son (and Van's nephew) BEANIE HARPER (Dennis Parnell). Also concerned about Meg's negligent behavior were Meg and Van's parents, SARAH DALE (Jane Rose, now Joanna Roos) and WILL DALE (the late Ed Jerome), and Meg's husband, CHARLES HARPER (Paul Potter), from whom Meg was then in the process of getting a divorce.

Unpredictable Meg was forever getting involved in some kind of unsavory activity, always with the idea of getting something for nothing. Once, for example, she was mixed up with a shady character by the name of MILES PARDEE (Joe Allen, Jr., now deceased), who later ran a gambling casino. But all Meg got from her adventurousness with Pardee was to become accused of murder. Another time Meg was romanced by a flashy, crooked gambling-casino owner named HAL CRAIG (Steven Gethers), who later turned out to be the murderer of his own twin brother.

Meanwhile the single and much more puritanical Van was more cautious about her love life. For a while she went to New York to try to become a cartoonist; there she met and married lawyer PAUL RAVEN (Dick Coogan). After many ups and downs in their marriage—one of the downs was his becoming involved in a shady deal with JACK ANDREWS (Donald Symington), Meg's second husband—Paul was in a plane crash and reportedly killed.

Meg and Van were still at loggerheads over Meg's morals. Eventually Meg—who married a third time to TOM CRAYTHORNE (Lauren Gilbert)—took Beanie and left Rosehill.

After some time had passed, with everyone thinking Paul dead, Van fell in love with a schoolteacher, BRUCE STERLING (Ron Tomme), and married him. After many years it was revealed, to the utter shock of both Van and Bruce, that Paul (now played by Robert Burr), was still alive! When Paul first showed up in Rosehill, he had a bad case of amnesia caused by the air crash, and he called himself Matt Corby. Van was torn between her two husbands—which one did she really love, Paul or Bruce? After much soul-searching she finally divorced Bruce—less over the question of Paul than because she had learned of Bruce's affair with another woman.

She was about to remarry Paul Raven when it was suddenly revealed that as Matt Corby (the name he assumed after the initial amnesia settled in) he had been married and had had a daughter, STACY CORBY (Cindy Grover), with his new wife. But Mrs. Corby had recently been mysteriously murdered. Paul Raven, alias Matt Corby, was unmasked as his wife's murderer and went to prison. Later he was killed while trying to arbitrate a prison riot, à la Attica. So Van, once with two husbands, now wound up without any husband at all. Little Stacy Corby, however, did stay with her.

During all the hurly-burly over Paul Raven's reappearance, Van and Bruce's best friends and confidants were their next-door neighbors CHARLES LAMONT (Jonathan Moore), owner of a bookstore, and his wife, social psy-

hologist DIANA LAMONT (Diane Rousseau). Charles's college-aged son by a previous marriage, BILL PRENTISS
(Gene Bua), a sensitive, musically talented boy, fell in
love with TESS KRAKAUER (Toni Bull Bua), a beautiful but
immature girl who didn't know exactly who she was or
what she wanted. Tess returned his love and married him.

The college romance had been complicated, however,
by another college-aged girl, SALLY BRIDGEMAN (Cathy
Bacon), who was unstable and fell wildly in love with Bill.
When the campus love triangle ended with Bill's marriage
to Tess, Sally went off the deep end and started taking
drugs. Through her addiction she met a college radical,
also on drugs, named JAMIE ROLLINS (Ray Wise), who
suddenly sobered up to the reality of drug danger when
Sally took an overdose and wound up with aphasia (the
loss of the ability to write). For a while Sally listened to
Jamie's warnings and kept away from her previous drug
habit, but when she learned that her mother, tavern owner
CLAIR BRIDGEMAN (Renee Roy), was having an affair with
Jamie's father, RICHARD ROLLINS (Larry Weber), who was
married at the time, she went into a deep depression and
ran away from home.

Tess and Bill were having severe marital troubles,
mainly because of their youth and Tess's total lack of ma-
turity. Wealthy industrialist JOHN RANDOLPH (Byron Sanders) took a shine to Tess and lured her away from Bill by
dangling the bait of travel and luxuries in front of her
eyes, and Tess divorced Bill for the glamour that John
Randolph could offer. Then, thinking she wanted love, not
riches, she divorced John and went back to Bill. Then she
divorced Bill again and went back to John—then finally
back to Bill, this time a much more grown-up, determined
young lady. But the police did not think much of the motives of Tess or Bill when John Randolph was suddenly
found murdered. Tess and Bill were both tried, but it
turned out that Richard Rollins, Jamie's father, was the
killer.

By now, Sally Bridgeman, rehabilitated by a psychiatrist, learned that she was pregnant with Jamie's child.
Jamie wanted to marry Sally, but, afraid that the burden

of a baby would interfere with his plans to become a lawyer, asked her to have an abortion. An angry and now responsible Sally refused both the offer of marriage and the abortion, but later, when their daughter, DEBBIE, was born, she relented and married Jamie.

Shortly after Sally left the drug scene, Stacy Corby, Van's ward, became involved in it. This time it was Sally who was giving Stacy advice to give up drugs, and also to give up the wild bunch of destructive kids she was hanging around with. Eventually she straightened out and was even able to accept the remarriage of Van and Bruce (by now publisher of a Rosehill newspaper, The *Herald*), which she had secretly opposed. At Van and Bruce's big, fancy wedding, the two of them, and Stacy, were the picture of happiness.

Tess and Bill Prentiss had been acquitted of murder only to face yet another horror—Bill developed a serious blood disorder, leukocytemia. Bill, a sensitive soul but never very practical, refused to accept the fact that he was dying and that he needed tedious and continuous medical care. Instead, he turned for help to a certain DR. KREISINGER (Leon B. Stevens), a quack who gave him bizarre treatments. Finally Dr. Kreisinger was exposed, but it was too late for Bill. He expired and his funeral was tearful. Everyone grieved for the wonderful Bill.

At the hospital Bill had been treated by two doctors: DR. JOE CORELLI (now Tony LoBianco, then Michael Glaser), who fell in love with Tess, and DR. DAN PHILLIPS (Drew Snyder) who was dating KATE SWANSON (Sally Stark), a singer working at the Club Victoria, owned by RICK LATIMER (Jerry Lacy). Rick was distraught because his wife, BARBARA LATIMER (Zina Bethune), had deserted him for parts unknown, leaving him with their son, HANK LATIMER (David Carlton Stambaugh). While Joe Corelli was getting nowhere with his plans to marry Tess because she couldn't forget Bill, Dan was more successful with Kate. He married her and she became pregnant. Rick Latimer, who wanted Kate for himself, thought Kate might have been carrying his child, for one night he had

-aped her. A blood test, however, revealed that the baby was really Dan's. Rick, ready to sink to outright deceit to get Kate, remained silent when he discovered that Dan's nurse, CANDY LOWE (Nancy MacKay, now Susan Hubly) —jealous of Kate and in love with Dan herself—had faked the blood test report to show that the baby was Rick's. After Candy gladly showed it to Dan, he divorced Kate.

A new arrival in town was the insidious BOBBY MACKEY (Richard Cox), Sally Bridgeman's cousin. He had met Bill Prentiss when Bill, who was dying, was temporarily residing in North Carolina. After hearing Bill play excerpts of the rock opera he was writing and talk about the fortune Tess had inherited from her previous husband, John Randolph, Bobby developed a scheme to bilk Tess out of her inheritance, which was to be set up as a trust fund for JOHNNY PRENTISS (Trip Randall), Bill and Tess's son. With Bill now dead, Bobby came to town and pretended he had never met Bill; but—because of ESP, he claimed—he was able to hum tunes from the opera and reveal all sorts of facts about Bill's life that he couldn't have known otherwise. He claimed that the same ESP would enable him to finish writing Bill's opera and get it produced with the help of his friend WALTER MORGAN (Richard McKensie). Of course Bobby was in cahoots with Walter Morgan, and the next step was to get Tess to agree to give them her $200,000 to get the rock opera produced. There's no honor among thieves, and Walter shot Bobby Mackey to keep all the loot himself. Tess, who inadvertently left her fingerprints on the murder gun, was tried for Bobby Mackey's murder. Walter Morgan, the murderer, had skipped town with the money.

When Bobby Mackey was murdered, Jamie was just passing his bar exam to become a lawyer. His whole career, he felt, was ruined because it was exposed that he had let his wife, Sally, persuade him to back her up in a lie to the police concerning her cousin Bobby's innocence before being killed. One day, after Sally and Jamie had argued a lot about her responsibility in the affair, she walked out on him, telling him in a note: "I'm taking our baby Debbie and leaving town." Months later, Sally sent Jamie a tragic telegram informing him that Debbie had drowned.

Kate Phillips gave birth to a beautiful little girl, REBECCAH, and was on the verge of marrying the deceitful Rick Latimer to give the baby a father. Then Dan, realizing that he still loved Kate and that he had divorced her out of false pride, begged Kate to come back to him, vowing that he would now accept Rebeccah as his own daughter. Kate was torn between Dan, whom she still loved but could not forgive, and Rick, whom she thought the father of her child. Rebeccah became gravely ill with meningitis, and it was Dan who saved her life. After Rebeccah's recovery, it was learned that she had been deaf from birth. Dan was able to help Kate cope with her daughter's deafness. Then Candy Lowe, who realized she could never make Dan love her, confessed that Dan, not Rick, was Rebeccah's real father, and that Rick had known all along that she had falsified the blood test. After Candy's confession, Kate decided to tell Rick off and remarry Dan. For a while things looked bright for the couple—until Kate, still singing in Rick's Club Victoria and starting to achieve great success with her first record album, became stricken with what seemed to be throat cancer. Although Kate survived her illness, her life was touched with tragedy when Dan and Rebeccah were both killed in a dreadful car accident.

Dr. Joe Corelli was, meanwhile, feverishly working to dig up evidence to show that the woman he loved, Tess Prentiss, was not guilty of the murder of Bobby Mackey. When Tess was finally found guilty of second degree murder after a prolonged court battle, and everyone had lost hope, Joe suddenly brought a man to the court who confessed how he had helped Walter Morgan arrange an alibi for the murder of Bobby Mackey. Tess, at long last, was exonerated but left so shattered by her ordeal that she felt she could never again find the peace of mind she would need to be a good mother to her son Johnny. After re-

jecting Joe Corelli's proposal of marriage, the emotionally
torn Tess left Johnny with Charles and Diana Lamont—
Johnny's grandparents—and went on a "vacation" to Mexico; she later wrote to the Lamonts saying that she didn't
intend to return.

The responsibility of having to care for their grandson
on a permanent basis began to cause a rift between
Charles and Diana, who were never a completely stable
couple anyway. Soon Charles began to react to his increasing marital problems with a classic case of impotence.
Diana talked him into seeking help at the Clinic for Sexual Dysfunction (a sex therapy clinic), run by a DR. TED
CHANDLER (Keith Charles). Charles resisted treatment and
Diana, feeling frustrated, began a brief but painful affair
with the younger Jamie Rollins.

Van's mother Sarah became inconsolable after the
death of her second husband, ALEX CALDWELL (originally
the late Fred Stewart, later Charles White). Soon she herself was stricken with a brain abscess and seemed close to
death. As she bided what she thought were her final hours
and Van sat at her bedside, she asked to see her estranged
daughter, Meg, who had been living outside of Rosehill
for seventeen years. Van and Bruce investigated and
discovered that Meg had last married a man named
Eduoard Aleata. After they wrote her a letter, a young
girl named CAROLINE—or "CAL"—ALEATA (Deborah
Courtney) turned up at Van's doorstep. She said she was
Meg's daughter! It turned out that Cal was a love-starved
girl who, like her stepbrother, Beanie Harper (now grown
up and played by Christopher Reeves), had been much
neglected by her mother and had run away from home. She
had read Van's letter to Meg and thought that she'd find
love in Rosehill with her aunt.

Sarah Caldwell did not die, but instead had a miraculous recovery after brain surgery. She was of course happy
to see Meg, who came to Rosehill looking for her daughter, but sad that Meg's character hadn't really changed.
Meg was still a troublemaker and still attracted to corrupt,
devious men. Her decision to remain in Rosehill, in fact,

was colored by the sudden romantic interest in her on the part of the town's politically corrupt mayor, JEFF HART (Charles Baxter). Mayor Hart's subordinates (and henchmen, really)—PHIL WATERMAN (Michael Fairman) and HOWIE HOWELLS (Ed Crowley)—tried to kill Van and Cal by locking them in a meat freezer at the local meat-packing plant, after they went there to complain about the strange tasting meat Cal had been served at school. There, Cal had inadvertently overheard that the school cafeteria "beef" was really horsemeat. Bruce and Jamie Rollins found Van and Cal before they were frozen to death, and Van pressed charges. But Jeff Hart, fearful that Van and Bruce might uncover the corruption in his local government, persuaded Meg—with whom he was now having an affair—to try to keep her sister quiet. Failing that route, Jeff attempted to have Bruce murdered, to further intimidate Van. Soon after, Meg married the unscrupulous Jeff Hart, and, once again, Van and Meg were at loggerheads over morals.

11. ONE LIFE TO LIVE

Ever since *One Life To Live* started on July 15, 1968, the drama's many devotees have been thrilling to an endless series of stories of ethnic intermarriage and romance—between the Rileys (Irish-Americans), the Siegels (Jews), the Woleks (poor Polish-Americans), and the Lords (wealthy WASPS). The serial's originator, Agnes Nixon, and the ABC daytime television executives who gave the green light to her ideas, are all to be commended for their courage and intelligence in taking the traditional serial—filled with ye olde romance, heartbreak, tears, and laughter—and crossbreeding it with the contemporary realism of our big cities.

"It was certainly a risk," says Mrs. Nixon. "As long as I can remember, the networks and producers have always had a parochial philosophy about daytime serials: 'Stay away from anything controversial.' And I myself, as a writer, became tired of all the put-downs by the critics of the serials who said we never did anything relevant. I asked myself, 'Do we deserve it?'"

When ABC gave Agnes Nixon full control over this, her very first serial creation, she realized a lifelong dream: to break the traditional no-no's and say something socially important with the serial form. "I've always had the feeling that we have the responsibility to educate when we can."

No serial, however, can hold an audience on just a steady diet of education and social importance, and it is to Mrs. Nixon's credit and the credit of the show's current writers (she sold the serial recently to ABC, who are the producers now), that *One Life to Live,* with or without social consciousness, is just one heck of a good story. The actors, with the help of skilled directors, do a superb job of portraying the serial's clearly defined and convincing characters in a continuing story that is consistently well plotted. Consistency is also found in the show's underlying theme—namely that we are all alike inside, despite misunderstandings arising out of differences among various economic, social, and cultural classes.

The show's cast during its first year included:

GILLIAN SPENCER (Victoria Lord)
LYNN BENESCH (Meredith Lord)
ERNEST GRAVES (Victor Lord)
LEE PATTERSON (Joe Riley)
ANTONY PONZINI (Vince Wolek)
JAMES STORM (Larry Wolek)
DORIS BELACK (Anna Wolek)
ALLAN MILLER (Dave Siegel)
PATRICIA ROE (Eileen Siegel)
ROBERT MILLI (Dr. James Craig)
ELLEN HOLLY (Carla "Benari" Gray)
LILLIAN HAYMAN (Sadie Gray)
DONALD MOFFAT (Dr. Marcus Polk)

The Story

Among Llanview's most prominent families were the Lords, headed by VICTOR LORD (Ernest Graves), wealthy owner of Llanview's newspaper, *The Banner.* A widower, Victor had been blessed with two daughters, but he had always really wanted a son to carry on his name. So he did the next best thing. He began to treat his oldest daughter, VICTORIA LORD (originally Gillian Spencer, then Trish Van Devere, and currently Erika Slezak), as if she were the son he never had—dominating her and instilling in her a sense of duty and family pride. She grew up to be a beautiful, strong-minded woman, and a great asset to Victor as *The Banner*'s bright chief business executive. Her only problem: she was torn between a sense of duty and independence, and her need to be near a strong man.

When JOE RILEY (Lee Patterson) first came to work at *The Banner,* Vicky was immediately attracted to this hard-living, hard-drinking, handsome loner with an enormous talent for writing. They were both working as reporters at the time and competed with each other for stories, but it was all in fun. After many spats and quarrels that were really caused by their tremendous attraction to each other, they were married at last. Joe was everything Vicky had ever longed for in a man, and Vicky was happy.

Their idyll ended, however, with the sudden screech of automobile wheels. Joe was in an auto crash and presumed dead, and Vicky's world was shattered. She turned for comfort to a fellow executive at *The Banner*—stable, conservative STEVEN BURKE (Bernard Grant).

Vicky's younger sister, MEREDITH LORD (Lynn Benesch), was frail, suffering from a debilitating blood disorder. Meredith fell in love with DR. LARRY WOLEK (Mike Storm), whose different background—a poor Polish-American from the wrong side of the tracks—caused her father to disapprove of a union between the two. Meredith, he felt, had been brought up properly and could never be happy with someone like Larry. But the couple persisted, and eventually Victor Lord, a sensible man at heart, was forced to accept the situation. After their wedding, Victor, knowing that Larry didn't have much money, generously asked them to live with them at Llanfair, the family estate; but Larry wanted to remain independent of his domineering father-in-law, so he and Meredith instead moved into a garage apartment on the estate.

Later, Meredith became pregnant—against doctors' orders—and she had twins. Only one, DANNY WOLEK, lived. The death of one of her babies, and the warning of doctors that she should never risk childbirth again, sent her into a postpartum depression. At this point it was thought wise for her to undergo psychiatric counseling—and she was successfully treated by none other than DR. JOYCE BROTHERS (playing herself).

Larry's family, the Woleks, were an amazing example of the American Dream come true—no matter how poor you are, with enough hard work you can become as successful as the next man. There were three Wolek children, ANNA WOLEK (Doris Belack), the oldest; VINCE WOLEK (Antony Ponzini); and Larry. At first, all the Wolek children, whose parents were dead, lived together and gave one another a helping hand. Vince, tough on the outside but with a heart as big as California is long, owned the B & W Trucking Company and put his younger brother, Larry, through medical school. Anna, a wise and wonderful woman, would do anything to help her brothers out of difficulty.

As a youngster, Anna Wolek was in love with Joe Riley, and in that regard she was no different than any other woman with whom Joe later came into contact. Later Anna entered Llanview society (just like Larry) when she married DR. JAMES CRAIG (Nat Polen), a widower with a daughter, CATHY CRAIG (Amy Levitt, and now Dorrie Kavanaugh). Cathy had a severe adjustment problem as an adolescent and was by that time becoming a drug addict. With the help of her parents, and therapy sessions at Odyssey House—a real rehabilitation center for young addicts—Cathy kicked her habit. (These scenes were actually taped on location at the real Odyssey House in New York City.)

Joe Riley's sister, EILEEN (Alice Hirson), fell in love with DAVE SIEGEL (Allan Miller), a lawyer. The fact that he was Jewish and she was a gentile posed certain problems for the two, which they worked out in time. They had a son, TIMMY SIEGEL, and a daughter, JULIE SIEGEL (Lee Warrick), an over-sensitive girl who became involved in an unhappy affair with callous JACK DAWSON (Jack Ryland). When Julie tried to kill herself over the affair, she was saved in the nick of time by handsome DR. MARK TOLAND (Tom Lee Jones). Soon Mark and Julie became romantically involved and were wed.

Julie loved Mark but was still haunted by her guilt feelings over her affair with Jack Dawson. Julie's subconscious began working overtime, making her frigid with Mark. When her lack of sexual responsiveness began to wreak havoc on her marriage, Julie started seeing DR. POLK (Norman Rose), a psychiatrist, to help her overcome her sexual coldness toward Mark. However, running into Jack Dawson every day at *The Banner,* where Julie began working as a secretary, wasn't helping her problem.

At first, her mother, Eileen, didn't think that seeing a psychiatrist was any way for Julie to solve the problem. But then, Eileen Siegel hadn't been thinking clearly since her husband, Dave Siegel, had died of a heart attack. An "up" person at heart, but always on the verge of hysteria when faced with the distress of those around her, Eileen was finding herself overcome by emotional burdens, among them the loss of her husband and the problem of her daughter, Julie. Slowly, gradually, she began taking tranquilizers and pep pills to get through her day. It wasn't long before she was addicted to them.

Making Eileen's emotional state worse was the sudden death of her close friend, Meredith Wolek. Always fragile, suffering from a blood disorder, Meredith was assaulted by burglars who had broken into her house. After they knocked her down, she suffered a cerebral hemmorhage and later died in the hospital. Her husband, Larry Wolek, was shocked and devastated. He and his son, Danny, moved in with his sister, Anna, and her family.

Joe Riley was not dead, after all. A lovable waitress in a Llanview restaurant, WANDA WEBB (Marylin Chris), had fallen in love with him, although neither she nor he knew at the time that he was Joe Riley. After the auto crash Joe suffered amnesia and had been wandering ever since. Suddenly Joe collapsed in her restaurant with an aneurysm, and when he was rushed to the hospital, everyone in Llanview—including Vicky, now Mrs. Steven Burke—knew that Joe Riley was alive.

Vicky didn't know which husband she wanted—Joe Riley or Steven Burke. In a way, she loved them both, but each for different reasons. Her decision was to stay with Steven—even though she still loved Joe, perhaps even more than Steven. Joe's presence at *The Banner,* where he was once again working as its top writer, was sending Steven Burke into a panic over the fate of his marriage and was making Vicky more and more uncomfortable about the decision she had made. Finally, Vicky asked Steven for a divorce to marry Joe.

Joe Riley was now Vince Wolek's roommate. Vince, who gave up the trucking business to become a policeman, was falling head-over-heels in love with Wanda Webb. Vince, the perpetual bachelor, and Wanda became engaged.

Vince's black friend and fellow police officer was LT. ED HALL (Al Freeman, Jr.), who at long last was marrying CARLA GRAY (Ellen Holly), Dr. Jim Craig's pleasant secretary. A light-skinned black, Carla for a long time would not admit to being black and even rejected her mother, SADIE GRAY (Lillian Hayman), in order to pass for white. Carla now accepted her blackness and was proud of it. Carla and her new husband were making plans to adopt JOSHUA WEST (Laurence Fishburne), a rebellious boy who was involved with youth gangs. For Carla, the adoption of a young black "alter ego" was yet another way of reconciling herself to her own painful past.

A newcomer to the Llanview Hospital was DR. DORIAN CRAMER (Nancy Pinkerton). She lived alone with her sister, MELINDA (Patricia Pearcy), who was crippled in a riding accident. Attractive Dorian, who had become an overprotective, domineering keeper of her sister, had made up her mind because of her duty to her sister she could never marry. However, when she met Dr. Mark Toland—who was growing increasingly sexually frustrated because of Julie's frigidity—she couldn't help herself and began an affair with him. The couple met secretly in an apartment they had rented, but Dorian's already troubled sister, Melinda, found out about the apartment and the secret meetings and became even more deeply disturbed. Like Julie, she began to see Dr. Polk, the psychiatrist, but could not bring herself to tell him what was really bothering her. Even newly widowed Larry Wolek, who had become her only real friend in Llanview, was unable to find out Melinda's dark secret.

There was yet another dark secret in Llanview. While Joe Riley desperately hoped that Steven Burke would grant Vicky her divorce so that she might once again become Mrs. Joe Riley, he was unaware that Cathy Craig was pregnant with his child. Before Vicky had given Joe reason to hope that they might be reconciled, he had gone to New York with Cathy to try to help her write her first novel, not realizing that Cathy was deeply attracted to him. Lonely and distraught, Joe allowed Cathy to seduce him into a brief affair. Now, with Vicky again in Joe's life, Cathy decided that she would suffer the terrible burden of her pregnancy alone.

12. SEARCH FOR TOMORROW

Search for Tomorrow—whose backstage history ha been chronicled in Chapter X—is still television's answe to radio's old *Romance of Helen Trent, Stella Dallas, M. Perkins,* and others. In its twenty-three years on television *Search* has seldom strayed from the theme of heroic self sacrifice, best demonstrated by the exemplary life of. it heroine, Joanne Tate—played since the serial started o September 3, 1951, by Mary Stuart. Through the years Jo has given help and moral support to her many friends neighbors, and relatives. But it has always been Patti, Jo' only child, who has been the center of Jo's life.

Patti was played longest by Lynn Loring, who origi nated the role when both she and the character she playe were six years old. After ten years, Lynn was replaced b Abagail Kellogg in 1962. Over the next few years, Pa Harty, Trish Van Devere, and Gretchen Walther playe the part; then came Melissa Murphy in 1966, and Me linda Plank in 1967. Two years later Leigh Lassen took over the role and has had it ever since.

In the current story-line, Jo is happily married to Dr. Tony Vincente, and Patti is married to Dr. Len Whiting Jo has a sister, Eunice, who is married to Doug Martin, lawyer. Scott Phillips, his son, is also a lawyer and is mar ried to Kathy, another lawyer. Jo's best friend, Stu Bergman, is a recent widower. He and his son, Tommy live with his daughter, Janet, and her wealthy psychiatris husband, Dr. Wade Collins.

The Story From The Beginning

At first Henderson's JOANNE GARDNER BARRON (Mary Stuart) wondered how she could keep on going after the sudden death of her husband, KEITH BARRON (Johnny Sylvester), in an automobile accident. But she could not permit herself to wallow in grief, for she had a six-year-old daughter, PATTI BARRON (Lynn Loring), to look after. Courageously, the young widow took a job in Henderson Hospital as the only means she had of supporting her little girl.

Of course, she could have turned to Keith's wealthy parents for help, but Joanne knew that MRS. IRENE BARRON (Bess Johnson) wanted to take Patti now that her son was dead. Her conviction that she and her husband, VICTOR BARRON (Cliff Hall), could provide for Patti better than Joanne grew into an obsession. She tried everything she could to win Patti's affections. Later, after Irene tried but failed to gain custody of her granddaughter, she lost her mind and kidnapped the little girl. The law finally made Irene return Patti to Jo, but not before she took flight with the child and led everyone on a long chase through the woods.

Jo's best friends were STU and MARGE BERGMAN (Larry Haines and the late Melba Rae), a good-natured, sympathetic couple who always knew how to laugh, even when the going got rough. Marge and Stu spent many hours in Jo's kitchen, having coffee with her and talking over personal problems. Priceless friends, they were always around when Jo needed them. They had two young children: JANET BERGMAN and JIMMY BERGMAN. (Janet was played as a child by Ellen Spencer, then by Sandy Robinson until 1961, and by Fran Sharon until 1966; then Marian Hailey continued the role, and Millee Taggart, the current Janet, took over in 1971). Jimmy Bergman, however, was really the son of Stu's dead brother, and he was later taken by the brother's second wife and her new husband. Janet Bergman became Patti's best friend. Later, Marge and Stu had another child, TOMMY BERGMAN (played originally by Peter Broderick, and currently by Ray Bellaran).

After Patti was once again safe at home, Joanne was free to turn her attentions to ARTHUR TATE (played from 1955 to 1966 by Terry O'Sullivan, except for six months in 1956 when Karl Weber took the role). Joanne had met Arthur at Henderson Hospital, where she was working and the two soon fell in love. Arthur's lawyer and friend NATHAN WALSH (George Petrie), also found himself deeply attracted to Joanne, but he put aside his feelings when he realized that Jo was in love with Arthur. Later, Walsh became one of Jo's most trusted allies who would offer his support—whether as a friend or as a lawyer—when a crisis arose.

Jo and Arthur, in ten years of courtship and marriage, certainly endured enough crises to last any other couple a lifetime. On the day of their wedding, for instance, a mysterious woman named HAZEL (Mary Patton) came to Joanne Barron's Motor Haven—which Jo and Arthur had bought and were running as a business well before they were married—and claimed to be his wife. In truth, this woman looked exactly like the woman Arthur had once been married to, but he thought she had been killed in a fire many years before. Of course, this wasn't Hazel Tate at all, but rather her twin sister, Sue. She had been hired by the local syndicate to upset Jo and Arthur's marriage plans so that it could gain control of the Motor Haven to use as a front for a dope-peddling operation.

Jo and Arthur were stymied by Hazel's apparent return from the dead, until Nathan Walsh discovered her true identity. To trick her into admitting the truth, Arthur, Jo, and Nathan faked a fire and hired an actress to impersonate the dead twin sister, Hazel. Distraught on "seeing" her dead sister, Hazel rushed out into the woods, where she was later found murdered. The D.A. immediately accused Joanne of the murder, and she might have stood trial if Arthur and Nathan hadn't discovered the identity of the real killer. In the process of finding the killer, however, Arthur was shot in the heart and nearly killed. For a long time, he was an invalid. Depressed that in his condition he couldn't be a real husband to Joanne, he refused to go ahead with their original wedding plans.

Meanwhile, the syndicate wasn't about to give up their efforts to gain control of the Motor Haven. Their next ploy was to send to Henderson a woman named ROSE PEABODY (Lee Grant, Constance Ford, and finally Nita Talbot), who was supposed to gain the friendship of Arthur and Jo and then figure out some way of ruining Jo's reputation so that she would have to sell the Motor Haven, paving the way for the mob to take it over.

To win Jo and Arthur's friendship, Rose pretended to need help with her mute brother, WILBUR (Don Knotts). Soon she and Wilbur were staying at the Motor Haven as guests of the people she was supposed to destroy. One day Rose poisoned the soup that Jo would be serving to a group of workers, but at the last moment she couldn't go through with the horrible deed and poured the soup down the drain. Eventually, psychiatry proved that Wilbur became mute as a reaction to the shock he'd endured many years before after almost killing their foster father who had tried to sexually molest Rose. When Wilbur was made to realize why he became mute, he suddenly found his voice again. The happy brother and sister then left Henderson.

Joanne finally convinced Arthur to marry her despite the complications caused by the gunshot wound. But shortly after the wedding fate had more trouble in store for them. Joanne became pregnant about the same time that Arthur was having severe financial troubles with the Motor Haven. He was forced to turn for help to his wealthy aunt, CORNELIA SIMMONS (Doris Dalton). She moved to Henderson and, like Jo's previous in-laws, became Jo's enemy. Aunt Cornelia would have liked nothing better than a permanent separation between Jo and Arthur.

Duncan Eric, Jo and Arthur's infant son, was born, but was killed when he ran into the street and was struck by a car. As if things weren't bad enough, Jo's mother died and her father, FRANK GARDNER (Eric Dressler and later Harry Holcombe) and newly widowed sister, EUNICE (played first by Marion Brash, and currently by Ann Williams),

arrived in Henderson to further complicate the lives of th
Tates.

Eunice—an unstable, selfish woman—was attracted t
Arthur, who returned her attentions. They had an affai
Later, Eunice suffered pangs of guilt and told Joanne th
whole story. Taking this turn of events as an opportunity t
separate Jo and Arthur forever, Aunt Cornelia offere
Arthur a job in Puerto Rico, where she had most of he
business interests. Torn by shame because of his unfaithful
ness to Jo, Arthur accepted the offer.

Arthur was away for a while. He returned to Hender
son some months later to find some startling occurrences
Aunt Cornelia was found murdered. Eunice and her nev
boyfriend, REX TWINING (Larry Hugo), were tried and
found guilty. But the real murderer was found by ALLISON
SIMMONS (Ann Pearson)—Aunt Cornelia's daughter—t
be her mother's housekeeper, HARRIET BAXTER (Viki Vi
ola). After they were exonerated, Eunice and Rex wer
married and moved to Puerto Rico. Jo's father, Franl
Gardner—who had been managing the Motor Haven i
Arthur's absence—also found happiness by marrying Stu
Bergman's widowed mother, thus making Jo and Stu sor
of relatives.

Best friends Janet Bergman and Patti Tate, by now ir
their late teens, were having adult problems of their own.

Janet fell in love with BUDD GARDNER (George Maharis)
Jo's nephew. They were married and had a son, Chuck
When Budd left home and was later reported to have diec
in an accident, Janet allowed herself to fall in love witl
DR. DAN WALTON (Martin Brooks, Phillip Abbott, and fi
nally Ron Hussman). Janet married Dan, not realizing
that Budd was still alive. While she and Dan were still or
their honeymoon, Budd returned to Henderson. Out of hi
mind with jealousy and anger on hearing of the marriage
Budd tried to force his way into the Bergman's home
Later, in a chase with the police, he was injured in a ca
crash and would have died had Dan Walton not gotten te
him in time to save his life. Janet, realizing that she wa

ill legally Budd's wife and that he needed her, returned
o him, even though she now loved Dan.

Budd, still the unstable type, soon got into a fight with
tu Bergman, who came to his apartment and pleaded
vith Budd to give up Janet. Stu was knocked unconscious.
Vhen he finally came around, Budd's body was lying
ead on the street many floors below the apartment. It
ooked as if Stu, in a rage, had thrown him out the win-
ow, so the police booked him for homicide. Later Joanne
iscovered a drainpipe that Budd had pulled from the side
f the building in his attempt to flee the apartment with-
ut being seen, having thought he had killed Stu. With
his evidence it was shown that Budd had died an acci-
lental death and Stu was cleared. Janet and Dan Walton
hen left Henderson so that Dan could practice medicine
n Chicago.

Patti, deeply disturbed by the troubles that her mother
nd stepfather were having, decided to go off to Arizona
o live with her grandparents. While there, she fell in love
vith an older man. When she discovered that he was al-
eady married, Patti was destroyed and returned to Hen-
lerson, deeply depressed. Once back at the Motor Haven,
he soon became romantically involved with young,
levil-may-care TED ASHTON. One night when Ted was
lriving wildly, he and Patti were in a serious accident,
nd Patti wound up in a wheelchair. Doctors could find
iothing medically wrong with her, however. Her paralysis
vas caused by all the emotional traumas she had suffered.
Psychiatrists tried to help her, but in vain. One day Ted
Ashton, as wild and unpredictable as ever, broke into the
Motor Haven and threatened Jo with a gun. Seeing her
nother endangered was the shock Patti needed. She got
ut of her wheelchair and walked over to Ted Ashton in
n attempt to save Jo's life. Distracted by Patti, Ted
lropped the gun; Jo retrieved it and called the police.
Patti's immediate problems were over.

Alcoholism suddenly began to plague Henderson. Ar-
hur, distraught over the past and over his inability to
:ope with Tate Enterprises, began to drink. So did FRED

METCALF (Tom Carlin, Donald Madden, and David O'Brien), Allison's newspaperman husband. Arthur's drinking and his frustrations at work combined to cause a serious heart attack, which caused him to become bedridden. Fred Metcalf, an emotionally insecure man who was intimidated by both his wife's money and by his domineering mother, AGNES METCALF (Katherine Meskill), drank his way to a divorce, despite the help he was receiving from Alcoholics Anonymous.

While Arthur was recuperating from his heart attack, a man by the name of PETER RAND came to Henderson from Puerto Rico and began harassing Joanne. Rand claimed that Arthur had fathered the illegitimate son of his daughter, Marian, when he was living in Puerto Rico. Naturally Jo was shocked, but she dared not imperil Arthur's health by confronting him with the accusation. Eventually, under pressure from Peter Rand, Jo had to tell Arthur, who promptly denied everything, though he admitted to himself the possibility that he might have had relations with Marian while he was drunk and then forgotten the whole thing. After Marian arrived in Henderson, a parental suit was filed against Arthur Tate. But as the case was about to go to trial, Marian confessed to Fred Metcalf, to whom she was attracted, that a man named Hal Hansen, who lived in Puerto Rico, was the real father of her son. When the truth came out, Peter Rand dropped all charges against Arthur.

By then Marian was in love with Fred Metcalf, and he thought he also loved her. However, he knew he really still loved Allison, his ex-wife, and it turned out that she also still loved him. Fearful of making a mistake, Fred suddenly left Henderson for Chicago just before he was supposed to marry Marian. But JOHN AUSTIN (Frank Scofield), a good friend to both Fred and Allison, realized they still loved each other and brought Fred back to Henderson. So, despite all of their past difficulties, Fred and Allison were finally able to find happiness together.

Patti continued to follow a self-destructive life pattern. She fell in love with an older married doctor named EV-

ERETTE MOORE (Martin Brooks) and, after spending one
night with him, became pregnant. When Everette's wife
committed suicide, Patti would probably have married
him—but only for the sake of her child. She had begun to
realize that her attraction to this older man was neurotic.
However, she was in an automobile accident and suffered
a miscarriage, so she no longer had to consider marriage
to Everette. The accident also made it impossible for her
to bear another child.

Arthur Tate dropped dead of a heart attack. Joanne
was once again a heartbroken widow, so DR. BOB ROGERS
(Carl Low), a doctor at Henderson Hospital, offered her a
job as a librarian there to help take her mind off Arthur's
death. Dr. Rogers soon became a close, dear friend of
Joanne's.

The story of SAM REYNOLDS (originally Bob Mandan
from 1964 to 1969, briefly George Gaynes, and finally the
late Roy Shuman) now began to interweave into the fabric
of the life of Joanne, her family, and her friends. Sam
Reynolds was a wealthy business tycoon who, before Arthur Tate's death, had started acquiring some of Henderson's business firms. One of the businesses he had taken
over was Tate Enterprises, much against Arthur's will.
This caused Arthur much grief and may have contributed
to his untimely death. Jo therefore held a grudge against
Sam Reynolds, who was nonetheless irresistibly attracted to her. At that point, Sam would have given anything
to undo the pain he had caused her and Arthur in the
past.

After a year, Jo was still resisting Sam's many attempts
at proving his good faith. One day, Sam suffered a near
fatal stab wound in the liver while saving Patti from a
knife-wielding dope fiend at the hospital. Then Jo's whole
attitude toward Sam changed from bitterness to love. All
along she had been secretly fond of Sam, a dynamic and
handsome man of basically good character.

After Sam and Jo finally declared their love for each
other, Sam sadly admitted that he wasn't free to marry because of his scheming wife, ANDREA WHITING REYNOLDS

(Virginia Gilmore, later Joan Copeland), refused to give him a divorce even though they had been separated for many years. So ruthless was Andrea that she had turned their son against him—going so far as to convince the boy to use *her* maiden name. Everyone in Henderson knew the young man as LEN WHITING (Dino Narizzano, currently Jeff Pomerantz), never suspecting he was Sam Reynolds's son.

While Jo and Sam were trying to straighten out their own lives, their children were becoming romantically involved. They had met at Henderson Hospital, where Patti worked as a nurse and Len was a bright young intern. Finally a wedding date was set. Jo and Sam and all their friends were deliriously happy about the forthcoming marriage—happy, that is, until Andrea Whiting arrived on the scene and schemed to break up the relationship.

Sam, in a last desperate effort to break free in order to marry Jo, threatened to sue Andrea for divorce on grounds of deception. Andrea decided to kill him rather than let him marry Jo. She already knew that Sam, as a result of his stab wound, had developed a rare blood condition and was dependent upon an experimental drug, Hemadol, which becomes lethal for the patient if he imbibes liquor ("Hemadol" is a fictitious drug). Inviting him over for a drink, Andrea intended to slip him a cocktail comprised of liquor and a few drops of the drug; but the drinks got mixed up and Andrea almost died. Sam was then tried for attempted murder. The trial was spectacular and suspenseful, climaxed by Andrea's breaking down on the witness stand and admitting that she had had an affair with another man, LARRY CARTER (Hal Linden), while married to Sam and that she was to blame for the death of Len's twin brother. One night, instead of taking care of the child at home, Andrea had been out cavorting with Carter; a fire had started and killed the little boy. After the trial, Andrea received psychiatric help and voluntarily granted Sam Reynolds the divorce he had been seeking for years.

Although the court's decision was good for Jo and Sam,
who could now marry, Andrea's revelation was shocking
for Len. Not a strong-willed or emotionally secure man
anyway (in fact, quite like Patti), Len went into a depression, giving up medicine and his plans to marry Patti. He
began doing manual labor in a factory, trying to forget the
horrors he had heard during the trial. After a while, however, he met a girl named GRACE BOULTON (Jill Clay-
burgh), who was dying of a brain tumor. Inspired once
again to renew his Hippocratic oath, Len saved the girl's
life with an impromptu piece of surgery—he removed a
fishbone from her throat with a bent spoon! He also had
an affair with her. The relationship was temporary, however, and soon afterward Grace left for California.

At the hospital where Len was again practicing, he and
Patti continually ran into each other. After saving the life
of a sick child together, they declared their love again and
were married. Meanwhile, Grace Boulton, who never told
Len that she was pregnant with his child, died in childbirth in California. Patti, who had suffered another miscarriage even though she had been warned by her doctors
never to attempt another pregnancy, became depressed
over losing her baby and began taking addictive pep pills.
She almost wrecked her marriage to Len. Finally, Len
and Jo talked her into adopting a child—Grace and Len's
child, whom Jo had been taking care of secretly. Neither
Len nor Jo told Patti that she would be adopting Len's
own son, who was eventually named Chris.

Jo's sister, Eunice, who returned from Puerto Rico after
the dissolution of her marriage to Rex Twining, now married lawyer DOUG MARTIN (Ken Harvey) and became
much more stable and unselfish. When Eunice married
Doug, neither she nor he knew that the young Vietnam
veteran named SCOTT PHILLIPS (Peter Simon) was in reality Doug's illegitimate son. After Scott's parentage was revealed, father and son eventually became close. Meanwhile, Scott, by now a law student, made the mistake of
marrying a girl named LAURI (Kelly Wood), who was as
materialistic as Scott was idealistic. After the mistake be-

came apparent to both, they divorced. Lauri took her illegitimate son, ERIC LESHINSKY (Chris Lowe), and became
involved with an unhappily married professor, JIM
(Michael Shannon). Meanwhile, Scott fell in love with a
fellow law student, pretty KATHY PARKER (Courtney Sherman). A born careerist, Kathy desperately wanted to become a successful lawyer. When she learned that she was
pregnant with Scott's child, she secretly had an abortion.
Later, she and Scott were married.

Just before Sam and Jo were to be married, Sam was
asked to go to Africa on a special assignment for the
United Nations. He was gone longer than Jo expected.
While Sam was absent, Jo was the victim of a catastrophic
automobile accident—caused by her sudden realization,
while driving, that Len was the father of Grace Boulton's
baby. DR. TONY VINCENTE (Anthony George) was responsible for saving her life at Henderson Hospital, but at
the time he could do nothing about the total blindness that
the injury had caused. While all of Jo's family and friends
worried over her condition, news came that Sam Reynolds
had died in Africa. Fearful of what the shock would do to
her in her present state, Jo's family held back the news. In
time, however, she found out and suffered a dreadful depression.

Jo's blindness was finally cured, after which she sought
to take her mind off Sam by working as a volunteer at the
Rec House, a center for underprivileged teen-agers, where
Dr. Tony Vincente also worked. At first mutual troubles
made Jo and Tony seek solace in each other's company.
In Tony's case, he was unhappily married to MARCY (Jeannie Carson), a spoiled rich girl who used a pretense of
being crippled and confined to a wheelchair to hold on to
him. In Jo's case, first it was the news of Sam's death,
then her worry when she learned that Patti had been taking drugs as a result of the emotional shock of losing her
baby. So Jo and Tony had good reason to turn to each
other. And their relationship did not remain platonic.

But Tony was already married, and both of them felt
torn by guilt. Then one night, Tony came home to find his

housekeeper on the floor, unconscious. The housekeeper had seen Marcy standing. To try to keep Tony from learning that she wasn't crippled at all but merely pretending, Marcy had tried to kill the housekeeper. Now, finally knowing the truth, Tony divorced his wife. It looked as if he and Jo could find happiness together.

They weren't in each other's arms very long before Sam Reynolds turned up—on the eve of their engagement party. The report that her fiancé had been killed in Africa had been erroneous, to say the least! Jo, of course, loved Tony Vincente, but she couldn't just brush Sam off, especially when he told her that during his long absence from Henderson he had dreamed night and day of being in her arms. Now he wanted to marry her. Prodded by his need for her, as well as by the urging of her family and friends, Jo broke off with Tony and made plans to marry Sam. But then a strange thing happened. Her blindness returned—this time, a psychosomatic symptom of her inner conflict over her love for Tony vs. her desire not to hurt Sam. Jo began seeing a psychiatrist to cure her blindness.

When their wedding day arrived, Jo was still blind, but Sam—who knew that she loved another man and whose African ordeal had caused severe, near-psychotic personality changes in him—insisted that they not put off their marriage. At the office of the justice of the peace, Jo suddenly changed her mind and begged Sam to take her home. He pretended to agree, but then kidnapped her and drove her to her brother-in-law's deserted cabin in the woods, calling her family in Henderson to assure them that the wedding had gone as planned and that they were now on their honeymoon. Jo, confused and stunned, was even more confused when a strange young couple, calling themselves simply "George and Sarah," broke into the cabin and shot Sam with a gun they found. Later, after they had fled, Jo, still blind, was found in a state of hysteria hovering over Sam's body.

Back in Henderson, the family was growing concerned because they hadn't heard from the honeymooners. Tracing Sam's phone call to Doug's cabin, Tony Vincente and Doug Martin, Jo's brother-in-law, went up to the cabin

and found Sam dead and Jo unconscious after a bad fal
in the woods. When she awoke her sight had miraculously
returned. Later, with the help of Jo's camera, which had a
picture of "George" (taken jokingly by "Sarah" before
Sam's murder), and with her memory of his voice, the
murderers were apprehended. Tony and Jo were finally
able to walk down the aisle together.

Her mother now out of danger, Patti should have been
happy with her husband, Len, and little Chris. But EMILY
HUNTER (Louise Shaffer, then Kathryn Walker), the
neurotic daughter of Dr. Bob Rogers, started trying to
break up Len and Patti's marriage because of her attraction
to Len and a mysterious vendetta against Patti. By using
her pretended friendship for both of them, she was able to
cause them to separate. Then Emily began arranging
"mistakes" for Patti to commit in her role as a mother
hoping to cause Patti to lose custody of Chris. Finally
after Len and Patti were reunited, realizing they still loved
each other, Emily was still desperate to hurt them. She
kidnapped Chris. The house Emily took Chris to was set
afire, but Len and Patti, with the help of Andrea, arrived
just in time to save Chris. Emily, the Iago-like villainess,
was consumed in the flames. After things had quieted
down, Patti and her husband decided to start fresh in
Seattle. Andrea, too, became happier because, by saving
Chris's life, she had settled the score with her own guilt
for having caused the death of Len's twin brother years
before. Soon after the departure of Len and Patti, she too
left town.

Henderson suddenly became a sad place the day that
Marge Bergman died. She and her husband, Stu Bergman,
had been Joanne's best friends for more than twenty-three
years.

Deeply affected by the untimely death of his wife, Stu
tried to pick up the pieces of his life and become, if he
could, both father and mother to his son, Tommy. Eventually he hired a housekeeper, ELLIE HARPER (Billie Lou
Watt), a close friend and cousin of Scott Phillips. Stu and

Ellie began growing fond of each other. Obviously she wouldn't mind becoming Stu's next wife.

It was really a double tragedy that struck Stu's family. Not only did his wife pass away, but Dan Walton, the husband of his daughter Janet, also died, leaving her to care for their teen-aged daughter, LIZA (Kathy Beller), and their son, GARY (Tommy Norden). After a respectful period of mourning, Janet took up her life again, and she fell in love with the handsome, wealthy psychiatrist, DR. WADE COLLINS (John Cunningham). Liza, however, considered the relationship between her mother and Wade a betrayal of her dead father's memory. After bringing her mother to the point of nearly breaking off with Wade, Liza finally accepted him as her stepfather after he skillfully forced her to examine her own motives in objecting to her mother's remarriage. Janet soon after became Mrs. Wade Collins. Later, Stu sold his house and moved with his son, Tommy, into Janet and Wade's huge house.

Handsome, well-to-do lawyer JOHN WYATT (Val Dufour) came to Henderson, indirectly causing all sorts of trouble. The very first thing John did was to buy a failing magazine, previously owned by CARL DEVLIN (David Ford), who built the magazine up from scratch. Carl, remaining on the magazine as a figurehead boss, deeply resented the young executive, FRANK ROSS (Andrew Jarkowsky), whom John Wyatt had placed in the office. Carl also didn't much care for the new freelance writer John hired—Jo's own sister, Eunice Martin. Eunice's husband, Doug Martin, wasn't keen on the idea of her new job, either, for it threatened his identity as breadwinner and he feared that John Wyatt was more interested in his wife's affections than in her writing. After many arguments over Eunice's new job, Doug moved to a hotel.

At the same time, Carl Devlin was becoming rather psychotic with suspicion that the younger executive, Frank Ross, would push him out of his job. In the heat of fury, Carl killed Frank. He immediately became paranoid and thought Eunice had seen him commit the murder. When she announced that she was going up to John

Wyatt's cabin to think through her problems with Doug Carl Devlin, now completely insane, decided to follow her up there and do away with her as well.

Meanwhile, Jo convinced Eunice's husband, Doug, that there was nothing between Eunice and John and that he should return to his wife. She told him that Eunice had gone to the cabin, so Doug decided that he'd follow her up there too. Both men, Carl Devlin and Doug Martin, were beaten to their destination by MARION (Pat Stanley)—John Wyatt's secretary—who got to Eunice first in order to warn her not to become involved with John Wyatt. Marion said that she loved him and wanted him for herself. Eunice, who never wanted John in the first place, agreed and said she was going back to Doug; she would let Marion wait for John at the cabin.

The whole episode reached a climax when Carl, mistaking Marion for Eunice, murdered Marion, and later, when Doug Martin arrived, tried to kill him too. Doug didn't die, but the shot he received paralyzed him from the waist down. Carl Devlin was caught and pronounced criminally insane.

Kathy Phillips, being "liberated," was still adamant about not having children and was furious when her husband, Scott, agreed to adopt Eric Leshinsky when his mother, Lauri, was killed in an auto accident on the first night of her honeymoon. Since everyone considered Kathy practically a villainess for not wanting Eric, she acquiesced and made a reluctant attempt to be his mother. Meanwhile, she was working as a lawyer in John Wyatt's office. John's plans to win Eunice Martin's love were aided, ironically, by Doug Martin himself. Realizing that he would be confined to a wheelchair indefinitely, Doug, not wanting to transform his wife into the guardian of an invalid, forced Eunice to divorce him. Eunice loved Doug, but she reluctantly started giving in to John Wyatt's attentions. When Doug suddenly left Henderson, giving Eunice the impression that he would never return, Eunice accepted John Wyatt's proposal of marriage—more out of fear of being alone at this low point in her life than out of true love for the wealthy lawyer.

All of Jo's attention was suddenly turned to Patti's new problem. Although the doctors had warned her that she would be risking her life if she ever attempted to have another child, Patti was overjoyed that she had become pregnant again and decided that she would not have her pregnancy aborted. Despite Len's objections to her decision, she found a doctor outside of Seattle—a DR. WALTER OSMOND (Byron Sanders)—who specialized in delicate pregnancies. Patti, far from Len and her family, was, as usual, becoming emotionally unstable. So she was brought to Henderson Hospital, with nurse STEPHANIE WILKINS (Marie Cheatham) assigned to look after her as Dr. Osmond's representative there. However, Stephanie Wilkins was an old flame of Tony Vincente's and it looked as if she might begin to pose a serious threat to Jo's happiness.

13. THE SECRET STORM

To the shock and dismay of millions of devoted viewers, *The Secret Storm* was canceled on February 8, 1974. CBS evidently felt that viewers weren't devoted enough, for the show's ratings were ailing for several years before the final blow. The serial, which began February 1, 1954, lasted exactly twenty years and one week. Although the reasons for the serial's poor ratings were sundry, essentially *The Secret Storm* had been mismanaged and made less appealing to viewers ever since its production was transferred from American Home Products to CBS itself in 1969. Perhaps the worst move the producers made was the decimation of the Ames family, whose problems had captured the imagination of the audience (and therefore got the ratings) for many years. By the time of cancellation, only Amy Ames was left of all the original tormented clan members. Successful serials, such as *As the World Turns,* simply do not get rid of major long-standing characters so cavalierly.

Oddly enough, the ratings of *The Secret Storm* were on the rise shortly after CBS announced the impending termination. Much of the credit for the improved ratings must go to the wonderful story line revolving around the romantic problems of Amy Ames, and to Jada Rowland's exquisite and moving portrayal of an orphan girl searching for happiness in a world filled with cruel, cunning people. Like Rosemary Prinz, Jada's achievement in the world of the serials has been exceptional.

When the show premiered in 1954, it had the following cast:

PETER HOBBS (Peter Ames)
JADA ROWLAND (Amy Ames)
JEAN MOWRY (Susan Ames)
WARREN BERLINGER (Jerry Ames)
HAILA STODDARD (Aunt Pauline)
MARJORIE GATESON (Grace Tyrell)

)verview

Today *The Secret Storm,* as a mere title, could just as asily fit one of the other fourteen daytime dramas. It had)ecome just a *general* show name, little more than a work-ng title. But when *The Secret Storm* began under producer toy Winsor's expert packaging, the words in the title were especially appropriate. The show really did offer viewers a ecret storm of desperate inner conflicts and hidden emo-ions—all outwardly manifested by the continuing melo-lrama of the family of Peter Ames.

And *melodrama* is a good word to use. Certainly, on Winsor's program there were more shocking deaths, sud-len bouts with insanity, illnesses, and embattled love ffairs and relationships than on any other daytime drama. toy Winsor envisioned the Ames family as having a never-seen but electric-fast pulse—rather reminiscent of he bizarre families one sees in modern horror films. Viewers became accustomed to and interested in the nerve-wracked Ameses from the very first episodes. The serial, for example, opened with a death so devastating in ts effect that it left the Ameses in a state of confused be-vilderment, which not even tears could express. Hence: heir secret storm.

The concept was a stroke of absolute genius, proved by he fact that six years after the show started, few daytime levotees dared spend a weekday without peeking in to ind out what new tragedies and entanglements were be-alling the long-suffering, fascinating Ameses.

Unfortunately, the show shed its basic theme. For a few years, however—before *The Secret Storm*'s cancellation—)roducer Joe Manetta did improve the story by making orays into controversial areas: a priest gave up his frock to marry; Amy had herself artificially inseminated; there was talk of impotency—and the like. Nevertheless, the show had ceased to be faithful to its title.

The Story

The sudden screech of automobile wheels set off a tragic chain of events in Woodbridge. ELLEN AMES was taken to the hospital in critical condition, and she died two days later. Her whole family—husband PETER AMES (Peter Hobbs, then Cec Linder, and later Ward Costello), eighteen-year-old daughter SUSAN AMES (Jean Mowry, most recently Judy Lewis), sixteen-year-old son JERRY AMES (Warren Berlinger), and nine-year-old daughter AMY AMES (Jada Rowland)—was devastated by the loss of Ellen. But it was Peter and Jerry who took the blow hardest. Young Jerry, overcome by anger and grief, made an attempt on the life of the man who caused the automobile accident that took his mother's life. Jerry was sent to a reform school. Peter himself began to show symptoms of temporary insanity. Everyone in the Ames family felt they had to look after him.

Susan Ames became the new mother figure, and as time went on she became bossy, domineering, and fearful of any changes in the status of the family—especially concerning any possible remarriage plans of her handsome father. Ellen Ames's, sister, always known to the Ames family as AUNT PAULINE (Haila Stoddard), also resented any plans Peter might make toward remarriage—unless, of course, *she* was to be part of his new marriage plans. Pauline had always been jealous of her sister and in love with Peter herself.

So when Peter became interested in the housekeeper, Susan did everything she possibly could to prevent a marriage from happening. And Aunt Pauline did even more. She turned up with BRUCE EDWARDS, who claimed to be the housekeeper's long-lost husband, and this naturally threw a monkey wrench into the romance of Peter and the housekeeper. Later, when Bruce Edwards was killed in a gangland shootout—Aunt Pauline had by now gotten involved with some shady criminals—Peter fell in love with beautiful MYRA (June Graham) and married her. But Myra's and Peter's families mixed like oil and water, and the marriage was short-lived.

By the time Amy was a high-school senior, she fell in love with rebellious KIP RYSDALE, son of the wealthy AR-THUR RYSDALE, who had recently become Aunt Pauline's new husband. Amy's family and Kip's family both wanted them to get married, but it turned out that Kip was already involved with the daughter of his high-school Spanish teacher. After Kip accidently killed the girl and had to go to prison, Amy said she forgave Kip for being unfaithful and would wait for him. But while Kip was in prison she wasn't able to keep her promise. Now a freshman at Woodbridge College, she was attracted to her history professor, PAUL BRITTON (Nick Coster). Paul returned her interest but was already married, although unhappily, to TERRY BRITTON. He said he was staying married to Terry, only for the sake of their son. Amy then threw caution to the wind and had an affair with Paul, resulting in her pregnancy. When Paul found out, he offered to divorce his wife and marry Amy, but she refused him, saying she wanted a marriage based on love, not on forced circumstances. Amy swore she'd raise her baby alone.

But that wasn't to happen. Kip Rysdale came out of prison, learned of Amy's condition and asked her to marry him, if only to give her baby a name. Amy, now fearful of going it alone, accepted the proposal. After becoming Mrs. Rysdale, however, her true love for Paul Britton came back to haunt her, and she couldn't have relations with her new husband. Finally, after Paul returned to Woodbridge newly divorced from his wife, he convinced Amy not to continue with her sham marriage but to marry him instead. Amy divorced Kip and she, Paul, and their little daughter, LISA BRITTON (Judy Safran), became a happy family.

Amy's father, Peter Ames, also found happiness with his third wife, VALERIE (Lori March), who had a grown daughter, JANET HILL, now divorced. Peter's marriage was happy—until tragedy again struck the family and Peter died of a heart attack while away on a business trip. The family's presence in Woodbridge was slowly diminishing. Jerry Ames had gone off to Paris to live with his wife, HOPE, a talented painter.

For a long time Amy Ames's best friends were KEN STEVENS (Joel Crothers) and JILL STEVENS (Barbara Rodell), brother and sister. Ken fell in love with LAURI (Stephanie Braxton)—a weak, piano-playing, neurotic type—and he later married her. Jill married HUGH CLAYBORNE (Peter MacLean). Jill and Hugh Clayborne, and Jill's brother (and Lauri's husband), Ken Stevens, were all killed in a plane crash. Instead of tearing her apart, the horrible incident brought about a drastic change in Lauri's character. She was suddenly a new person: stronger, better able to cope with life. She gladly took up the job of becoming the mother of CLAY STEVENS (Jamie Grover), Ken's son from a previous marriage.

Amy Britton was now to encounter her sharp-fanged arch rival, BELLE CLEMENTS (Marla Adams). Beautiful Belle had had a daughter who died in a boating accident in which Amy was also involved. Belle blamed Amy for her illegitimate daughter's purely accidental death, and she swore that she'd get even with Amy by stealing the affections of Amy's husband, Paul Britton. Since Paul had once been married to a blonde who looked just like Belle, he was easy bait for this scheming viper; and Amy was no match. After Paul divorced Amy, Belle soon became Mrs. Paul Britton.

Amy was literally dumb-struck by what Belle had done to her. People worried about her when she began to have hallucinations, to play with dolls and pearls and the like. Amy had to see a psychiatrist, a DR. IAN NORTHCOTE (Alexander Scourbi), who cured her and eventually married Amy's stepmother, Valerie Ames.

Attention was also being paid to the problems of Amy's sister, Susan, whose husband, ALAN DUNBAR (Jim Vicary), was listed as killed in action. Susan then remarried newspaperman FRANK CARVER (Larry Luckinbill). To her shock, it turned out that Alan Dunbar had not been killed at all but had been a P.O.W. and was now back in Woodbridge, warped by his war experiences. Alan got involved in a drug ring headed by DAN KINCAID (Bernard Barrow), who was running for governor of the state at the same time. Belle Britton, who by now was becoming bored as the wife of a professor, met Dan and suddenly saw herself as a wealthy governor's wife. And Dan was spellbound by Belle. Belle divorced Paul Britton and married the man she thought would turn out to be the state's next governor.

Amy now became the daughter-in-law of her hated rival, Belle. Amy had fallen in love with Dan Kincaid's lawyer son, KEVIN KINCAID (David Ackroyd), and married him. But despite their new, forced kinship, Amy and Belle continued to be arch enemies.

All Belle's plans to become First Lady collapsed when Dan's underworld connections were revealed and he was sent to prison. But Amy and her sister, Susan, were also drawn into the wreckage when Amy's husband, Kevin, was shot by one of his father's mafia friends and paralyzed from the waist down. Susan was accused of murdering her first husband, Alan Dunbar—who was actually killed in a general shootout with Dan's drug-dealing friends. During the trial Susan's husband, Frank Carver, stood by her. After her acquittal, they left Woodbridge.

Before her husband, Kevin, had become a paraplegic and impotent as a result of the shooting, Amy Kincaid mistakenly thought that she was pregnant and had told Kevin the good news. Now, with Kevin in a wheelchair and not wanting to depress him further with the news that she wasn't carrying his child after all, Amy asked her friend, DR. BRIAN NEEVES (Jeff Pomerantz, later Keith Charles), to arrange for her to be artificially inseminated. He agreed but, because he fell in love with her himself, he supplied his own semen. It was to have been a secret; but nurse MARTHA ANN ASHLEY (Audre Johnston), a cohort of Belle's, told Belle, and she in turn threatened to tell Kevin unless Amy forked over enough cash. Amy came up with the blackmail money, which Belle needed to keep her dashing new lover, ROBERT LANDERS (Dan Hamilton), happily supplied with racing cars, his great passion. Little did Belle suspect that Robert Landers was really Dan's illegitimate son. The only person who had that information was Belle's one-time ward, JOANNA MORRISON (Ellen Barber), who was in love with Robert herself. It was becoming apparent that Dan and Robert, now enemies because of Belle's affair with Robert, would soon have to confront the reality of their father-son kinship.

Kevin, however, already found out that Amy had been artificially inseminated with Dr. Brian Neeves's own sperm. He forced Amy, who was just having her baby, whom she called Danielle, to move out of the house and in with her stepmother, Valerie, and her husband, Ian. Kevin, only thinking of Amy's happiness, made her divorce him and began trying to encourage her to marry Brian, the real father of the child. Amy—confused and unhappy—began having an affair with Brian.

After the death of her husband, Ken, Lauri Stevens couldn't believe it but she was falling in love with a priest. His name was Father MARK REDDIN (David Gale), who, despite his devotion to the Church, found himself drawn to Lauri. The two fought their feelings for a while, but finally Mark decided he wanted to be Lauri's husband (and the father of her stepson, Clay Stevens) more than he wanted to stay in the priesthood. Mark and Lauri were wed and seemed happy—yet Mark couldn't seem to forget his vows to the Church. He seemed to be torn between two worlds, though Lauri at first had no suspicion that he wasn't completely satisfied with their life together. Subconsciously, however, she may have felt it, for soon after when they moved into an old house, Lauri became obsessed with the idea that it was haunted by its previous owner, Georgina—and even thought that *she* was Georgina's reincarnation. Her delusions were fed by a young handyman, Eric, who was psychotic and had murdered Georgina and her children years before.

Mark, too, was showing signs of deep emotional stress;

he was becoming an alcoholic, rather than face his true desire to return to the Church. One terrible night, all of Lauri's and Mark's problems were resolved by a scourge of death and violence. Mark had gone to pay a call to his old church superior, MONSIGNOR QUINN (Sidney Walker) and found him on his deathbed; Mark, despite himself, was miraculously transformed into a priest again as he prayed all night for the soul of the dying prelate. Meanwhile, young Eric, the psychopath, had broken into Lauri's bedroom and was about to strangle her when he suddenly saw the image of his past victim, Georgina, coming at him through a big standing mirror. He jumped through it and was gashed to death by the broken glass. The horrible violence of that night brought Lauri to her senses; she was able to see that Mark really belonged with the Church. Mark was also transformed by his own ordeal and knew that he had to return to the frock. As they parted, they vowed that they would never forget what they had given one another.

Robert Landers finally discovered that he was the son of Dan Kincaid and the brother of Kevin Kincaid. He then went to Italy in pursuit of an important racing Grand Prix so that his new prestige would make Dan feel proud of him. Before the race, however, he stopped off in London to give moral support to his brother, Kevin, who was secretly undergoing a dangerous operation to restore his legs. Although Kevin, who now knew of Robert's real parentage, had previously rejected him, Robert was determined to prove that he could be both a good brother and a good son.

Meanwhile, Amy, who found out why Kevin went to London so abruptly, refused to marry Brian. She realized that she would never be able to love anyone else but Kevin. Brian was hurt, but not destroyed. One afternoon, shortly after turning Brian down, Amy came home to find Kevin sitting in her living room. He begged her not to come to him; he got up on his own feet and walked toward her. He almost made it, but fell on the floor a few feet away. Amy, deliriously happy at Kevin's return, fell down with him, hugging and kissing his face. Moments later, Valerie came in, followed by Amy's daughter, Lisa. They, too, fell to the floor, forming a circle of happiness. Kevin, Amy, Lisa, and little Danielle would never again be parted.

At Kevin's mysterious urging, Dan Kincaid paid a visit to Robert Landers and his pregnant bride-to-be, Joanna Morrison. When Robert told his one-time rival, Dan, that he was his illegitimate son, Dan was stunned. He looked into his son's eyes, and they both realized that they had many years to make up for. Dan was now blessed with two sons, and although his wife Belle was leaving him and Woodbridge to take up a glamorous singing career, it was apparent that he was destined to remain a most happy man indeed.

14. SOMERSET

What is now called *Somerset* was originally called *Another World—Somerset* and was offered to viewers (at its debut on March 30, 1970) as the second half of a full hour of the older serial. The situation was fascinating indeed. Characters from the parent and the new infant show would go back and forth on the two programs (traveling from Bay City to Somerset, and vice versa) just to remind viewers that what they were seeing was in reality the *same* program, merely expanded. But it soon became obvious that the only real connection between the two serials was Procter and Gamble's desire to get *Another World* habitués also to acquire the *Somerset* habit, and as quickly as possible.

The two Procter and Gamble shows couldn't have been more different in format. *Another World* had always been the product of Irna Phillips's interest in turbulent interpersonal relationships: romance, marriage, the effect of tragedies on people's lives. *Somerset,* on the other hand, was clearly an attempt on the part of the soap company to duplicate its success with the chiller-type, crime-fighting theme on its other serial, CBS's *The Edge of Night.* P & G even hired *Edge*'s head writer, Henry Slesar, to put his inimitable "mystery" imprint on their new series. Whole story-lines began revolving around the slow poisoning of a beautiful young girl by her psychotically jealous rival, the mysterious murder of a millionaire, and the infiltration of a crime syndicate into one of the town's biggest companies. The serial was, in effect, another *Edge of Night* who-done-it.

329

Unfortunately, the Nielson Ratings never showed that the viewers were ready for this second mystery-serial, despite its excellent acting and well-contrived stories. At the time that this book was going to press, Proctor and Gamble had let Henry Slesar go and had replaced him with Roy Winsor, who gained fame as the originator and first producer of *Love of Life*, *The Secret Storm*, and *Search for Tomorrow*. Presumably Mr. Winsor would employ his special talents to transform *Somerset* into a more traditional soap opera. "I'm writing *Somerset* as simply a story about a town," he said.

When *Somerset* premiered, various actors playing characters on *Another World* would show up at random in the neighboring town, and quickly leave again. Some of them, however, such as Jordan Charney, Ann Wedgeworth, and Carol Roux, remained in Somerset. The show's original regular cast members were:

JORDAN CHARNEY (Sam Lucas)
ANN WEDGEWORTH (Lahoma Lucas)
CAROL ROUX (Missy Matthews)
ED KEMMER (Ben Grant)
GEORGANN JOHNSON (Ellen Grant)
PHIL STERLING (Rafe Carter)
RALPH CLANTON (Jasper Delaney)
LEN GOCHMAN (Peter Delaney)
MARIE WALLACE (India Delaney)
DOROTHY STINNETTE (Laura Cooper)
WALTER MATTHEWS (Gerald Davis)
PAUL SPARER (Rex Cooper)
WYNNE MILLER (Jessica Buchanan)
ALICE HIRSON (Marsha Davis)
GARY SANDY (Randy Buchanan)
DOUG CHAPIN (Tony Cooper)
SUSAN MacDONALD (Jill Grant)

The Story

When SAM LUCAS (Jordan Charney) got the idea to move his law practice from Bay City to Somerset, where he'd have a better chance of prospering, his wife LAHOMA

LUCAS (Ann Wedgeworth) went along with the idea. Once moved to Somerset, the Lucases had a daughter, Susannah. Sam took on a law partner, BEN GRANT (Ed Kemmer), who, along with his wife, ELLEN GRANT (Georgann Johnson) and their late-teenaged twins, JILL and DAVID GRANT (Susan MacDonald and Ron Martin), became best friends of the Lucases. Jill and David had grown up with TONY COOPER (Ernest Thompson, now Barry Jenner), whose parents were Delaney Brands' heiress LAURA COOPER (Dorothy Stinnette) and REX COOPER (Paul Sparer), a production manager employed by her father.

The rich and powerful Delaney family owned Delaney Brands, or rather it was JASPER DELANEY (Ralph Clanton) who really *owned* the company, having bought it and built it up when his children were infants. His way with them all had always been domineering. There were three Delaney heirs: PETER (Len Gochman), the youngest son, ROBERT (Nick Coster), and Laura Cooper.

Robert forever dreamed of being an architect but was instead cowed by his father into working for the company. Robert had also allowed himself to become entangled in a dreadful marriage with INDIA DELANEY (Marie Wallace), a shrewd, sardonic woman who had always gotten everything she wanted. One thing she wanted, for example, was to find a husband she could castrate and demean, and Robert filled the bill perfectly. However, when Robert met JESSICA BUCHANAN (Wynne Miller)—a nightclub entertainer at The Riverboat—and fell in love with her, he decided to end his sick marriage. But Jasper forbade a divorce—the scandal, he said, would hurt the family name.

By now, Laura Cooper had been brooding for months over some mysterious, shattering secret. Neither her concerned husband, Rex, nor her son, Tony, could understand why she was slowly becoming an alcoholic. Laura's secret was that Tony was really her illegitimate son by HARRY WILSON, a man with a shady past.

Laura would have been even more upset if she had known that Harry Wilson had been living in Somerset for some months now under the alias of Ike Harding, part owner of Somerset's nightclub-casino, The Riverboat. Jasper Delaney, learning of Harry's presence in Somerset and of his fathering Laura's son, threatened to expose Harry Wilson and his closetful of skeletons. Soon afterward, Jasper was found murdered; Harry had to keep him quiet.

The murder of her father and her suddenly discovering that Harry Wilson was living in Somerset were too much for Laura to bear; and her husband, Rex, fearful of her emotional state, committed her to a sanitarium. Meanwhile, their son, Tony, fell in love with PAMELA MATTHEWS and ran away with her. It was eventually revealed that Jasper Delaney's murderer was Harry Wilson, alias Ike Harding. Harry was later killed in a general shootout at the nightclub.

With things more or less back to normal in *Somerset*, two things still had to be settled: what would happen to Delaney Brands now that Jasper was dead; and who would pretty young Jill Grant turn to for love now that Tony Cooper, whom she had always secretly loved, had gone away with another girl? Jill's problems were more easily solved than were Delaney Brands'. MITCH FARMER (Dick Schoberg)—a disturbed boy with a possibly criminal past—was the one Jill gave her heart to, despite the objections of her parents, Ben and Ellen. At the time of her marriage to Mitch and her departure from Somerset with him, they were still fearful for her.

As for Delaney Brands, Jasper's death—and the departure from Somerset of his sons, Robert (who divorced India), and Peter—made it advisable for the company to be sold. It went to a shrewd, cool operator by the name of LEO KURTZ (Gene Fanning). Unknown to anyone, Leo had bought the company with the funds of a big statewide crime syndicate that had been looking for just this sort of opening to get a foothold in Somerset.

Leo Kurtz's brother, DR. STANLEY KURTZ (Michael Lipton), was the doctor most sought by Somerset's wealthy families—including the Moores. At first EMILY MOORE

(Lois Kibbee) didn't know what to make of the strange, debilitating illness of her attractive young daughter, AN-DREA MOORE (Harriet Hall), nor did Dr. Kurtz, whom she consulted. Andrea's mysterious illness made her listless brother, DANA MOORE (Chris Pennock)—an unsuccessful writer—even more despondent than usual. Eventually it turned out that Andrea was being fed small amounts of poison in her food by the psychotic ZOE CANNEL (Lois Smith), who wanted to kill Andrea because she imagined that her husband, JULIAN CANNEL (Joel Crothers), was in love with her. In reality, Julian's boredom with Zoe was caused by the fact that he had only married her for her money, which she obtained by dint of the marriage of her father, PHILIP MATSON (Frank Schofield), to wealthy Emily Moore.

When Dr. Kurtz had cleverly figured out a way to stop the poisoning—not knowing that the poisoner was Zoe— Zoe was equally clever in figuring out another plan to do away with Andrea. She invited Andrea and her boyfriend, David Grant, to her cabin. After David left to drive to town for some groceries, she grabbed a gun and was just about to shoot Andrea when Zoe's brother, CARTER MAT-SON (Jay Gregory), came storming into the cabin. He said he learned about Zoe's treacherous scheme from a crooked manager at Delaney Brands, in whom Zoe had confided. In a panic, Zoe shot and killed her own brother. Soon after, she was committed to an asylum. Shocked by the tragic event, Emily left Somerset with her husband and son, leaving behind Julian and Andrea, who was now out of danger.

Julian, with the help of Andrea's money, bought Somerset's failing newspaper. Once a gifted pianist, Julian again contributed something to the world when he began to use his newspaper to expose the crime syndicate that had recently bought into Delaney Brands.

For a while, however, no one suspected that Leo Kurtz was just acting as a front for the mob. Sam Lucas, who had left his law practice to become president of Delaney Brands, was warned by Ben Grant, the company's lawyer, that there was foul play in the way the company was treating its employees and customers. Only then did Sam begin to suspect that something was wrong. For one, Rex Cooper, the production manager, had been paralyzed from the waist down in an obviously set-up "accident." But Sam was reluctant to believe that Leo Kurtz was involved with criminals, and only through his wife's prodding did Sam start listening to Ben Grant.

So the syndicate now decided that it would somehow have to make Sam and Lahoma break up. They planted irresistibly attractive CHRYSTAL AMES (Diahn Williams) as Sam's secretary, giving her specific instructions to lure him away from Lahoma.

Meanwhile, the ruthless plant manager of Delaney Brands, VIRGIL PARIS (Marc Alaimo), raped Tony Cooper's new wife, GINGER KURTZ (Fawne Harriman)—Leo Kurtz's own daughter. Hearing about it, Leo went wild and got the mob to bump Virgil off. After Ginger was accused of Virgil's murder, Leo tried to confess to it; but the police already knew that the killing was the syndicate's work and that Leo was its front man. For the latter, he went to prison.

Sam decided to send his wife Lahoma and their daughter Susannah out of town for safety and had already made up his mind that he would leave Somerset and join them when all of this was over. Later, however, Lahoma found she could not forgive Sam his unfaithfulness and so he went on alone to Bay City to join his sister, Ada.

Julian Cannel continued to try to run the mob out of town with exposé articles in his paper. Chrystal, now reformed, and Julian were slowly falling in love. The happiness of the new lovers, however, was tragically short-lived. Zoe Cannel—Julian's dangerously psychotic wife—had escaped from the insane asylum where she had been sent after attempting to murder Andrea Moore and killing her own brother. Still seeking to kill any woman who dared take Julian away from her, Zoe took a bus to Somerset and, after many weeks of hiding from the police, proceeded to Chrystal Ames's apartment with a gun. Chrystal was in the process of cooking dinner for Julian when Zoe barged in and murdered her in cold blood! Julian was shattered at his loss, and Zoe was returned to her mental institution, after once again leaving a tragic memento of her deranged mind.

Meanwhile, Ellen Grant's retired father, JUDGE BRAD BISHOP (Allan Gifford), came from Boston to live with his daughter and son-in-law. Ellen and Ben were quite happy to have the judge stay with them—but not at all happy with his new fiancée, attractive EVE LAWRENCE (Bibi Besch), a woman at least thirty years his junior. Although Eve sincerely was in love with Judge Bishop, Ellen and Ben's assumption that it was his material wealth that attracted her was understandable, as was the hostility of Eve's daughter, HEATHER (Audrey Landers), toward such a union. More pressure against the marriage came when MARK MERCER (Stanley Grover), the new plant manager of Delaney Brands (replacing Rex Cooper, who became the company's president when Sam Lucas went to Bay City), and his wife, EDITH (Judith Searle), arrived in Somerset from Boston. Edith, who knew that her husband Mark had been in love with Eve Lawrence for many years, set out to destroy Eve's reputation in Somerset with ugly rumors about Eve's "stealing" her husband. Among those who heard the gossip was the old judge himself, who, disillusioned, broke off his engagement with Eve and took his grandson, David Grant, on an extended European vacation. The Mercers managed to patch their marriage up, while their young son GREG was growing interested in Eve's daughter, Heather, despite the objections of his mother, Edith.

Happily married Tony and Ginger Cooper gave up their Somerset apartment and moved with their year-old son, JOSEPH REX, to a suburb called Whispering Beaches, where they rented a cottage. Their landlady turned out to be an ex-patient of Ginger's uncle, Dr. Stanley Kurtz—a woman by the name of MRS. BENSON. Tony and Ginger's idyll in the country was becoming a little strained when they learned that Mrs. Benson, an eccentric astrologer, would deal with them *only* on the basis of a careful analysis of their natal charts vs. her own.

15. THE YOUNG & THE RESTLESS

In some ways *The Young and the Restless* is the most modern, elaborate, and "slick" serial yet produced on daytime television. Its cast simply reeks of California-tanned good looks, good health, good spirits. The sets are truly lavish, with much of the action taking place in an incredibly realistic-looking nightclub—obviously part of Screen Gems' expensive Hollywood filming facilities. There's a well-rehearsed feel to the acting. For the first time ever on daytime, nude or seminude scenes are shown; and there is at least as much lovemaking on the screen as there is talk of sex. The scripts abound with special contemporary sexual problems: premarital sex, sexual inhibitions, rape and the fears women have of testifying against rapists. All this is new, very new to daytime television.

But in some ways *The Young and the Restless* is not new or modern. Its theme concerns young people finding themselves, and love as well, in a contemporary world. But these young people don't go to peace rallies, join communes, or worry about the conflict between having to live in a practical world and needing to be creative. Instead, they are above all concerned with marriage and their relationships with their families, as has been true of young people on daytime serials since the early days on radio. It is important to realize that the young people on this show are not the young people of today.

Indeed, this combination of the young and new with the familiar and old-fashioned has made *The Young and the Restless* astonishingly popular for such a new daytime endeavor. Most serials have to be on the air for a few years to show signs of any ratings-growth, but this one is already beginning to satisfy the hopes of its network and producers. It may well turn out to be a big winner.

It premiered on CBS Monday, March 26, 1973, with the following cast:

> ROBERT CLARY (Pierre Rolland)
> ROBERT COLBERT (Stuart Brooks)
> LEE CRAWFORD (Sally McGuire)
> BRENDA DICKSON (Jill Foster)
> WILLIAM GRAY ESPY (Bill "Snapper" Foster)
> DOROTHY GREEN (Jennifer Brooks)
> TOM HALLICK (Brad Eliot)
> JAMES HOUGHTON (Greg Foster)
> JANICE LYNDE (Leslie Brooks)
> JULIANNA MCCARTHY (Liz Foster)
> PAMELA PETERS (Peggy Brooks)
> TRISH STEWART (Chris Brooks)

The Story

Chicago psychiatrist-neurosurgeon BRAD ELIOT (Tom Hallick) suddenly gave up medicine and left town, just minutes after the son of his fiancée died under his scalpel. He was torn by the idea that he had killed the boy. Later on, after he wandered into Genoa City and began working on a newspaper, he saw a news report come in on the wires: DR. BRAD ELIOT OF CHICAGO HAS BEEN KILLED IN AN AUTO CRASH. Brad realized that the man who had stolen his car and identification papers as he was leaving Chicago had been killed in a crash in that car. Here was the perfect way to "die" and start his life all over.

The paper he worked on was published by STUART BROOKS (Robert Colbert), husband of once ravishingly beautiful JENNIFER BROOKS (Dorothy Green) and the highly moralistic father of four exceptionally attractive daughters: LESLIE (Janice Lynde), LAURALEE (Jaimee Lynn Bauer), CHRIS (Trish Stewart), and young PEGGY (Pamela Peters). Stuart Brooks had taken a liking to Brad from the first moment he met him in a Genoa City restaurant. He not only offered him a job on his paper, but introduced him to his oldest daughter, Leslie, an aspiring concert pianist. It was indeed a strange act of trust and intuition on the part of Stuart, for Brad insisted on keeping his background a mystery, which should have put Stuart off. He was usually skeptical of the motives of his fellow men. But then Brad had a mysterious, unexplainable effect on most people. He instilled trust and he was always eager to help others.

Leslie Brooks, for example, was shy and socially backward when she first met Brad. She had spent so much time studying to be a concert pianist that she had completely neglected her social life, never going out with people her own age. With Brad's attentive help, she began to feel more attractive, more feminine. Her growing love for him, therefore, was understandable.

Chris Brooks, Stuart's second-youngest daughter, was the one who gave her father painful misgivings. Eager that this soft, vulnerable, and extremely trusting daughter meet and marry the right man—and not be taken advantage of by *any* male—Stuart became dead set against her interest in "SNAPPER" FOSTER (William Gray Espy), a medical student from a poor family. It was Snapper's seeming indifference to his daughter—even more than his low-class background—that angered Stuart Brooks.

And Snapper Foster didn't seem to know himself what he felt toward Chris. His main concern, before his personal happiness, was getting through med school and helping his mother, LIZ FOSTER (Juliana McCarthy), put his younger brother, GREG FOSTER (James Houghton), through law school. Liz's husband had deserted the family seven years before, leaving her to work in a factory and her two sons and daughter, JILL (Brenda Dickson), to fend for themselves. Somehow Liz managed, though often at the expense of her health. Jill had helped out by working as a beautician, although she would have liked to chuck it all and become a glamorous model. Liz wanted nothing more than to see her two sons professionally successful and married to smartly brought-up girls—like Chris Brooks.

Despite Snapper's antipathy toward marriage right now, Chris offered to sleep with him because she loved him. Snapper thought Chris wasn't ready for that. Instead, for a physical relationship, he turned to SALLY MCGUIRE (Lee Crawford), a young waitress at Pierre's, a popular nightspot in Genoa City. Sally's background was the complete opposite of Chris's. Her mother had committed suicide and her father had died an alcoholic; she'd already had an illegitimate child, whom she'd given up for adoption. In love with Snapper, she realized that all he could offer her at the time was an affair, and so when the club's owner, PIERRE (Robert Clary), offered to take her on a trip to Paris to meet his family, she accepted—but not before planning to conceive Snapper's baby. She had relations with him the night before departing with Pierre, and she didn't take her contraceptive pills. Becoming pregnant with his child might be one way, she thought, of making Snapper marry her.

When Stuart Brooks learned of Snapper's affair with Sally McGuire, his worst fears that his daughter was being taken advantage of by Snapper were realized. He immediately confronted Chris with his knowledge of Snapper's affair. But instead of turning Chris against Snapper, the information only confused her and made her doubt herself. Crying out that she needed time to think, she left home and took a room in a boarding house. She looked everywhere for a job, but couldn't find one.

Before long, however, Stuart contacted Greg Foster, who was just opening up a new law practice, and asked him to hire Chris as his girl Friday, promising to underwrite Chris's salary. Greg was all too happy to comply, for he had always been extra fond of his brother's girl friend. Now, together with her every day, he was falling in love with her, and she began to have similar feelings for him—until she learned of the deal he had made with her father. Hurt and angry, she chastised Greg and warned her father to stay out of her life for good.

Finally Chris faced up to herself and decided that it was time for her to try to compete with Sally McGuire on her own level—she would give to Snapper the same thing

Sally had given him. After setting the bedroom scene with soft music and lights, donning a sexy negligee and taking Snapper in her arms, she broke down and confessed that she couldn't go through with it. Snapper said he understood and respected her for the kind of girl she was.

But Chris was destined to lose her virginity—in the cruelest way possible. After being followed home one night by a man who forced his way into her apartment, Chris was brutally raped. Ashamed and shattered, she tried to keep Snapper from finding out, but couldn't. "I'm no good for any man now!" she sobbed. Snapper, feeling even more love for her than ever before, realized that the only way to help her adjust to what had happened was to make her his wife. At long last, Snapper proposed marriage to Chris. But at the same time Sally McGuire was learning that she was pregnant with his child, and was making plans to return to Genoa City to ask him to marry her.

Chris, instead of following the example of many rape victims and not pressing charges for fear of humiliation, bravely tried to have the rapist punished. She testified against him at the trial—facing a cross-examination by the defense attorney who tried to make it look as if she had willingly submitted to sexual intercourse. But it was all to no avail. Because the rape laws tend to favor the attacker rather than the victim (absolute corroboration of rape is normally needed, which is rather impossible without witnesses), the rapist went free and Chris's reputation was damaged.

So were her normal sexual responses. She now feared sex with any man—even her new husband, Snapper Foster. But Snapper proved his mettle by showing such patience and understanding during their first uneasy weeks of marriage that Chris was finally able to respond to lovemaking with him.

Crushed after hearing of Snapper's marriage to Chris, the pregnant Sally McGuire had no one to turn to and tried to kill herself. After Brad Eliot saved her life, she told Pierre that she was pregnant. Pierre, in love with her from the start, asked her to marry him and told her that no one else need know that the child she was carrying wasn't his. After they were married, however, Pierre's sister, MARIANNE ROLLAND, became jealous of Sally and, after making a few educated guesses, accused her of carrying another man's child. She then confronted Pierre with her suspicions and he admitted she had guessed the truth. A short time later, Pierre was attacked by a mugger and died in the hospital. Sally, still expecting Snapper's baby, was feeling more alone than ever.

Lauralee (or "Laurie") Brooks finally came home from college and took a job on her father's newspaper, working closely with Brad Eliot. Snobbish and immature, Laurie set her sights on Brad, even though her sister, Leslie, was deeply in love with him. At every opportunity, Laurie would attempt to undermine Leslie and Brad's relationship. She would take up much of Brad's free time with the excuse that she needed his help on a book she was writing. Then she would fail to deliver important messages from Brad to Leslie, or Leslie to Brad. Soon Laurie had Leslie believing that Brad was losing interest in her, and Brad believing that Leslie's career as a concert pianist would suffer if he pursued her. To Laurie, Brad was a potential conquest worth all her scheming.

Now that Sally needed his help, Snapper, with his wife's consent, began to spend a great deal of time with her. He had already been told of her past suicide attempt and feared what she would do to herself if she were left too much alone. Stuart Brooks, however, learned from Marianne Rolland that Sally was carrying another man's child before she married Pierre, and he surmised that the child had to be Snapper's and that Snapper himself had to know the child was his. He refused to believe that Snapper had married Chris without knowing that another woman was carrying his child. Despite Stuart's conviction that Snapper was once again betraying his daughter by seeing Sally, Chris nobly continued to believe in the integrity of her marriage and of her husband's unequivocal love for her.